THE CHOCOLATE BIBLE

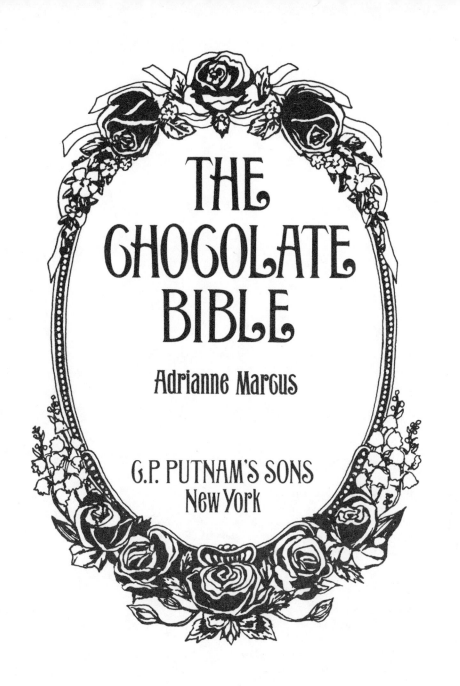

THE CHOCOLATE BIBLE

Adrianne Marcus

G.P. PUTNAM'S SONS
New York

Library of Congress Cataloging in Publication Data

Marcus, Adrianne.
  The chocolate bible.

  1. Chocolate.   2. Chocolate industry.
3. Cookery (Chocolate)   I. Title.
TX791.M36   1978   641.3'37'4   78-25784
ISBN: 0-399-12042-4

Printed in the United States of America

DEDICATION

The Chocolate Bible is dedicated to all those who were a part of it, and to these people in particular:

To Eve Merriam and William Dickey, whose insistence convinced me there should be a book for other lovers of fine chocolates, and one in which no chocolate traveler should be without.

To Melanie Annin, my good friend and chocolate companion through all the miles of this book. Her energy and good taste remained constant, and her help in bringing the various parts of this book to completion is gratefully acknowledged.

To my New York chocolate contact, Sheila Tschinkel, my continued thanks for all her help in procuring some of the best chocolates possible, and never faltering in taste or judgment as we sampled them.

To my Philadelphia chocolate friend and fine poet, Frank McQuilkin, who accompanied me to Hershey, Pennsylvania, and managed to enjoy a bit of the chocolate folklore of America.

And last, to the memory of the late L. Russell Cook, a man whose standards of excellence will always be reflected in the chocolate industry of which he was so much a part. He was respected, admired and a good friend of both small candy makers and large manufacturers alike. His encouragement, patience, and willingness to answer questions and instruct me in some of the intricacies involved with the production of fine chocolate were invaluable. My single regret is that he did not see the book at its completion, since he had so much to do with its inception. We will all miss him, and this book is dedicated to the standards he helped bring about: the finest chocolates that can be made anywhere.

TABLE of CONTENTS

5 THE GREAT EUROPEAN CHOCOLATE CHASE

THE
CHOCOLATE
BIBLE

1
CONFESSIONS
of a
CHOCOLATE
ADDICT

"When I die," I said to my friend, "I'm not going to be embalmed. I'm going to be dipped."

"Milk chocolate or bittersweet?" was her immediate concern.

This is the rhetorical response of one chocolate addict to another. We both know the answer. Bittersweet.

I approach the subject of chocolate with reverence and anxiety, not to mention tenacity and humor. Place any two chocolate lovers in one room and what you get is all of the above, plus passion. Place names, types of chocolate we have tasted, and what is still out there waiting to be tasted, will lead us by strange and exotic routes to the same destination, Chocolate. Any city, in any weather, at any time finds me ready to embark on another circuitous chocolate foray.

What brings me to this obsession? The remembrance of chocolates past. Each of us has known such moments of orgiastic anticipation, our

19

senses focused at their finest, when control is irrevocably abandoned. Then the tongue possesses, is possessed by, what it most desires: the warmth, liquid melting of thick, dark chocolate.

I confess. I will go to any lengths to obtain a particular chocolate. Even further, if more than one kind is involved. Few passions are worth this kind of effort and continued dedication, but chocolate is one of them. Two chocolate addicts can act with an amazing mobility. Nothing, short of death, which I've already made provisions for, will stop us. In our finest moments, we have had the best, and are always looking for more.

"Where are you going?" she inquires, noting the inclement weather, the beginning of a blizzard in New York.

"To Kron's," I reply, already planning a route that will allow me to arrive there midmorning to pick up my order, a careful assortment of hand-dipped chocolate candies, placed the day before. Then, two short wintry blocks away, at William Greenberg's Bakery, I'll purchase the bittersweet chocolate cake they have set aside for me. One final stop: Colette's. Four chocolate cakes are waiting there, and all of these will accompany me back to California.

"Wait a minute," my friend says, grabbing her coat and joining me. We are off, enjoying the mutual harmony of those who travel well together, even in blizzards.

If the carefully wrapped items were not occupying the vacant seat beside me, I would not be found sitting so demurely in the no-smoking section of the airplane for hours, heading to San Francisco. I guard the contents fiercely, for I know how chocolate picks up other odors, flavors. I willingly give up smoking for this other, much tastier habit, which accompanies me, hand carried across the continent. But this is the easy way.

I have driven the entire United States with my friend, and we have collected chocolates from places much harder to get to than New York, placed our chocolate candies in the cooler in the car's trunk, brought them back, more or less intact, in the dead heat of summer, with the odds against their survival.

I confess to countless chocolate trips. All of which have begun and ended lavishly in chocolate. My friend Melanie understands. We have traveled the long miles together, shared chocolate in all its lovely forms, saying yes to this one, no to that.

Eighteen thousand miles of chocolate. All gathered here for you. We have sampled Godiva in Downingtown, Pennsylvania, and Godiva in Brussels, Belgium. Nestlé's in Broc, Switzerland, and Nestlé's in New York. Hand-dipped chocolates from Salt Lake City have made their way into our mouths with as much ease as their elegant Viennese counterparts. Glazed Australian apricots half-dipped in glossy chocolate offered an intense delight, while the sophisticated novelty of gin encased in chocolate provided an intense experience of another type. And there was that moment when we swore allegiance to those Belgian creams: pureed raspberries blended in freshly whipped cream which had been coated with dark, biting chocolate.

All of these can be tasted and enjoyed. Some can be mail-ordered. We have gathered them all here for you, bringing together the multitude of different times, places and chocolate experiences to prove one thing: you can have your chocolate and eat it too.

But it starts long before—somewhere in childhood, perhaps with the first Hershey Bar when the incredible pleasure of chocolate imprints itself indelibly as a memory worth saving. Over the years the pattern remains; the self may grow more discriminating, but the taste is never forgotten. It is repeated. And the memories accrue.

I remember our drives up to the ocean. How once, by sheer chance, we happened to stop at a tiny general store in a town called Valley Ford. A California town so small its major distinction was the fact that its bank was constantly being robbed. What else was there to do in Valley Ford? The whole town consisted of a bank, a gas station, and the general store. One restaurant, I think, occupied a separate corner. We stopped at the general store for some reason, long since forgotten, and discovered they carried homemade chocolate candies. An incredible honeycomb came in two chocolate flavors, dark and light. Its molasses-webbed interior was covered with the deepest dark chocolate imaginable.

There were probably other varieties of chocolate candies, ordinary ones, and therefore forgettable. But not the honeycomb. That one alone was worth the trip. For years, when driving anywhere near that area, we would make it a point to head for Valley Ford and some honeycomb.

One Sunday we drove up to buy some with no more than our usual anticipation. We walked inside: there, in front of us, were three tiers of empty shelves behind the glass. Had they moved it? We looked; no, there was no candy anywhere. Nor would there be. The candy maker from the nearby town of Santa Rosa had died, and with him or her, the recipe. There has been no reason to stop in Valley Ford since then.

But chocolate addicts are resourceful. Cut them off from one source, they will find another. What is good, noble and desirable about us is the fact we will share the places we have found, the chocolates we love. We are equal not only in devotion, but in madness, as the passion comes upon us.

My New York chocolate contact and friend Sheila is to all outward appearances normal. Respectable. She holds a job of considerable stature. But she is one of us. She calls me quite unexpectedly late in the afternoon. I am in California. She is in New York, but no matter. What joins us is the subject at hand, the importance of chocolate.

"I've asked my brother-in-law," she begins, "who is going to Vienna next month, to get you a Sacher Torte from the Hotel Sacher. He's getting me one, also. I thought we should try it."

The wires crackle with this cross-country information. Then we both laugh. For neither of us has begun with casual amenities, the how-are-you's, but leaped into our conversation with what was crucial and uppermost in her mind—and now is on mine. She is, of course, an addict of equal persuasion.

"I did taste it once," I say cautiously. Whether it is the hesitancy in my voice, or the noncommittal nature of my response, she picks up the hidden clue.

"You're going to tell me it isn't as good as the Plaza's," she sighs.

"Have him bring them anyway," I reply in a burst of generosity, while my mind compares the remembered tastes, and leaps back to an evening in New York. I recall it perfectly. It is shortly after Christmas. I am seated in the elegant Palm Court, feeling quite delighted at being here, for I have made everyone join me, come blocks out of our way on this snowy evening to be here, convinced this is where we must have dessert.

I order Sacher Torte and espresso for all of us. While we wait, I look around to see if anything's changed. The Plaza is a childhood dream of mine of one who grew up reading *Eloise* and who, long past adolescence, finally arrived at the place to find it all just as she had imagined. Yes. The mirrors are still as I remembered, the palms, perhaps a little smaller, but the string trio plays softly, the marble tables are just as I envisioned, and when the waitress brings the cake, it is as I remember, the same. A dark, deep version of delight, apricot distinct between the layers. Yes.

My mouth agrees and my heart is content; all is as it should be. There is harmony, order in the universe after all.

Now the Sacher Torte will arrive from its place of origin and be judged by the standards of other Sacher Tortes. Wait, I will tell you about that later.

City after city, country by country, I hear chocolate rumors as they travel and we go to meet them. Someone will say, "You should try the chocolate in Yugoslavia; that's the best I ever tasted."

"Japan," someone else announces. "There's a place where they have good chocolate."

Everyone has his or her own chocolate specialty or a place that ought to be tried. There are more of us than I suspected.

We are as numerous as we are discriminating. I confess to that, also. As much as I love good chocolate, I have no difficulty throwing away bad chocolate. For there is chocolate and there is CHOCOLATE. We know the difference. Those who love it have little patience with others who can consume any chocolate, or even worse, devour all our delicacies with carelessness. It should be savored, melt on the tongue slowly. We know all chocolate is not the same. And the good ones are worth traveling for.

So how could I not try as many as possible? Go to as many of the places as time and energy permit? Just listening to the stories of other chocolate lovers compels me to want what they describe as their perfect chocolate moment. To have it as mine. And to those places I am unable to get to, I write. Send chocolates. I have heard of you. And they do. Even though I cannot get everywhere, everywhere can get to me.

Letter by letter, I ask each place about their chocolates, as I explain I am looking for chocolates of unusual character, distinction, and taste. As I write, more memories come back. Places that were only airports, stops between destinations. But even there, I sometimes found what I was looking for.

In the Dallas/Fort Worth airport, I am willing to clear security to get to the gift shop, to buy a candy made here, in Texas, by Pangburn's. A candy I remember from my childhood. I ask the clerk for Texas Bragg. It no longer exists. I am too late. But I buy a box of Millionaires before I leave. It is the least I can do. By the time I arrive at my destination, there's half a box left.

Other airports, other chocolates. This time in Washington, D.C., I am going to visit my sister, but before we leave the airport, she escorts me to the candy counter. Fannie May's. I select an assortment from the display case. Then taste a piece. Another. "Not bad," I remark, offering her one.

"What do you mean, not bad?" she says between bites.

"It tastes a lot like See's Candies," I explain as I reach for another. There is always a comparison, and See's is, in one sense, the Western equivalent of Fannie May's. The similarity is pleasing to me, for that day I want a candy that is chocolate and sweeter than usual. I am in that kind of mood.

As we drive toward the suburbs in my sister's car, I tell her I cannot stay in Washington very long, for I am going back to New York for the weekend: I have a date to try a new chocolate cake.

She laughs. "You're mad."

"That was never in question; only the degree remains to be discussed," I agree, as we pull into the driveway.

"Before you leave, be sure to give me the address of this place you're going. I have to be in New York next month myself," she adds.

Perhaps madness runs in families after all. Chocolate madness does.

Chocolate addicts learn to expect outrageous requests from others who are similarly inclined. After all, if you can't ask an addict for a chocolate fix, whom can you ask?

My daughter, packing to leave for a semester's study in England, waits for me to tell her what I want brought back. She overlooks the snide remarks about which one of us really ought to be going, and attempts once more to mollify me. "Is there something you'd like, something I can bring back?" she asks.

Hardly any hesitation on my part. "You could bring me back some chocolates."

"Any particular kind?" she inquires, her voice full of suspicion at such a generalized request.

"Oh, an assortment or two," I say, as the entire English production of chocolate passes before my imagination. But that is too greedy, even for me. "You won't forget to bring me those Cadbury Bournville Bars, I hope. The ones with the red label. Bittersweet. I can't get them here, and since you'll be right there . . ." My voice trails off, with hardly a tremor. Perhaps I can convince her to take an extra piece of luggage. After all, she is going to England, and the history of chocolate owes a great deal to the English. And they owe it to the Spanish, who tried to keep the whole thing a secret, to themselves.

The story of chocolate resembles the circular paths I sometimes have to take to get to it. For chocolate history begins on this continent, goes to Europe, and then comes back to be reintroduced to the same continent that discovered the uses of the cocoa bean. But when that happens, it is some hundreds of years later, and only the very beginning of chocolate candies as we'll come to know, love, and enjoy them.

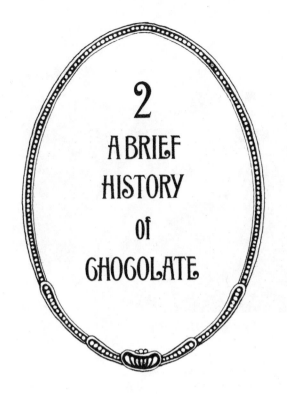

2
A BRIEF HISTORY of CHOCOLATE

If there had been chocolate in England at the time, the line would have read, "If chocolate be the food of love, play on." But there was no chocolate for Shakespeare, and while the English played with various other treacled confections, the Spanish, on the other hand, were busily enjoying chocolate.

After all, they'd had it to enjoy, in one form or another, since 1502, when Columbus brought cacao beans back to Spain on his fourth voyage. King Ferdinand's response to these strange brown beans went unrecorded, for his interest was more in the other items Columbus brought back, which were of known value, such as gold, silver, and jewels.

In time, these shiny cacao beans proved to be as much an indicator of wealth as jewels; in fact, they would be worth their weight in gold.

Halfway around the world, the natives of Central and South America knew this. The Mexican Indians included cacao beans in their ceremonies

Cocoa pod: fruit of the gods. (*Chocosuisse. Union of Swiss Chocolate Manufacturers*)

as a reminder of the gift that had been left them by their gracious god, Quetzalcoatl. The value which the Nicaraguans placed on cacao beans was equally high, for one historian reported it took a hundred or so beans to obtain "a tolerably good slave."

Cacao beans served as a standard of currency for Mayans and Aztecs alike, but in 1519 a ceremony took place that irrevocably altered the course of history for one of these tribes, the Aztecs. It was a ceremony that involved chocolate, and it took place between Emperor Montezuma II and his Spanish guest, Cortez.

As part of the initial formalities, Cortez was presented a golden goblet containing a substance so precious to the Aztecs that each goblet was used only once before being discarded. Montezuma drained the contents of his goblet first, and when the brown, frothy mixture was consumed, the golden container in which it had been served was thrown into the lake beside the palace. Cortez then tasted the mixture and turned to his interpreter to ask what substance they were drinking. The interpreter replied, "Chocolatl, which we would call bitter-water."

It was indeed bitter, Cortez noted, as he finished drinking it. The Aztecs used no sugar, although other spices were added to the beverage. Cortez was told he had just partaken of something quite special in this ceremony, for the Aztecs believed that chocolate conferred universal wisdom and knowledge to thank those who drank it. The Spanish were curious about the origin of the beverage, so Montezuma graciously took them over to some slender trees, forty to sixty feet high, that branched widely. He pointed out the downy branches and leathery leaves, under which the ripe pods, ribbed and wood, ranged in color from yellow-orange to purplish-red.

Montezuma ordered the women and children, the pickers, to bring some of the ripe pods down. When a pile of them were heaped at his feet, the thin foot-long pods were split open with stone knives. Through the interpreter, Cortez was told that the twenty-five or so whitish to lavender seeds inside each pod would now be scooped out, piled into baskets, and allowed to ferment naturally before being pounded into a paste.

The Aztecs believed the gods of the air had brought down these beans from the heavens of paradise. They showed Cortez the final steps in the process, how the beans were pounded and the paste combined with hot water and whipped to a froth.

Soon after, Cortez wrote back to Spain with the information, *"Un taza de ester preciosa brebaje peremete un hombre de andar un dia entero sin tomar alimente."* Freely translated, he told them what the Aztecs knew and believed, that drinking a cup of this beverage daily conferred upon the consumer great quantities of energy. According to written records, Montezuma always drank a full goblet of chocolate prior to entering his harem. He was known to drink fifty or so portions of this beverage daily.

Modern science, would, in time, add proof to what the Aztecs knew and practiced. Chocolate does confer energy. Its active ingredients are caffeine and theobromine. Both exert a stimulant effect on the central nervous system. But this fact was not known at the time the Swedish botanist Linneaus gave the cacao trees their official name, *Theobroma cacao,* the name by which they are known to this day. The scientific label does bear the same reverence the Aztecs and other tribes imparted to the gifts of this remarkable tree that has been under cultivation for at least three thousand, and possibly well over four thousand years. Just as the legends and uses of the cocoa bean made it sacred to those people in whose regions it grew, Linneaus took the Greek word *theos,* meaning God, and combined it with *broma,* meaning food; thus, "Food of the Gods." We receive our gifts of chocolate, just as the ancients did, from trees whose pods contain the heavenly cocoa beans.

Depending on the time or culture into which chocolate was

introduced, it has been considered a stimulant, an aphrodisiac, a medium
of exchange, or a revered substance. And each culture altered chocolate to
its particular taste. The Aztecs added spices, such as vanilla. The bitter,
stimulating taste was what the Aztecs preferred. The Spanish, however,
did not care for this bitterness. They added sugar, and with this
variation, sweet, hot chocolate became the Spanish court's favorite
beverage. The Spanish nobility experimented even further, added other
spices, until any number of various concoctions, each with chocolate as
its base, were prepared and served. Some proved to be of questionable
gastronomic bravery, but most were lavishly enjoyed and consumed.

The Spanish were not only fashionably taken with chocolate, they
were aware of its financial potential. They made sure that cocoa, or cacao
beans, were planted in all their overseas possessions. The business of
chocolate began. The Spanish had such a firm hold on their secret that for
almost a century it remained a monopoly; the nobility maintained a
closed corporation.

It took an Italian visitor, Antonio Carletti, to break their secret. In
1606, he brought the recipe for this new beverage to his native Italy.
From there, the method traveled to Austria, and then to the rest of
Europe. Every country responded with as much enthusiasm as Spain had.
As chocolate grew in popularity, it gained a reputation for having certain
powers. Physicians began prescribing chocolate as a bromide, a cure-all
for their patients. Others, less concerned with its curative abilities,
suggested chocolate's primary virtue to be that of a stimulant, and even
more particularly, an aphrodisiac. Whatever the goal happened to be,
chocolate was the way to get there. *The* beverage. And only the new
chocolate-moneyed generation, the aristocracy, could afford to enjoy it.

In France, the court of Louis XIV adopted this beverage as eagerly as
their Spanish counterparts. This might have been due to the fact that the
two courts were joined by the betrothal of Spanish Princess Maria Theresa
to Louis. She valued chocolate to the extent that she presented it to Louis
as an engagement gift, suitably packaged in an expensive, ornate chest.
Chocolate quickly became a mark of success, a firm indication of one's
wealth. Silversmiths and porcelain manufacturers such as Limoges were
called in, commissioned to create elaborate chocolate services. What they
produced was as extraordinary as it was costly. Madame de Pompadour
was reported to have the most expensive porcelain chocolate service ever

Antique chocolate pots. *(Candy Americana Museum; Wilbur Chocolate Company)*

created. It was, after all, a way of showing both status and standing in the court. Those who had it, flaunted it.

The nobility consumed the substance which cost them dearly, and which left nothing to show for itself except a thin brown froth on the bottom of an exquisite china cup. Their servants could wash the cups, but not afford the beverage that had gone into them.

At this same time, chocolate made its appearance in England. One date stands out in chocolate history: 1657. It was in 1657 that a Frenchman with all the right ideas made *the* crossing of the Channel to open his shop in London, the first chocolate house, and introduced the English to the pleasures of this beverage. English lords and ladies could pause, have a cup of this beverage, or even purchase a bit of solid chocolate to take home to prepare. But at ten or fifteen shillings a pound, chocolate was considered so expensive that it was limited to the nobility and the wealthy. Again, it was the upper class beverage.

The English government made sure it remained that way by placing a high import duty on raw cocoa beans. Just as the Spanish had discovered earlier, to their delight, chocolate was a sure way to increase government revenue. The excessive import duties and fees resulted in some smuggling. The penalties were not light, either. Anyone caught could look forward to spending at least a year in jail. Chocolate stayed a luxury available to the upper echelon of society. It took another century and a half before the tax was finally reduced enough to permit chocolate to be an affordable, popular drink for all classes.

The English, always ones to tinker, even at those prices, tinkered further. They added their variation to chocolate, a distinctively English touch: they added to their beverage, milk.

By the middle of the eighteenth century—1765, to be exact—chocolate completed the great circle. It returned to the continent from which it came, only this time it arrived in the United States. Cocoa beans from the West Indies were brought to Dorchester, Massachusetts, to be refined in the space rented in a grist mill. Thanks to John Hanan, chocolate manufacturing began when he convinced Dr. James Baker that this project deserved financing. Their product, advertised with the suitable guarantee, "Satisfaction or money refunded," is better known today as Baker's Chocolate.

In the nineteenth century, two events altered the history of chocolate in production and taste. C. J. Van Houten of Holland took out a patent to make "chocolate powder" by removing approximately two-thirds of the cocoa butter in chocolate. The "cake" that resulted from his process was considered more digestible and easier to mix with warm water. The partially defatted cocoa powder became the base for hot chocolate, even as we drink it today. Van Houten then introduced another variation, one he had heard about in an old story. A Mexican Indian "doctor" made chocolatl even more helpful for patients by mixing the chocolatl with sifted wood ashes. The brew was claimed to be healthier, more readily digestible, and was used as a cure or restorative, whichever was needed. Van Houten was enough of a chemist to realize the active ingredient in the sifted wood ashes was potash, and his process utilized this knowledge to alkalize the chocolate powder. His second contribution was a darker-colored chocolate, which was milder in flavor, and moreover, combined quite readily with hot water. His process came to be known as "dutching," and today we enjoy "Dutch" cocoa.

The true benefits of Van Houten's discoveries were found in the side benefits of his processes. During the pressing of the cocoa beans, the fat that was released was cocoa butter. Thanks to refining, it took only a short time before manufacturers and intelligent chocolate chemists realized they could mix the chocolate with sugar and cocoa butter to produce a thin paste that could then be molded into what we call the "chocolate bar."

Development followed development with increased rapidity. Varieties of chocolate were numerous. In Switzerland, Daniel Peter of Vevey was busy experimenting with fresh Swiss milk and chocolate. To his credit, "milk chocolate" resulted. He joined up with another Swiss firm, and today the bar he invented is known throughout the world under its familiar name of Nestlé. But Peter has not been forgotten. The large ten-pound bars that Nestlé continues to make as coating for candy makers and industrial users of chocolate all bear the name Peter's on each and every bar of coating.

Switzerland, Germany, France, England, America—each contributed both ingenuity and variation to chocolate. All praised it. In America, Thomas Jefferson declared chocolate to be superior for both health and nourishment to tea or coffee. With justifiable pride, France announced it was the first country to employ mechanical devices in the manufacture of chocolate. And Germany claimed Steinhude was the first place on record to manufacture chocolate.

But it is to England we return. At this same time, a young man who had applied his firm Quaker virtues and values to a coffee and tea business added what he thought of as a small sideline: chocolate production. His operation was so small that he roasted his own beans and ground them by hand with a mortar and pestle. Surprisingly, the public took to his product immediately. He sold enough chocolate to warrant renting a small factory in Birmingham, England. In just such a humble way, one of the world's largest chocolate manufacturers began: Cadbury's. In 1896, Cadbury's advertised something called "cocoa essence," and soon, joined with Fry, the company had more than a ready market for its products. Today, England remains one of the leaders in the consumption of chocolate. The Swiss consume more chocolate, per person, than any other country in the world.

In the 1900's, America began to enter the chocolate manufacturing business with the same tenacity as the European manufacturers. And

Cadbury's cocoa chemist. (*Cadbury Limited*)

Cadbury's factory (1889). *(Cadbury Limited)*

early in 1900, a new name appeared on the chocolate horizon, a name synonymous with American milk chocolate: Hershey's. Hershey and Nestlé are the two names that dominate the world of chocolate in America, but the names of other manufacturers in other places are just as well known to true chocolate lovers.

Their individual histories will be touched upon as we travel to those places and discover the best of all chocolate worlds. And since the making of chocolate is more or less standardized, with few exceptions, we can now see how chocolate is made. No matter in which country you find yourself, it all begins with the first and most important ingredient: the "Food of the Gods," the cocoa bean.

3

THE MAKING of CHOCOLATE

The "original" cocoa bean that Montezuma presented to Cortez was probably Criollo, one of the three broad groupings of beans now commercially grown. The Spanish valued Criollo so highly that they planted it in their overseas possessions.

Today, fine flavor grades such as Criollo and Arriba beans constitute only 10 percent of the world production. Forastero types account for 90 percent of all cocoa beans grown. This hardier variety gives a larger yield. The more exotic, or finer flavor beans, are blended with the forastero.

Cocoa beans vary considerably in taste. Each region produces a particular flavored bean. And to make chocolate, various types must be blended, according to the formulation the manufacturer wishes. Out of this blending, the different proportions of beans, comes the particular taste we associate with a chocolate we like.

It all begins in the growing regions. The beautiful and delicate cocoa trees grow in many parts of the world, but only within twenty degrees, north and south, of the equator. Here, temperature, rainfall, and soil conditions combine to permit the trees to reach their mature height of twenty to twenty-five feet. Of the small, odorless clusters of blossoms that form (as many as six thousand blossoms per tree), only a small percentage will be fertilized and come to fruition as ripened pods. Inside each of these pods, twenty to forty small almond-shaped beans nestle in white pulp.

The beans are grown in places such as Guatemala, Nicaragua, Panama, Costa Rica, Nigeria, Trinidad, and the Ivory Coast of Africa. The finest flavor grades, the 10 percent that produce the most distinctive tastes, include such rare and costly beans as the Maracaibo, which is grown only in the region of Lake Maracaibo in Venezuela. To the east, another bean, the Puerto Cabello, a light tan bean with a nutty flavor, is equally prized for its unusual taste characteristics. The inclusion of these beans in a blend will alter the taste of the basic chocolate and produce a flavor so distinctive that many chocolate lovers will pay a much higher price to enjoy it.

Ceylon, Madagascar, Brazil, Columbia, Ecuador—many countries grow and harvest the raw beans. But the largest producer for commercial purposes is Ghana in Africa. The Ghana bean—a Forastero type—is considered a staple, a "basic" cocoa bean, in the chocolate business. Interestingly enough, these cocoa trees are relative newcomers in the three-thousand-year history of cocoa. For it was only a hundred years ago that missionaries planted the first cocoa trees in Ghana, as an addition to their exotic gardens. Today, Ghana produces over half the world's crop of cocoa beans. The medium dark-brown beans are noted for one important fact: they lack distinction. Neither good nor bad, they produce a fine basic chocolate without a single predominating flavor characteristic. Good chocolate begins with good, basic beans; other beans may then be blended with the basics.

Nigeria is the world's second largest producer with a cocoa bean similar in taste to Ghana's; Brazil occupies third place; and the Ivory Coast, fourth.

Wherever they are grown, once the ripened pods are ready, they are picked, split open, and the small beans are removed. These are heaped into piles, covered, and allowed to ferment for two to nine days. Then the beans, which are still 60 percent water, are dried in the sun to remove excess moisture. The farmer can now bring his crop to a local official, or buying agent. Here, it is inspected, tested, and weighed.

Approved, the beans are rebagged and shipped from the collecting station to the nearest port. When enough of the beans are collected, the government declares the harvest closed.

A second inspection, grading, and weighing now take place. At this time the crop is purchased by dealers and cocoa merchants. Chances are, the crop has already been bought. For the making of chocolate starts long before the cocoa beans arrive at the chocolate factory. Months before, decisions have been made, orders placed as to which kinds of cocoa beans should be purchased, according to the availability of the crops, projected harvest types needed, and blends. In order to assure a particular manufacturer that the types of beans he wants will be available at the specific time he needs them, they must be bought well in advance.

Cocoa contracts and purchases are usually handled through commodity brokers, and orders placed with them. It is the business of buying futures. Anyone who wishes to go into the chocolate business would have to take out many "options" ahead of time, and this valid contract between buyer and seller makes sure the lots are available. However, one lot is thirty thousand pounds of cocoa beans. Hardly the place for anyone with the idea of chocolate making as a small hobby or sideline.

An informative booklet is put out by the New York Cocoa Exchange. For those who are interested in the way all this works, the Exchange will gladly send the booklet, upon request. But for now, I'd rather leave this in the hands of those more able to cope with tons of cocoa beans, namely, the big manufacturers such as Nestlé, Hershey, Wilbur's, Merckens, and Van Leer, who buy their cocoa beans well in advance.

From all over the world, the bags of cocoa beans arrive. They are stored in cool, dry, well-ventilated rooms, or taken out of their burlap bags and dumped into silos, depending on the manufacturer's preference and facilities for storage. When they are needed, they begin their journey into chocolate by being put through a cleaning machine. This removes all the extraneous materials, and now the beans become ready for roasting.

Science, skill, and above all, the art of the chocolate maker are crucial to produce the best results out of the raw beans. For the beans vary as to moisture content, age, ripeness, plus degrees of fermentation and curing. They are not uniform. First, the chemist or chocolate maker has to determine all these factors, for the roasting has to take into account what type of cocoa beans are involved, how long they should be roasted to reach the desired taste, and what kind or type of roast to employ. There is the additional question of which kind of chocolate is to be made from the raw beans. A fondant type of chocolate will require a low roasting heat. A "Dutch" type requires a higher temperature. For a natural-process chocolate, the skill of the chocolate maker can place the temperature at anything short of burning beans to achieve a particular, desired flavor.

And it is this particular flavor that is being sought. The artist in charge of all this is aware of that. He will be both chemist and creator, for he knows that for every unwanted flavor he drives off, he may also drive off a wanted flavor. However he proceeds, he proceeds carefully, and he always starts with good, basic raw beans. Nothing will save bad raw beans, not even the finest chemist. He checks the batches carefully, for the best chocolate comes from the best raw materials.

However it is done, there is nothing that smells as rich or as good as roasting cocoa beans. The smell of chocolate permeates everything, and for miles around the aroma is enough to make anyone's mouth water. During the roasting process, the outer shell of the bean is loosened as the inside contracts. The next step takes the beans into the winnowing machine, and here, the beans are completely cracked, the hulls blown away, and the important part, the small, irregular pieces, the nibs, which are the meat of the cocoa bean, are exposed. The nibs must now be blended, according to special recipes. The blending determines what type of chocolate is desired, as well as the flavor which the chocolate will have, from the most delicate, to the strongest.

The nibs vary in cocoa butter content from 50 to 56 percent. This cocoa butter is still locked inside the nibs. The next step, grinding, is done with a triple stone chocolate liquor mill, or similar machine, which usually consists of three sets of millstones that continually grind away to reduce the size of the nibs. By the pressure and heat generated during this process, the cocoa butter, which was locked inside the nibs, is also released. Now the thick ground mass is liquid and it has a name: chocolate liquor.

At this point a choice must be made. The chocolate liquor can go one of two ways. If the manufacturer is making cocoa powder, the liquor will be fed into powerful presses, which squeeze out most of the cocoa butter. These hydraulic presses can reach maximum pressures at times in excess

Turn-of-the-century roasting ovens. *(Hershey Foods Corporation)*

of 6,000 P.S.I. as the ram slowly compresses and forces the cocoa butter out, to run off into collecting devices. What is left is the hard cocoa cake, which is released, discharged, cooled off and sifted until it has been converted into cocoa powder.

But if the manufacturer makes the other choice, instead of cocoa powder he chooses chocolate bars; the chocolate liquor goes another route. It is now mixed with pulverized sugar, additional cocoa butter, and flavorings. If milk chocolate is being produced, the dehydrated milk is added at this stage. The mixture now has a thick, pastelike consistency. This is the moment at which it enters the series of rollers to be refined.

A modern high-speed refiner with five rolls can handle from 350 to 2,000 pounds of paste per hour. Once the controls are set by the operator, the pressure determined, the sole purpose is to produce a smooth, uniform chocolate by reducing the particle size to the exact dimensions required. Very smooth chocolate may be passed through a refiner more than once to make sure the texture is perfect.

Once this has been accomplished, the chocolate goes into the conche, a machine that kneads and mixes the chocolate over and over, sometimes

Chocolate being conched. *(Hershey Foods Corporation)*

for days. It is in the conching that the final flavor and texture of the chocolate are achieved.

Chemical changes occur in conching, since any remaining water and volatile acids are driven off by this process. The knowledge of the chemist/artist is once again crucial. He must know exactly how long to conche the chocolate, for if it goes too long, it becomes "oily." Chocolate that is too smooth will not be as palatable on the tongue as chocolate that has been conched just the right length of time. Precision is knowing exactly how long to continue the process; too long is as fatal to chocolate as not long enough.

If everything goes right, the conching has been completed, the chocolate is now warm, liquid, and can be fed into tempering equipment. After tempering, it is ready to be molded, made into bars, chocolate chips, stars, flakes, or large ten-pound coating bars. Whatever it is deposited into, and we shall use molds as an example, properly processed chocolate now passes into a cooling tunnel. The molds are agitated to remove any remaining air bubbles as the chocolate cools; and when all of the steps have been followed precisely, when the chocolate completes cooling it will have a high gloss that results from correctly made, tempered and cooled liquid chocolate passing into its solid state. The result will be perfect, glossy chocolate bars.

But the chocolate is not quite ready to be eaten. First, it must be aged. In the case of high-quality dark chocolate, aging develops flavors in much the same way good red wine improves with age. There are probably long scientific explanations of what happens in terms of oxidation and chemical interactions to cause the change in taste, but the simple delicious fact is that well-aged chocolate has a flavor that makes it truly fit for the gods. I have tasted six-year-old dark chocolate. It is richer than anyone would care to believe, and the dark, delectable aftertaste it leaves stays on the tongue for long minutes after the chocolate has been consumed.

Boldemann Chocolate Company crew. (*Boldemann Chocolate Company: Oscar Boldemann, Jr.*)

Milk chocolate, however, does not improve in flavor after an initial aging process of a few weeks. If you keep milk chocolate too long, it will taste flat. It holds up best the first few months.

Most dark chocolate is not aged more than three to six months. It is costly to hold it. But if you can obtain a ten-pound bar and put it away in a cool, dark place, away from dampness (and keep from eating it), a year later it will taste even better than when you bought it.

But most of us have limited storage facilities. Besides, when we buy chocolate, we want to eat it then and there. And this brings us to the places where the chocolate candies are made. We are ready to enjoy it, and the only question remaining is where do we get it?

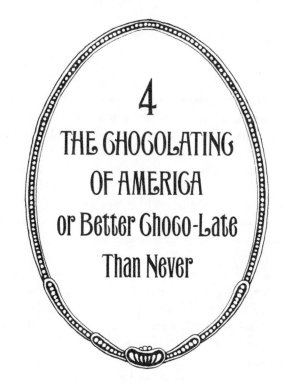

4
THE CHOCOLATING
OF AMERICA
or Better Choco-Late
Than Never

As you have gathered, there are no lengths to which devoted chocolate lovers will not go to obtain the chocolate candies they love. This statement can now be revised to: there are no highways on which two chocolate lovers will not travel in search of the ultimate chocolate dream. The great adventure begins: to find those places in America where the finest chocolate candies are made, and if we cannot see them all, to ask them to come to us. One way or the other, we wanted to compile a directory of chocolates and chocolate places. Early in June, we set out to drive across the United States with a huge cooler in the trunk of our small car for all the chocolates we would gather along the way. It was the chance of a lifetime: to see and taste as many chocolate candies as we and our cooler could hold in the next six weeks.

As with any adventure, it is good to begin with a particular goal. Ours was to get to Connecticut within a week, for Bob Munson was

45

running the last of the Bolton strawberries through chocolate and we had heard these were the ultimate chocolate-fruited confection. We had to get there before the strawberry season ended, which was in six days. Then we would go to Chicago to attend a joint convention of the people involved in the making of our favorite dream—the Retail Confectioners' International and the National Confectioners' Association. But the rest of our trip was somewhat unplanned. We would just go along, see as many of the small and large chocolate makers as we could, see and taste more than anyone thought possible, and perhaps stop, just short of gluttony. Melanie and I would take photographs and sample chocolates, of course, as part of this immensely important undertaking.

We had already been told by various large manufacturers we should expect to find differences between the chocolate we were accustomed to consuming on the West Coast and what we were heading toward in the East. We would be moving from the lighter, milkier chocolate candies to the darker, richer variety. Easterners seem to prefer darker chocolate, even bittersweet. We, as Westerners, supposedly prefer the lighter, sweeter chocolates.

With few exceptions, this proved to be true. Chocolate is regional. Just as the tastes of a region differ, so do the chocolates which are made there. Chocolates reflect the tastes of those who buy them. In California, where we begin, the transient population requires a great variety in chocolates, perhaps indicative of the various cultures that are intermingled in this most populous state.

As noble chocolate lovers, what could we do but share all this information? After all, it is important information and can save hours of research. Wherever you are, you should always be aware of what chocolates are in your immediate vicinity.

We were also curious about what chocolate candies we would find elsewhere. During the growing up of America, each town, or almost each town, had its individual candymakers. The rapid growth of the candy industry, the ease with which most of us buy commercial candy bars, their relative inexpensive cost in comparison to the handmade, as well as the decline in the art of chocolate dipping and small candy makers were facts cited to us. We were told there are fewer places now than there used to be. What we found tends to support the decline in numbers, but not in quality. We found a great many places. Places where chocolate candies are hand-dipped, handmade, and crafted are still available. A few of these

Robert Strohecker begins his chocolate business in Reading, Pennsylvania
(*Harbor Sweets; Ben Strohecker*)

produce enough chocolate candies to be considered more than regional candy stores. They sell their products to department stores all over the country. From the smallest regional candy store to firms approaching the size of commercial plants, the care that goes into the making of chocolate candies is an art. All try their best to create a product that is distinctive. The chocolates differ from region to region. And making them is an art. Like any art, it will endure, even in the era of mass production. From places such as Los Angeles, where Swiss chocolates are made and where Edelweiss coats their fruit under a heaven of chocolate, to Salt Lake City, where two brothers—C. Kay and Paul Cummings—have two separate candy stores, each making candy in a class all its own, right through to small towns we had never heard of: Vermilion, Ohio; Lititz, Pennsylvania; each place had its kind of chocolate. All are worth their weight in gold.

As I mentioned, some mass-produced pieces were great. Critchley's mints, in New Jersey, are a fine example. Godiva, from Downington,

Pennsylvania, has an enviable selection of chocolate candies. Harbor Sweets, in Marblehead, Massachusetts, ships its distinctive chocolate candies all over the country to customers who write and ask for them. Wilbur's candy bars, from Lititz, Pennsylvania, are now available in California. Wherever we went, we were looking for the best, and we found it, wherever or however it happened to be made.

What delighted us were all the others just like us: those chocolate lovers who were equally picky. There is a large discriminating public that wants good chocolate. There are places that imaginatively provide chocolate lovers with just what they are looking for. You can buy almost anything in chocolate—from a foot-and-a-half-high ornately decorated duck to a chocolate pizza, from fresh fruits such as strawberries and blueberries dipped in chocolate to gherkins similarly treated. Creams, caramels, marshmallows, jellies—you name it, they have it.

And we were lucky enough to enjoy it; to have our chocolate and eat it also. As to the question that comes up time after time, which place makes the best, it depends. On what you want. That is not a diplomatic answer, that is *the* answer. Somewhere ahead of you, on a road you did not expect to take, in a town or city in America, there is a chocolate candy you have been looking for. Your chocolate heart's desire.

CALIFORNIA

SAN FRANCISCO, LOS ANGELES
See's Candy Shop, Inc.

The inveterate chocolate traveler divides America into zones; not time, but candy. There's Fanny Farmer in the East, Fannie May as you move westward, and See's, the standard chocolate time of the West. Until just a few years ago, See's was only California time, but slowly and steadily they've expanded into the surrounding western states. You can now buy See's as far east as St. Louis. No matter where you find them, in whatever new location, it's still the same old See's, black and white, the shops straight out of the twenties.

It's more than just old time's sake that makes their name synonymous with what western tastes desire in candy. Any box I've ever bought, prepacked to my exact specifications, has been fresh, with those large centers still moist and lovely. See's won't sell what isn't in prime condition. They're the only candy firm I know that will ship their candy anywhere in the United States all twelve months of the year and guarantee their candies will arrive in good condition.

All of their products come out of two factories, one in Los Angeles, and the other in South San Francisco. They employ from one thousand people in midsummer to over four thousand at their peak season, mid-November to mid-December. But 70 percent of their candies are made in a northern California plant, so I list them as San Francisco rather than Los Angeles.

What's really surprising is the amount of hand work which they still do. In the age of abundant technology, candy factories have found it easier to run their centers through enrobing machines. Yet See's continues to dip its bonbons by hand. They're probably the only large company which insists on doing this hand work. The firm employs a great many women, not only to dip bonbons, but to hand-roll their cream centers so that the fruits and nuts remain whole before being coated in chocolate.

It is precisely this kind of effort that is needed to produce their characteristically large-centered pieces. A pound box of See's contains about twenty-five of these lovely chocolate delights, compared to the typical box from another company which will contain thirty-one or more pieces. There is also another difference which is immediately apparent upon opening one of their boxes: light chocolate candies predominate two to one over dark. This reflects the Western taste and preference for lighter, sweeter coatings.

There is also a heavy emphasis on fruits and nuts in See's rich, creamy centers. This, too, is Western. I have found some pieces that seem to me even more distinctive and regional. One of my favorites is the crystalline square with Spanish peanuts and peanut butter, all coated with Nestlé chocolate. When you bite into it, it shatters into exactly what it's called—Peanut Crunch. In the dark milk pieces, the superb Guittard coating See's uses sets off the centers. One particular piece, which is a favorite of my Eastern friends, is treated in just this way, but it isn't apparent at first. The Marshmint won't even show its chocolate until you take it out of the box; for it has been placed emerald side up, green mint jelly showing, in the assortment. Marshmallow beneath the mint gives way at last to a chocolate bottom. I am not as much a devotee of this piece as friends of mine, although I do like the jeweled touch it gives a box of chocolates.

I am for the creams, and See's uses 36 percent butterfat cream and pure butter in these beauties. Their Raspberry is an example of richness that could make a miser weep, since it's impossible to hold on to this piece. Red raspberry is mixed into buttercream, and then black raspberry jelly is added to that before the whole thing is coated with dark milk chocolate. You have to eat it. Then go on to the Bordeaux. That is as good an example of the lighter chocolate as well as a buttercream-brown-sugar piece. When I really want to be impressed, or to impress someone else, I head for their specialty pieces such as the chocolate cream. It almost fills the palm of my hand. I don't know if anyone else makes these; since See's does a good enough job I've never looked anywhere else.

Specialty items are the rule. Each candy season comes appropriately feted with such extravagances as pumpkins, Easter eggs, turkeys. Whatever is called for. Chocolate lover though I am, I wouldn't let a Halloween pass without an assortment of See's bonbon pumpkins. Each one is a hand work of art, and as much a treat for me as for any wandering goblin.

Back at the chocolate and nuts division, I recommend their fudge. They'll cut it to any size you desire. Right next to it is the Rocky Road, a marshmallow, chocolate, and nut experience also cut to whatever size you want. The pieces See's makes with chocolate and nuts are all good—fresh and thick coated in chocolate, nuts are hard to pass by. This goes for their California Brittle as well, right on through to the chocolate-covered walnuts and almonds.

The box you get, bearing Mary See's picture on the cover, points to a certain unfailing pride in this fifty-year-old candy tradition. Until very recently, there was a member of the See family in the firm's management. Although the last member has retired, nothing else has altered. Their commitment to its candy makes a great many Westerners believe See's is the finest moderately priced box of chocolate available anywhere. It beats any drugstore variety by a mile. And since the West is a vast territory, even in candy, this ought to tell you something about the great number of pieces they offer and the numerous combinations they've invented to please most of us. What's nice is they're still busy inventing more.

See's Candy Shops, Inc.
3424 South La Cienega Blvd.
Los Angeles, Calif. 90016
Tel.: (213) 870–3761

Mail orders accepted all twelve months of the year to anywhere in the United States. Write and ask for their list; it will give you a lot to choose from.

OAKLAND
Hooper's Confectioner's, Inc.

I have been known to go miles out of my way just to visit Hooper's pink cottage-like store in Oakland. It seems, at first glance, to be conspicuously misplaced, set back a bit from the gray business fronts that surround it. When I walk inside, the fantasy continues. The whole store shimmers with crystal and gifts: chocolate gifts, one great candy after another. Well, I don't actually "visit." I go to buy some of the tremendous selection Gordon Hooper makes. His chocolates are indecently rich. Just because he insists these lavish candies should labor under quite ordinary names such as Mocha or Raspberry Cream or Vanilla you should not be fooled. The minute you sink your teeth into those centers, with 40 percent fresh cream he uses to make them, you know these candies are not calculated to be anything but extraordinary. Any berry piece he cares to create I care to eat.

Hooper's Truffles are another masterpiece of understatement. Nowhere on the box is there a description of what to expect when you unwrap the foil and pop one into your mouth. By the time the smooth center melts away, you are already unwrapping another mint or lemon truffle to replace it. They are exquisitely smooth blends of chocolate and fresh flavor. I end up with a pile of foil and a chocolate smile all over my face every time I enjoy them.

The only resistance I have to anything he makes is the cherry cordials. But I have to be truthful. That is because my daughter always gets to them before I can. And you can't take candy from a child. Not in the store, anyway.

I confess to one other thing. I fell madly in love with a foot-high decorated hollow-mold duck (in chocolate, naturally) created for Easter. I brought it home to photograph. It is still here, untouched. I can't imagine anyone having the audacity to eat this work of art, and there doesn't seem to be any reason to do so, considering all the other candies Hooper's makes. There's something for everyone, whether they want a sweet milk chocolate piece or a bittersweet. One member of my family, who prefers to remain nameless, bought himself two pounds of Hooper's fresh roasted nuts and declared them the best he's ever had.

Hooper's chocolate Santa.
(*Richard Steinheimer*)

My favorite time to visit is at holidays. As befits the season there are always appropriate chocolate spirits to go with the festivities. Easter has ducks, easter eggs, and chickens, all created right there. And for Christmas, there's Santa Claus, even bigger than my duck, done in chocolate and piped in red and white decoration.

It's a wonderland, that cottage, at any time. Whenever I get there, I find it holiday enough to enjoy celebrating with at least a pound of his incredible creams. If you are in the Bay Area, do what I do. Go over and "visit." It's well worth the trip.

Hooper's Confections, Inc.
4632 Telegraph Ave., or
P.O. Box 3064
Oakland, Calif. 94609
Tel.: (415) 654–3373

There's mail order available; ask Gordon Hooper to send you a catalog, which will show you what can be ordered. Some of his candies are also available in local department stores. But whatever you do get, don't forget to try his Truffles and chocolate-covered creams.

VALLEJO
Lileds

Can a young man from the world of stocks and bonds find happiness as a candy maker in a small northern California town? Well, Hank Barner seems to be doing just that, and turning out some remarkably good candies in the process. His decision to go into business for himself wasn't one of those "let's get back to the earth and live organically ever after" routines, although he uses the best Mother Nature provides, including 40 percent real cream in pieces such as his Plum Pudding.

"If you really use good ingredients, you have to work hard to butcher them up," he says, "and so I use the best." After serving an apprenticeship for six weeks under the tutelage of Ed Jensen, who started Lileds in 1936, Hank has been in the continuous process of learning by doing, and the results are tasty conclusions of effort well spent.

I asked him if there was a difference between how he felt as a novice and how he feels now. He laughed and pointed to a batch of caramel he was cooking in a copper kettle. The caramel would eventually become the centers for chocolate candies. "At least I don't have to wonder each time I begin a batch whether or not it's going to come out exactly right, as I did in the beginning." And I agree, reaching over to enjoy another piece of candy.

His Plum Pudding I mentioned earlier is one of my favorites. It is an eggnog buttercream with plump raisins that have been soaked in sherry. This special piece is all Hank's—I've never had it anywhere else.

It takes a great deal of enthusiasm as well as skill to succeed in the candy business. The long work day begins at seven or so each morning, when Hank arrives, and he works straight through until six thirty or seven each night. This hasn't dampened his feelings about what he's producing, since he obviously enjoys it. So do his customers, for they line up to buy candy and the rich ice cream he makes right there in the shop. The ice cream isn't a minor sideline either; he places the same care in producing it that goes into the candies. If you try his coffee ice cream what you taste is the best mocha java beans ground fresh made into a strong infusion before being blended with cream.

Drifting back to the world of chocolate, I suggest you try his Bordeaux, the almond buttercream with nuts. If you happen upon his French Creams, I'd like to offer my suggestion that you permit them to reach 70 to 75 degrees before eating them. I usually recommend that chocolates be kept no warmer than 65 degrees, but these creams only come to full flavor when they are warmer. The whipped and softened chocolate will literally melt away into your mouth the moment it leaves your hand.

Hank's centers are hand-rolled, and he coats them with the finest chocolate available. Most of the time he uses Nestlé's. At Easter, he produces the molded rabbits children love, and one other piece I care about, a chicken in a basket. All are available in chocolate, but you who are more adventuresome can have your chickens in butterscotch.

I do heartily concur with his decision to leave the gray flannel world for this new one; it's going to pay dividends to all of us, and at a growing rate of interest.

Lileds
1318 Tennessee St.
Vallejo, Calif. 94590
Tel.: (707) 643–7425

He'll accept mail orders during most of the year; write and ask for price list and be sure to have some of the Plum Puddings.

NUT TREE
Nut Tree Candy and Foods

Whenever friends from the far reaches of the East or Midwest come to visit, I try to make sure they see all the special sights for which the Bay Area is noted. When they are finished gasping at the giant redwoods and the spectacular scenery, I then insist that they're going to try something which I consider equally important—a trip up to the Nut Tree. The usual response to this suggestion is a blank stare and the inevitable question, "Where's that?"

"On the way to Sacramento, on Highway Eighty," I reply, and if pressed further, they get my version of mileage, California style— "About an hour or so away from here." Then, Californian to my very wheels, I trundle them off into the car and away we go. So far, I've yet to strike out, for no matter where they have eaten, including the best San Francisco can offer, I know they haven't been to a place like the Nut Tree.

California is synonymous with fruits, nuts, and other natural delights. The Nut Tree started out years ago as a small wayside stand selling just that—fruits and nuts. But it's come a long way since then. Over the past fifty-seven years, what used to be a small restaurant at which one stopped going to or from the Sierras, is now a reason in itself for going there. The signs along the way herald the number of minutes left until you reach it.

Once there, it's worth the effort. A meal begins with fresh pineapple flown in from Hawaii, served inside its own hull and accompanied by a light marshmallow sauce on the side. Their salads are beyond comparison, and the one that bears the name Fresh Fruit will have such niceties as papaya, kiwi fruit, and figs arranged exquisitely on a plate with homemade nut bread. A tiny vanda orchid also graces the plate.

Everything they serve is fresh, from the vegetables, which vary according to season, to the deep-dish pies. The diverse nature of their menu permits everything from Chinese barbecued spareribs with sweet ginger glaze to fresh salmon or tamales. After all, the taste of California is as varied as its regions.

And we are blessed by such riches, I think, until I get to dessert. Then I have a small quarrel with them. Granted, the fresh fruit pies are marvelous, but their chocolate cake, which should be equally so, isn't. It used to be. But not lately.

Nostalgia, as I define it, is a funny critter. It reminds us of what we've had and would like to enjoy again. I remember that chocolate cake as very special. But lately, if I were blindfolded, I'd be hard put to declare it was chocolate.

Nut Tree candies. (*Richard Steinheimer*)

Luckily, that's not the case with the Nut Tree's candies. Art Mayland is busily presiding over the candy kitchen and he maintains a strict and loving watch over how things are combined. His results are consistent and luscious. The fudge, which I have loved from the first time I tried it, is still beyond compare. And his new piece, the Vanilla Chocolate Bark, is a chocolate dream, with almonds and chocolate set to perfection by just the right addition of vanilla. I even like the Rocky Road here, which surprises me, for most versions of that candy are relatively light on the chocolate and consist mainly of marshmallow and nuts. Not the Nut Tree's. It's full of crunchy nuts, light puffs of marshmallow with the dark delight of chocolate.

Still, it's the fudge that captures my heart and mouth. I always buy some, remembering it won't keep over a few days. Which means I get to enjoy it as soon as I've finished supper. The other chocolate candies are also good. And their packaging is so well done that it's worth buying a box and displaying it in the house like a good piece of art. It's that pretty and more.

Some of the pieces are hand-dipped, and all of them are beautiful. I've bought their candy bars, which feature large postcards as covers; they say "California" all over in a classy design. Another novelty item I enjoy are the large gold coins containing chocolate. They're unusual and exotic, bearing the symbols of California as well as the Nut Tree. My friends adore receiving them from me.

How can I describe a place that keeps changing and getting better year after year? The Nut Tree boasts its own landing strip, just out back, beyond the toy store, which makes it convenient for those who want to fly up and have a spot of lunch. Let me say it's all done in good taste. And certainly the best that California offers.

Nut Tree Candy and Foods
Nut Tree, Calif. 95688
Tel.: (707) 448–6411

I'm sure they'll be glad to mail order if the weather isn't too hot. Do write and ask for a price list and enjoy what is available for the time of year you happen to be enjoying.

BURLINGAME
Preston's Candies

For the traveler arriving at San Francisco airport, it is only a matter of minutes to Burlingame, where on the main street, Broadway, a small candy store called Preston's Candies makes the finest Honeycomb I've ever had the privilege of worshiping. *Devouring* is too crass a word for this delicacy, for the divine molasses and chocolate confection literally melts as you bite through the chocolate surface into the crystalline, airy center.

That center is the color of the mythic California tan. It is all sun and golden hills, a fine chorus of the Beach Boys and surfing music. It is California candy, and indeed other places call this confection Seafoam or Sponge, but here it is called Honeycomb. Art Preston has created the perfect crisp light center. Then he has enrobed it in either light or dark chocolate. And his customers come from all over to buy it, as much as ten pounds of this candy alone, at one time.

The way I came upon it is a story all its own. Many years ago in the town in which I live, San Rafael, California, there was a small candy store called Moore's. It was on the main street and they sold what I came to believe was the perfect Honeycomb. Their going out of business was such a loss that I renounced other candies which only had the name Honeycomb but none of its high attributes. No one even approached the remarkable center I remembered, that puff of molasses and honey. So when Art suggested I taste his Honeycomb, I was understandably cautious. I bit into it. Amazed, I took another bite, and I turned to him and said, "Do you know, this is the first piece of Honeycomb I have had in years that even begins to match some I used to buy years ago. There used to be this small candy store in San Rafael that made the best . . ."

He looked at me and replied, "Moore's?"

"How did you know what I was going to say? This tastes exactly the way I remember it!" I said, finishing off one piece and reaching fast for another.

"It should," he answered, smiling. "I used to make the centers for them."

How can I tell you about my joy in finding that a nostalgic experience could be so easily and completely recaptured? I admire Art Preston's fine candy touch. It is more than apparent in the aforementioned goody, but there are others which I then went on to enjoy. His Argentine is a smooth creamy caramel in which a filbert nut has been encased. The whole chocolate surprise blends perfectly. And a new piece with which he's delighting the chocolate audience is called a Chocolate Mousse. He takes a light chocolate and whips it until the center is ready to float, then adds nuts and fruits to anchor this extravagance down before coating it in either light or dark chocolate.

If you are an ice-cream fancier, you can't get much fancier than his, which he makes right there. Nor his candies, which are also made on the premises. Novelty chocolates, such as alphabet letters, and chocolate baseballs are also bought at the front counter, after being freshly made right in the back of the shop. But it is the Honeycomb that propels me down the freeway to Burlingame. As I drive past the San Francisco airport exit, I know I am almost there. Just one more off-ramp. A pound or so later, the Honeycomb is tucked safely at my side, I'm flying home, the Beach Boys on the tape deck, the sun riding the coastal hills, and I feel the world is as it should be, all sweetness and light.

Preston's Candies
1170 Broadway
Burlingame, Calif. 94010
Tel.: (415) 344–3254

Art will gladly fulfill your mail-order fantasies, providing the weather is cool enough to guarantee his chocolates' safe delivery. And it usually is. Don't forget to buy at least a pound of his Honeycomb.

Guittard Chocolate Company

I went to Guittard Chocolate in Burlingame to ask all sorts of questions about a product I thought I knew little about, only to discover I'd been enjoying it for years. It happens to be the coating on one of my favorite candies, Art Preston's Honeycomb. See's Candies also uses Guittard. That drove the point home: Guittard's chocolate is exceptionally good. As if that weren't point enough, I happened to mention to my eldest daughter that I'd been down and visited Guittard. This was said in a tone of delight. She paused, looked at me, puzzled, and replied, "Oh yes. We've been using their chocolate chips for years."

I went over and looked in my own cabinet. There they were, complete with the little Dutch girl right on the front of the package. I hadn't even connected the name with what I'd been buying and enjoying all this time. I simply called them "the good ones." Since the grocery store always had them in stock, I automatically reached for the configuration I knew and had been buying them for more years than I care to mention. Forgive me, folks at Guittard. If that store had ever run out, I'd have learned your name a lot sooner.

Guittard, after all, has been around over a hundred years, and during all this time, it's remained a family-owned business. It started with Etienne Guittard, who left his uncle's chocolate factory in Paris to come to California just after the gold rush. He discovered chocolate was scarce, here on the frontier, so the next time he came to California, he came to stay. In 1868 he put to use what he'd learned in his uncle's factory and started Guittard Chocolate in San Francisco.

Guittard continued to grow in spite of the great San Francisco earthquake of 1906, which almost put everyone out of business. They built a new plant and kept on making what they do so well, their chocolate. In 1955, Guittard moved to their new factory in Burlingame, near the San Francisco airport. The area was just being developed at that time and the road was named after them, Guittard Road, which makes them easier to find.

Their plant was the first new basic chocolate plant to be built in this country in twenty-five years and it permitted Guittard to operate on a continuous rather than on a batch-by-batch basis as the cocoa beans arrived from such places as Ecuador, Venezuela, West Indies, the Gold Coast of Africa, and the East Indies.

Guittard is still better known to those in the candy, ice-cream, and baking industries than to the general public, which knows them primarily by one item: their chocolate chips.

I wish they made candy bars. But if you are the fiend for chocolate I am, you could perhaps procure a ten-pound slab of their fine chocolate and it would hold you for at least three months, if you portioned it out carefully. For special occasions—and chocolate is always one of those—I'm grateful for the fine quality of Guittard, the firm whose name we all ought to remember.

Guittard Chocolate Company
10 Guittard Rd.
Burlingame, Calif. 94010
Tel.: (415) 697–4427

You could write and ask if they'll ship you a ten-pound bar. It's worth a try. They even have a cocoa tree growing in their lobby.

Guittard antique Santa mold. *(Adrianne Marcus)*

Boldemann Chocolate Company

"There's a difference between chocolate and candy," Oscar Boldemann, Jr., said, "and it's important to remember. There's chocolate, which comes solid, like a bar, and then when you take it and wrap it around nuts, sugar, corn syrup, that's candy." This was my first lesson in discovering that chocolate and candy are viewed quite differently by someone in the chocolate industry than by the rest of us, who use the word *chocolate* to mean candy. Dod Boldemann, as he's called, is a good teacher, since he's been in the chocolate business all his life. Although you may not recognize his chocolate by its name, you've probably tasted the product they make in tollhouse chips or as one of the coatings on your favorite chocolate candy. Boldemann sells primarily to bakers, candy makers, and confectioners, who buy the chocolate in ten-pound bars or bulk cocoa and then reuse it, making their own specialties.

Boldemann's was a family business, dating back to the 1880s when it was in San Francisco. Today, it's part of Blommer Chocolate, one of the biggest chocolate manufacturers in America, but Dod still has his office. He's more than happy to talk about chocolate and how Boldemann got into the business almost by accident. The firm was looking for a product to make up in bulk, in order to procure a better shipping rate, even back in the 1880s, for freight was as expensive an item then as it is now. Chocolate was the bulk item it chose. As second-generation in the business, Dod has been involved in chocolate all his life and has watched the industry change. "The nickel candy bar I used to eat when I was a kid is now twenty or thirty cents, but you have to remember cocoa beans, which were really inexpensive back then, are now up to two dollars a pound." He's watched other changes happen: from a high point of well over forty large chocolate manufacturers, only twenty-two still remain. Increasing costs, large-scale production demands and the expensive nature of cocoa beans have caused some companies to merge and others to go out of the business, unable to compete in this highly competitive market.

In the early 1950s, Blommer Chocolate Company was looking for a West Coast plant in which they could expand their operations. Henry Blommer, Sr., and Dod were old friends, and it was a natural merger as Boldemann sold the common stock of the company to Blommer to become a division of that large operation, one of the five biggest in America.

Antique Boldemann ad. *(Boldemann Chocolate Company; Oscar Boldemann, Jr.)*

Antique Boldemann truck. *(Boldemann Chocolate Company: Oscar Boldemann, Jr.)*

But it wasn't until 1971 the plant left San Francisco for Union City, across the bay, and opened production in its new 161,000-square-foot concrete building. Here, all the newest production equipment and machinery are on one floor, making it one of the largest single-story operations anywhere. And all of it devoted to the one sweet conclusion: chocolate. Chocolate coatings continue to be the major portion of Boldemann's business, and its bittersweet version is one I prize highly— and with good reason.

Before I left, Dod reached into the steel cabinet beside his desk, brought out a large ten-pound bar, and broke it into pieces over the top of his desk. "Here's something I don't think you've ever had," he said, offering me a large chunk of chocolate. Never one to refuse, I bit right in, and savored something I can't begin to describe. "Like it?" he asked, as I reached for more. All I could do was nod. "That's six-year-old chocolate," he announced, smiling. "I told you I didn't think you'd ever tasted anything like that." He was right, and I got my second lesson in chocolate right from the master chocolate maker: Dark chocolate, like good red wine, improves with aging, and if you can ever manage to get your hands on some bulk bittersweet coating, just put it away and let it age. It will become better and better as the years go on.

At that point, I evidenced the complete dedication that is the mark of a true chocolate addict. I asked for a bit more to take home with me and Dod complied. I simply wanted a portion of this ultimate chocolate treasure he had so lovingly saved to share with someone of equal persuasion.

But I needn't have worried. Hank Blommer, Jr., the general manager of Boldemann's, witnessed this exchange. After he took me through their plant and extended my education in the making of chocolate, he presented me with the chocolate addict's dream of a lifetime: my own ten-pound bar to take home and age. And it's still there, downstairs in my chocolate cellar, getting better and better, with only four more years to go.

Boldemann Chocolate Company
1515 Pacific St.
Union City, Calif. 94587
Tel.: (415) 471–4300

As you can tell, I'm more fond of their bittersweet coating, but they make a complete range from the lightest, sweetest milk to the darkest, deepest bittersweet, as well as an item you can buy in a great many stores—Pokies, which are chocolate drops in colorful sugar coatings. They might be willing to sell you a ten-pound bar to have and to hold, if you write. Tell them I sent you.

SAN FRANCISCO
Ghirardelli Chocolate Company
In California, one of the world's most beautiful cities splendidly aligns itself into a series of spectacular views, so a visitor's introduction to Western chocolate might take place at Ghirardelli Square, once a chocolate factory, now a posh stagger of shops.

Ghirardelli still produces chocolate, although not at Ghirardelli Square, where it has a shop. The century-old firm was bought out by Golden Grain and now makes chocolate in San Leandro, California. I did go through their production facilities, and wish I could change my opinion of its product, but I can't.

As much as I'd love to defend San Francisco for its taste, Ghirardelli's serves to remind me that bad chocolate is bad chocolate anywhere, no matter what the view. Their label says "finer chocolate," but I refuse to believe it.

My husband, who remembers Ghirardelli's from his childhood, obviously doesn't share my dismay, for I've seen him buy and consume the raisin bars and Flicks, neither of which I'll eat on any day. The only way I've found Ghirardelli's chocolate edible is melted, over ice cream on the sundae made at the shop. It's my last desperate attempt to consume it. Otherwise, every bar I've bought has been grainy in texture, mediocre in taste, and despite the addition of nuts, mint or what have you, the packaging is the most tasteful part of the whole item. Their cocoa is passable, but not exceptional. I don't care for Ghirardelli's chocolate products, and not having been brought up on them, I don't have my husband's good memories to convince me I should try them again. Their advertising is splendid. I wish their product were equally tasty.

Ghirardelli Chocolate Company
1111 139th Ave. West
San Leandro, Calif. 94578
Tel.: (415) 483–6970

Alhambra
Just Desserts
Carl's Pastry Shop
Three Mills Creamery

For a city that prides itself on sophistication, in both food and viewpoint, it's sad to note that San Francisco has few candy stores or places where good chocolate products are made. Alhambra, on Polk Street, makes a variety of candies, and they are of good quality, thanks to John Prongos, who has been in the candy trade since 1930. Unfortunately, he's planning to retire in a few years and doesn't expect that anyone will succeed him. He began working at Red Poppy, a candy store just up the street that closed because of lack of business only this past year. For now, John continues to make his candies. His marshmallow covered with chocolate is one of the nicer pieces he produces.

His brother Charles has another candy store on Irving Street, where he makes an assortment of chocolate candies plus ice cream. The creams are nice, but there are no exceptional pieces, since San Francisco consumers don't seem to demand the exceptional in chocolate. Both firms use Guittard and Merckens chocolate.

Alhambra and Three Mills are two of the best candy shops San Francisco offers. Each has been making chocolate candies for a long time. In any other city, there would be a demand for quality chocolates, locally made. But not here. For just around the corner from Alhambra the worst chocolate cake I've ever eaten anywhere continues to enthrall the natives. It's at Just Desserts, and what it lacks in character and taste, it makes up for in price. I've seen it served at the finest parties, and I avoid it whenever possible.

If you really want a good chocolate cake when you're in San Francisco, it's worth the time and trouble to head over to Carl's Pastry Shop on Eighteenth and Guerrero, out in the Mission district. They make the best chocolate cake I've ever found in the whole city of San Francisco. It's called Fudge Rose. Be sure to ask for it by that name, since it's made to order. Dick Amandoli's Fudge Rose is chocolate through and through, with a lovely mocha between layers and a good fudge coating over all. The motto in his window, "What is a birthday without a cake?" makes me wish I had more than one birthday a year.

You have to call in the morning to order it, then you can pick it up that afternoon. I find it tastes best at room temperature, which brings out the full flavor. So if you refrigerate it, take it out at least an hour before you plan to serve it.

San Franciscans ought to support their good local chocolate places, such as Carl's and Alhambra. Otherwise they'll continue to get exactly what they seem to favor—their proper and Just Desserts.

Just Desserts
1469 Pacific Ave.
San Francisco, Calif. 94109
Tel.: (415) 673–7144

Carl's Pastry Shop
600 Guerrero St.
San Francisco, Calif. 94110
Tel.: (415) 552–1141

Alhambra Candy Company
2206 Polk St.
San Francisco, Calif. 94109
Tel.: (415) 474–9925

Three Mills Creamery
836 Irving St.
San Francisco, Calif. 94122
Tel.: (415) 681–1255

Princess Delight Confections

The best homemade candies in San Francisco can be found in a tiny store just next to the Larkin Theatre on Larkin Street. Peter Lojkovic, who has fifty-four years of candy making behind him, creates them. During his career, he has seen most of the little candy shops vanish, but he has remained not only constant, but faithful, producing special items such as chocolate-covered raisins (fine seedless muscats, plump and juicy under a coat of Nestlé's), Raspberry Honey Jellies, and the best nut buttercrunch I have ever tasted. Toasted cashews or the equivalent on top, then chocolate, and a firm, buttery, almost smokey-tasting crunch just underneath all this. Of the five of us who tried it, the decision was unanimous: it was the best commercially made candy of its type we had ever tasted.

His raisin clusters, coated in chocolate, are an experience worth repeating. You get about six pieces in each cellophane packet to enjoy. I chose the dark coating, which set off the plump raisin taste perfectly.

Mr. Lojkovic refuses to go to cheaper coatings. He likes pure chocolate, and he applies it lavishly to his candies. I am not as fond of the French Chocolates as I am of his nut pieces. Even the clusters of cashews, coated in chocolate, have a nice, crunchy, toasted taste that is unusual and memorable. He is open only from two in the afternoon until eight at night, so get your chocolates then. It's a tiny place, and he handles it all himself, making his chocolates in the morning and selling them in the afternoon. It's so nice to have him making chocolates in San Francisco, and how happy I am to have found him!

Princess Delight Confections
820 Larkin Street
San Francisco, Calif. 94108
Tel.: (415) 885–6910

GLENDORA
Mackinac Island Fudge

This is too good for me to keep secret, since I've been buying Mackinac Island Fudge for years, and everyone who has ever tasted it reacts exactly as I did the first time: where can I get more? You can get it only in California, and what's even more difficult, only during certain months of the year for a few days at a time.

Mackinac Island Fudge means it is summer. For the local fair and the fudge come to town together. Every July, I wait for the first notice of when the Santa Rosa Fair is going to begin, because I know John Marzolino will be there, with his fudge kitchen set up, turning out batch after batch of the best fudge in the world. I bring home five or six pounds at a time, wrapping it carefully, putting it away in my freezer so I can have some for special occasions when nothing else will do.

John Marzolino is the candy maker, and his fudge recipe appears in the 1960 *Cubelet,* a magazine put out by C and H Sugar. It's simple, as it states, "Take 4,000 pounds of C and H Sugar, 400 gallons of pure high-test cream, 20 bushels of shelled English and black walnuts, plus 4 gallons of assorted flavoring extracts," and that's where it ends. I think they left out all the Guittard chocolate wafers that are then added, and the cooking time.

I've seen John cook that fudge in a large copper kettle. It only takes ten to twelve minutes to get all those ingredients to the right temperature, plus two people to lift up the heavy kettle, tilt it, and pour out the molten fudge onto its marble slab. Then someone has to grab a large paddle and begin to run around the marble table, folding the fudge back in on itself until it reaches just the proper consistency. This may take a few hundred batches to get down pat because you also have to take into account the weather and humidity. Anyone who has made fudge already knows that. Within a few hundred batches, as I said, you may have a perfect batch to enjoy. But rather than do it over and over, I'd prefer watching John do it, just as he has, for twenty-three years.

The process by which he makes his fudge so very different from anyone else's is called Slab Fudge, for the final cooling and mixing of the candy take place on that marble slab, instead of in its copper kettle, the way most candy makers do it.

However he manages to do it, he does it the best. Batch after batch brightens the days of all sorts of people. Starting in January, if you happen to find yourself at the Convention Center in Anaheim, California,

Pouring Mackinac Island Fudge. *(Adrianne Marcus)*

you can buy some of his fudge. In April John takes his portable fudge kitchen on the road. June to November, it's available at some of the fairs in California, and that's when the rest of us enjoy it.

My favorite of all the kinds he makes is the chocolate nut fudge. I also tried a new one, peanut butter fudge, and I liked it, but nothing can replace the chocolate nut fudge. And besides, he isn't planning to replace it. That one is King of the Road.

Since no preservatives are used, you get it fresh, daily, right there, where it's made. It goes out as fast as he can turn it out. Once anyone tastes it, they come back for more. All winter I watch my fudge supply dwindle; by March, there's not a scraping left. I'm thankful when July comes. Four months is too long to be without it.

Mackinac Island Fudge
7860 Glencoe Heights Dr.
Glendora, Calif. 91740

I'll bet if enough of us wrote to him, he would make it available to us by mail. As of now, it isn't, but we could change all that. It's great fudge.

PALM SPRINGS
Fun-in-the-Sun Candies

In late January, the weather closes in. At that point, it's time to take the cure, join the exodus back to the sun. For me, the closest place that guarantees this is Palm Springs.

I confess to all sorts of illusions, from chocolate right on through to the perfect place. And Palm Springs is one of those illusions. Under its benevolent and exquisitely blue sky, there are palm trees, enough to permit an exotic touch, all the desert and continual falling of sunshine I need wherever I look, and the weather, steady and holding at 70 degrees. The San Jacintos gleam ruggedly at the edge of town, their masterful peaks arranged delicately with snow. That would be enough for most people, but Palm Springs has the final touch I need. A perfect candy store.

How often do we have the chance to have all of our illusions done correctly? Palm Springs may well be the ultimate in packaged illusions, and June Mennell helps contribute to that by packaging the great chocolate extravaganzas made in her shop to your exact request. Behind each counter of glass is a virtual glistening of delights, all waiting to be tasted. Start with the dates. They are mammoth, beneath coats of deep chocolate. The dates themselves are tender and moist, and must hold together by sheer willpower, waiting to be enrobed in chocolate. Then go on. Try the Fallen Leaves. These drift into a box in a swirl of marshmallow and nuts, with chocolate through and through, as well as over them. If you have room, then you should have a few of the chocolate creams. They are rich as anything you could imagine.

Even their Honeycomb is exceptionally good. The dry air of Palm Springs must allow it to rise to its crisp, natural conclusion, and then, encased in chocolate, it remains in that state of suspended delight until it's eaten. Their chocolate-covered fruits are equally commendable. Before I leave, I buy at least two assortments to bring home with me. When I return to the fog and rain of northern California, I keep the sunshine at hand by simply reaching into the box and having one or two pieces. It's one way I've found to have my illusion and eat it also.

Fun-in-the-Sun Candies
232 North Palm Canyon Dr.
Palm Springs, Calif. 92662

They'll ship their candies only during those months they are open, during the winter.

Jo's Candy Cottage

If you think about the craft involved in hand-dipping chocolates and the fact that one is still considered an apprentice at this trade after ten years, you can begin to appreciate the care and skill that go into each box of chocolate candies Frank and Mary Vukmanic produce. They offered to teach me the craft, but I've been too busy enjoying the fruits of their labor to take time away from my first skill, which is all-consuming, and which you already know about.

Their candies have contributed to furthering my chocolate education, as well as to adding a bit of chaos in my life. Until the moment I had tasted their Honeycomb, I had sworn allegiance to Art Preston's, whose Honeycomb is the delight of northern California. Now I must declare a dual allegiance: for Jo's Candy Cottage makes one the size of a monumental surfing wave, and I can ride right on through the chocolate and molasses crest into the very heart of it, letting it take me by sheer energy to where I belong. It's in Manhattan Beach, California.

Their Maple Nut coated in milk chocolate could save any castaway. There's also a Chocolate Cream Nut, which conceals its pleasure under a coat of dark chocolate, and is truly a piece to which you can resort at any time.

I've never wanted to ride the pipeline in Hawaii, since surfing requires skill as complicated as hand-dipping chocolates, but their chocolate piece with a huge pineapple center will call it all to mind. It's included in their regular assortment. Even if you don't come upon that particular piece on first try, you won't be disappointed, for each caramel, nut, nougat, Bordeaux is all you've ever hoped to enjoy, and all yours, in that deceptively simple box.

For some of their special pieces, such as the Honeycomb, you must order by name since they are too large to fit into the regular box. The giant Bordeaux is another. They are the size of chocolate treasures, and the only thing that could tear you away from enjoying them is the Almond Crunch. They also offer a peanut butter piece, which can be had in either white coating or chocolate. It, too, is the size of an enormous candy bar, and its meltaway center is a peanut butter lover's dream. My favorite piece? It would be easier to say which isn't my favorite, but I haven't come upon one yet. If I knew how to surf or hand dip, I could stay there long enough until I found one I didn't like.

Jo's Candy Cottage
213 Manhattan Beach Blvd.
Manhattan Beach, Calif. 90266
Tel. (201) 774–7507

You can call and ask Frank or Mary to recommend an assortment; even their general assortment is exceptional. But I'd also have them ship a few of their specialty pieces, such as the Honeycomb. Letters will be promptly answered, and they'll be glad to send you a listing and prices upon request.

LOS ANGELES
Allen Wertz Candies

Chocolate, the Food of the Gods, has more natural connections with The City of the Angels than anywhere else I know. During my childhood, Saturday was movie day. Chocolate bar in hand, I would sit back and enjoy a western and a horror film (always a double bill) each week, and was thereby granted my hours of immunity from the real world. I have always been grateful to southern California for any and all their illusions, past and present.

Los Angeles is where they do it with style. A box of candy from this mecca is one you can take to the movies. It is easy to spot in a dark theatre, and Allen Wertz makes it even easier, with their gold box adorned only by their name and the weight of the contents. Inside, there is a whole cluster of enjoyment, given form and substance by chocolate. When the film begins to lag, look down, see if you can spot the piece that's in the gold fluted cup. It is filled to the edge with dark, shining chocolate. Peel off the tiny cup (quietly), bite into the best bittersweet Merckens chocolate possible. Let it flicker on your tongue as it dissolves.

The coconut is a fine counterpoint. I found the creams, however, too sweet. A trip to the water fountain is necessary after two of the creams. The one cream that is not as sugary-tasting is the lemon. A sweet coating sets off the tart, exciting center. They have done this lemon cream properly. The flavors both blend and contrast.

Their caramels are best if you are watching a heavy tragedy. The candies are of medium density and do not require too much attention. The real drama is in their nut nougat rectangles, which have an edge on the caramels. Wertz's English Toffee has a nice flair (gold foil wrapped). I wish there were more chocolate coating on the Toffee for me to sink my teeth into. The Toffee can play a nice supporting role, but the square chocolate piece with nuts inside gets star billing.

Should you happen to have a few pieces still left at the end of the movie, just take them home with you. They'll hold up for at least three more movies, or a couple of weeks, whichever comes first.

Allen Wertz Candies
3970 Los Feliz Blvd.
Los Angeles, Calif. 90039
Tel.: (213) 663–2296

Give them your most promising illusions, chocolate-covered, and let them fulfill them. Write for price list and pieces available.

BEVERLY HILLS
Edelweiss Candy Kitchen

Leading the chocolate parade is Edelweiss, a winner in every category. From presentation through the multiple pleasures of chocolate in all its forms, I wish I could present them as the major event they are.

Edelweiss deserves all the flourishes, accolades I can give them. Each box is so out of the ordinary, so beautifully packaged, if I didn't know how luscious these candies were, I'd hesitate to remove one single gem from its resting place. They are that perfect.

Pomp and circumstance come to their natural chocolate glorification when a master such as Hermann Schmid turns his Swiss chocolate training into these American beauties. He has taken the lowly snail and exalted it, made it golden, for under the clear cover an entire box of individually gold wrapped chocolate snails are curled. These molded escargots reveal a taste of milk chocolate heaven. Make it a slow dissolve of chocolate, sugar, honey, molasses, dried fruits and fruit peel, egg whites, coconut: All these marvels and more are listed as the ingredients on this box. Each looks as if it had been turned to gold by the Midas touch, and under the gold, each is exquisitely edible.

Edelweiss's chocolate candy assortment. (*Adrianne Marcus*)

Edelweiss's singular flaw is their modesty. How else could I explain their glossy red box with its unassuming title, "Chocolate Covered Fruits"? I never expected glazed Australian apricots, large as cross-sections of an apricot planet, to have individually been dipped up to their equators in Nestlé dark chocolate. Nor was I prepared for their taste, larger than fantasy, as my mouth held the tart sweetness of the dried fruit and the dissolving warm chocolate all at once.

This kind of magic permits more magic to happen. In their kitchens, an eighty-year-old dipper named Geraldine was dipping smaller apricots in chocolate. She happened to dip one first in caramel. Hence, the Geraldine was named in her honor. This smaller apricot is no less exciting than its Australian relative, but it is different. Touched with caramel, the apricot blends into a chocolate shape, hand-dipped and overwhelmingly tasty.

Edelweiss can turn a plain prune into a star. They stuff it with pecan and apricot, immerse it in chocolate, and it shines right next to its companions, the orange peel, long and lovely, and the figs, dates, and pineapples. Each one of these jewels has been given the right direction and touch, and each is flawless, even by Swiss standards.

No box Edelweiss makes is less than distinctive. Each furnishes an array of chocolate candies that must be seen and enjoyed to be believed. Ask them to be sure to send you at least a box of theirs, marked Our Unusual Marshmallows. Whatever incantation they murmured over the cooking kettle turned the marshmallow into a white cloud, then it was coaxed down onto a marble slab to be cooled and cut into shape. Various coatings surround these; and you can have your marshmallow treated to toasted coconut and chocolate, or mint truffle. They are also available in pastel coating. But the Toffeemallow is the one I would be sure to request. With this one you sink your teeth through a chocolate and English toffee coating to encounter a center of marshmallow. Its white perfection matches the lightness of the above mentioned clouds, and you, too, can gasp in pure admiration at what you've just enjoyed.

In Edelweiss's Assorted Chocolates, I discovered a lemon cream with pure ground lemon peel at its tingly center. A coffee cream-caramel softness was the next piece, and it matched the best of Belgian chocolates. Edelweiss's treatment of coconut is always superb. In one piece, which is not too sweet, coconut is mounded like pure snow captured, just barely, by a chocolate shell that comes halfway up the side of the piece.

For all the candies Edelweiss creates—nuts, clusters, chews, crunches—I have nothing but superlatives. This is quality and craft, all the way.

At the risk of being considered more a glutton than a chocolate gourmet, I still have to mention one more. Order the European Praline Assortment. Inside that box are the small dusty orbs of cocoa surrounding creamy, dense chocolate centers. Swiss Truffles are also in the box, each wonderfully rich, as the chocolate-coated circles embrace a chocolate center which is immensely flavorful. Whether your favorite turns out to be the French Cocoa Truffle, with its powdery exterior or one of the others, it really won't matter. You will have them all, and the best of all chocolate fantasies, fulfilled by Edelweiss.

Edelweiss Candy Kitchen
444 North Canon Dr.
Beverly Hills, Calif. 90212
Tel. (213) 275–0341

Ask for a list of all they make, and then you have the difficult task of trying to choose from so many great candies. The only items they won't ship are the stem cordial cherries and the chocolate-covered fresh strawberries (in season). But you can't blame them for protecting these perishables, and you can always get them if you happen to be in Beverly Hills during the right season.

CANOGA PARK
Confections by Sandra

When Sandra and Ellen Katzman approached Neiman-Marcus early in 1978 with the idea of creating a specialty candy item out of chocolate for the Neiman-Marcus catalog, they were told to come back to Dallas in May with all their finished products. A week before Ellen was scheduled to leave, Sandra had an idea: she wanted to do a Monopoly game. She asked Ellen to call up Parker Brothers and ask permission. Ellen tried to dissuade her, saying they'd never be given permission, and indeed, when she finally called the attorney for Parker Brothers, he said no. Ellen then asked him if it would be possible for them to send him a sample of what they were doing and let him decide from that whether or not to grant permission. They sent it and the day he received it in the mail, they were given the go-ahead. As a result of chocolate genius, plus ingenuity and persistence, the opening page of the 1978 Neiman-Marcus catalog featured Sandra and Ellen's creation: an entire chocolate Monopoly game, offered to the public for six hundred dollars.

When I asked Ellen how they managed to mail this extraordinary gift, Ellen replied, "Very carefully." You can see why when you see the actual pieces; even the tokens are perfect re-creations: everything is in chocolate, from Chance to Community Chest, to the entire chocolate board. The item is indeed both faithful to the game and to chocolate.

The sisters are fourth-generation Californians and they have developed their own molding process which allows them to reproduce anything, with any amount of detail, in candy. From Christmas cards to wedding announcements, personal monograms to calling cards, whatever you can think of, they can do. All done in Nestlé coating, each piece is amazingly intricate in design and execution, and tastes as good as it looks: spectacular.

Aside from the novelty items they make, they also offer a complete line of chocolate candy, from almond bark to chocolate-dipped dried fruits. I am partial to the giant pears nestled in chocolate.

They also sent me a calling card: the letter "A" in chocolate; actually the letter is as beautifully scrolled and illuminated as a parchment letter would be, but this one is on a small square of chocolate, and the raised design, the letter, is complete with the fanciest Victorian scrollwork I've ever seen.

Write and ask them what they can offer you in the way of new chocolate experiences.

Confections by Sandra
22330 Sherman Way, C-3
Canoga Park, Calif. 91303
Tel.: (213) 345–6261 or (213) 888–4947

They do accept mail orders; write and ask for a complete listing and prices, or make a suggestion as to what you'd like in chocolate and see how extravagantly they manage to fill your request.

OREGON

Van Duyn Chocolate Shops, Inc.

The knowledgeable and head candy maker, Martin K. Herrman, learned his craft in Germany many years ago, and he busily applies his knowledge gleaned from the old world in this newer setting. The basic principles of chocolate, fine ingredients and careful blending of centers with coating involve years of learning and craft. To handle chocolate properly, one always wishes for a master in the trade.

Knowing this, I looked forward to a distinctive assortment. When the box arrived, I was surprised to find the flavors and tastes of Oregon differed considerably from mine. People in Oregon seem to want more sweetness in candy and less contrast. Out of the entire box one piece came closest to matching what I hoped to find, the chocolate piece with the fruit center. There was also a very jellied oval, and I'd suggest trying this one with an after-dinner cup of coffee or tea.

What I didn't find in the other pieces was a sense that the coating was more than an encapsulating force over a center which lacked contrast. There was nothing distasteful, but neither was there anything truly memorable that made me want to go back to the box and hunt for another piece identical to the one I had just tried.

Again, this serves as a reminder that tastes differ. The folks in Oregon prefer their chocolates blander than I do. The quality of Mr. Herrman's ingredients is never in question; he uses good chocolate. But my tastes go more toward the unusual in chocolate candies, those uncommon wonders. The box I tried was a nice, sweet assortment, without very many pieces I'd consider out of the ordinary.

Van Duyn Chocolate Shops, Inc.
P.O. Box 12227
Portland, Ore. 97212
Tel.: (503) 287-1143

Kelly Westrom, the president of Van Duyn, will receive your requests at the above address and pass them along to be filled from one of their sixty candy shops.

WASHINGTON

LONG BEACH
Milton York Fine Candies
Milton York makes all of their candies by hand. Since they use no preservatives, it's best to enjoy your assortment promptly. You might

begin with their Ragged Robins, which are pecans and caramels dipped in light or dark chocolate. This particular piece has always been a favorite of candy lovers in the Northwest, and Milton York has been pleasing them for almost one hundred years.

They'll be glad to furnish a whole box of these candies, or include them as part of their regular assortment, which contains almonds and chocolate, butter toffee and other chocolate-coated pieces.

My favorite is still their Cranberry Jell which is a perfect addition to the holiday season. I don't know of any other place that makes a cranberry jelly, and these go so well at Christmas or Thanksgiving that I am sure to order them fresh just before the holidays. They're shipped by air, and they arrive here in splendid shape, and add to the festivities. My request is usually dark, rather than light chocolate, but they come both ways.

Milton York Fine Candies
Long Beach, Wash. 98631
Tel. (206) 642–2362

Write for a list of all the chocolate candies they make, and you can order from their large assortment exactly the ones which will please you. I do suggest their Cranberry Jell should be included.

TACOMA

Brown and Haley

A few miles from Tacoma's busy port, the Brown and Haley factory is equally busy, getting ready to surround their crisp buttercrunch centers with creamy milk chocolate. When that's done, they innundate them with fresh roasted California almonds, then each is individually wrapped in shiny gold foil. Down the assembly line, they are packed into place in the familiar pink container, and then it's complete: Brown and Haley Almond Roca, ready to be enjoyed.

Their motto, easily remembered, was the chant, "Brown and Haley makes 'em daily, 'cept Sunday." It used to be printed on the Smart Cards, which were cardboard inserts that came with their Mountain Bars. You can still get the candy, but not the inserts. Fred Haley, the second candy generation of the firm, had just come in from a long, invigorating walk, reminisced with me about these cards, for hardly a week goes by that someone doesn't ask about them. Just in case you never saw one, they featured a random assortment of extraneous information on one side, such as a difficult word in English, a word or phrase in French, the meanings of both, plus some fact of little known relevance such as the number of legal holidays in Tangier, as well as a geography lesson and a mathematical question. On the flip side was a joke, a cartoon, and the answer to the mathematical puzzle. Because of increasing costs, the Smart Cards were discontinued, but I miss them, although I still have a Mountain Bar now and then for old time's sake.

Candy lovers have long memories, and for them, Brown and Haley continues to make their complete assortment of boxed chocolates available, but these aren't as easily come by as their Almond Rocas, those finger-sized goodies in their familiar pink containers. I always looked forward to hearing the "whoosh," which meant I'd gotten the can open, but they tell me their new process has eliminated that sound, although the foil-wrapped candies inside are still vacuum-packed fresh. My memory must be working overtime, for I still manage to hear the sound

Brown and Haley ad.
(*Brown and Haley*)

whenever I open the container—and yes, the candies are as fresh as the day they were packed. They are always a perfect gift for a friend, or even better, for yourself, and they are available just about anywhere. Try your favorite department store that features good candy or your local drugstore. The pink container is instantly recognizable, as are the instantly enjoyable fresh crunchy Almond Roca inside.

Brown and Haley
P.O. Box 1596
Tacoma, Wash. 98401
Tel.: (206) 593–3037

Their general sales manager, Nick Herb, will be glad to advise you in case you're having any difficulty finding their products, and will let you know where you can buy their assortments, as well as their registered trademark, Almond Roca, that buttercrunch delight.

CASHMERE
Liberty Orchards
There is a quality called pride that I thought had almost vanished from America. It still exists, however, in Washington State and it still means something to the people who are happy about where they live and what they do. They are proud of their area and the candy they make, and for that reason, I am including a product that is indigenous to that area. A candy that has its slogan "The Unique Fruit Confection of the Far West."

The candy is not chocolate. But it is so special I think you should know about what Liberty Orchards makes: Aplets, Cotlets, and Grapelets. They are all made in the tiny town of Cashmere, Washington. I landed at Wenatchee, the nearest airport, where Dick Odabashian, the vice president of Liberty Orchards, met me. As we drove from Wenatchee to Cashmere, he pointed out the places I should take note of in the valley, and I heard in his voice a glowing respect for the land on which he lives and works. This is prime apple-growing country and the valley is ringed by the high reaches of the Cascade Mountains. We pass by the largest apple juice manufacturing plant in America, Treetop, then the largest apple warehouse, Blue Star. We arrive a few minutes later in Cashmere, a small town with one main street and a train station. People greet each other by name here. It's the home of Liberty Orchards.

The apple orchards of Cashmere go up the sides of the surrounding hills. The valley must have seemed exotic to the two Armenian friends, Mr. Tertsagian and Mr. Balaban, when they arrived here in 1916 and saw this same valley in full apple blossom display. They decided to live here, and tried any number of things to make a living in this, their new home. A restaurant did not work out. The apple orchard they bought and named Liberty Orchards to show their faith and belief in America did not produce quite as much as they had hoped. But they continued to believe. In this valley. In this promised land. Something would happen, and something did.

They made candy for friends. Called Lacoom in Armenia, and Turkish Delight in other places, the candy was a way to utilize all those apples. They cooked the apples into a thick pectin, added walnuts. And from one small kitchen, one large dream, a whole industry began. Aplets and Cotlets became the product they made.

It might have remained a small local industry had not the pride I mentioned earlier come into the story. As each box of candy was packed, a slip was added to the box which informed the consumer if this unique product of the Northwest was enjoyable, they should also try Brown and Haley, another unique product of the region. When Mr. Haley found out about this, he was surprised and delighted. From then on, Brown and Haley made Aplets and Cotlets available to their customers also. Washington State is that kind of place. People helping one another.

Now, over half a century later, the product, very much like the area out of which it comes, has not changed all that much. The package is different, but the candy and the pride with which it is made remain stable. The original Aplets and Cotlets have been joined by a newer candy, invented for the Spokane World's Fair, called Grapelets.

Some employees have been with Liberty Orchards for more than thirty-five years. As I walked through the factory, they took the time to show me the huge kettles where the apples are simmered. The smell of apples is everywhere. Here are the tables on which the huge slabs of candy are separated, made into smaller pieces. At peak periods, over nine thousand pounds a day are made.

The candy is now shipped all over the world, thanks to a new package invented by the firm that extends its shelf life of the candy for up to nine months—without the addition of a single preservative. Major department stores such as Bloomingdales carry their products.

Once Aplets, Cotlets, and Grapelets were available only in the Pacific

Northwest. I can remember back in the olden days, buying and sending these candies back East. I wanted my friends and relatives to have a chance to taste something I felt was unique to the West, and a candy I had never found anywhere else.

And when I came to Cashmere, to the place that's known as the Vale of Cashmere, and saw the Columbia River as it winds through the valley, the apples hanging full on the trees, and above all of that, the peaks of the Cascade Range, I knew that my original intention had been correct. The candy would have to be as special and spectacular as the place, for it has to match the region. So each time you open a box, just below the lightly dusted sugar surface, taste all of those tangy apples and walnuts locked together, and enjoy what I do: a small taste of Washington pride in each box.

Liberty Orchards
Cashmere, Wash. 96815
Tel.: (509) 782–2422

If you can't find these at your favorite department store, do write and ask Dick Odabashian to send you a price list. It's unique and tasty, and you can think of it as your chocolate bonus, one more proof of how unselfish chocolate lovers are, to want all the best a region can offer.

CANADA

ONTARIO
Laura Secord Candy Shops

My box of Canadian candy arrived while I was in Italy. By the time I returned home to enjoy it, the virtue of freshness by which a box should be judged had passed. This is not bad news. For it tells me something about Laura Secord candies which I like: they will not keep. This means they are made and sold fresh and should be enjoyed that way. So I have to beg off judgment on these, since neither the candies nor I were at fault, just a missed connection.

I can tell you a few things about them, however, which might be of interest. You can make your own judgment from the facts. Their shops in Canada were the prototypes for our own three major candy chains: See's, Fannie May, and most directly, Fanny Farmer. Frank O'Connor, who started Fanny Farmer, was the same man who started Laura Secord. The black and white shops that we think of as the trademark of each of these firms were his idea to begin with, in Canada.

The range of candies Laura Secord produces is about equivalent to any of those marketed in America: chocolate-covered caramels, crisps, toffees, chips, creams, and fudge, to name a few. Their buttercreams are closest to our water-fondant-based ones, with fresh butter added. They do seem to use a bit more food coloring in their centers than I have seen in ours, but they maintain as tight a control over quality and freshness, I've been assured, as any products produced in the chocolate candy market.

With over 225 stores in Canada, Laura Secord candies are available in almost every town. If my previous experiences with Canadian candies are correct, I suspect you will find them a bit sweeter than some of ours, for Canadian tastes are inherited from English candy tastes, and verge more toward the sweet than bittersweet side of the candy counter.

As I said, they are readily available in most places in Canada, and I am sure they will be glad to ship you whatever you wish to import.

Laura Secord
Laura Secord Walk
P.O. Box 1812, Station "D"
Scarborough, Ont.
Tel. (416) 751–0500

Do write and ask them the various assortments they offer; they'll respond promptly with a mailing list and prices.

BRITISH COLUMBIA
Echo Chocolate Boutique

Georges Huwyler began making his chocolates as a sideline, since his job at that time was both impressive and demanding: he was the pastry chef at the famous Harrison Hotel. He modestly describes what happened as he made his chocolates available: "Since the chocolates went well, I opened my own store, started to make also some nice cakes and French pastries, and built up a nice little shop. Of course, I long ago quit my job at the hotel."

He is being much too modest, for having tasted his chocolates, I'm sure there is more than a ready market for them. Some may be born to chocolate; others may have chocolate thrust upon them; but Georges occupies a category all his own: He was born to make these chocolates and share them with all of us.

He does it so well and with such good humor. Take those little chocolate candies he calls Sasquatch-Kisses, after that elusive creature who hangs around the backwoods, scaring tourists right out of their Winnebagos. We call him Bigfoot in California. No matter what the creature is called, it would take only one of these Sasquatch-Kisses to convert the hardiest disbeliever, and a whole box of them could bring the Abominable Snowman down from the Himalayas to join the search party. Georges takes the finest Belgian chocolate coating Callebaut ships him, brings a center of whipped chocolate to meet it, and creates mound after mound of chocolate texture, flavor, and freshness. They melt away in a superb example of creamy indulgence.

His B.C. Truffles are a bit different from their Swiss cousins, but no less gloriously rich. Other chocolates show he is equally adept at adding nuts in just the right amount, and there is a princely souvenir chocolate wafer that he has directed with a printed marzipan label. Of course, one of these lovelies features Sasquatch as its portrait.

I wish I could share with you all the cakes and pastries he makes, but I haven't tried those as yet. If they are anything like the chocolate candies he produces, they would be reason enough to visit Harrison Hot Springs. I do plan on that, and when I get there, it won't be to take slides of the Canadian sunsets, as spectacular as they are, but to visit Georges's boutique. I need a firsthand view on how chocolates such as his are made. After the samples I enjoyed, I can't see how anyone traveling near there could possibly miss a trip to his shop: It's the kind of scenery chocolate lovers will go miles out of their way to see.

Echo Chocolate Boutique
P.O. Box 231
Harrison Hot Springs, B. C.
Tel.: (604) 796–9256

He'll mail all of his chocolate candies, except during the summer months; just write and ask for a price list and selection. Don't forget to order at least a box of the Sasquatch-Kisses.

UTAH

Cummings Studio Candies

Still dazzled by the blinding white salt beds of western Utah, I can't drive into the city of Salt Lake without remembering how I first came upon it, years ago, when I approached it from the east. As I drove down the eastern reaches of the Wasatch, I suddenly saw below me an incredibly white city, gleaming and shimmering in the distant clear air like a pure vision. There was that moment when I first knew what Brigham Young meant when he stood looking at this same valley and announced, "This is the place."

Salt Lake City is the place. The home of the finest chocolate candies in the Beehive State, Salt Lake City can boast that it has the best you will find anywhere. The people who live here already know this. They consume more candy per person than people anywhere else in the United States. They have a lot of reasons to do so.

Paul Cummings is one of the reasons. He makes candies. That's equivalent to saying Vladimir Horowitz plays the piano. Or Beverly Sills sings. It's an understatement. Cummings' reputation is all art, and he could rest on his performance with just one single piece of candy, his Three-Color Opera Cream. He begins with the finest chocolate, which is made only for him by Merckens, the chocolate people of Nabisco. This chocolate, made to his specific recipe, is very, very special, for its lavish taste has the smallest hint of exotic smokiness to it. The center of his three-color cream is hand-dipped to produce a chocolate candy of such extraordinary taste I could praise it with every superlative I know and still not match it. It's smooth as silk, with its mingled center of chocolate, berry, and vanilla rippling through under the thick chocolate coating.

In the back of his shop, two women sit and hand-dip his candy centers. Paul creates the centers, but the women dip them. At one time, hand-dippers, women, were considered the queens of the trade. They served long apprenticeships, learning on the cheapest centers before they were allowed to dip the finest ones in chocolate. Today, there are only a few hand-dippers left, and this is still a woman's field.

Hand-dipping is an art that takes years of practice to perform as quickly and beautifully as these women do. They prepare tray after tray of

Hand-dipping chocolates at Cummings Studio Candies. *(Adrianne Marcus)*

perfect chocolate candies, with hardly a drop of chocolate wasted. Each motion is gracefully executed, as a woman scoops up chocolate from the heated basin in front of her and kneads it until it reaches just the correct temperature, which she knows by touch. When it is cool enough to hold the right shape, she will quickly place a center into the middle of the chocolate mass, spinning the center over to coat it thoroughly. Then, with one swift motion, she will draw her finger up to mark each piece with its proper initial, or "string," as it's called, the design on the top that indicates the flavor of the particular piece she is dipping. This is the way one can tell what pleasure lurks under the surface—for example, the fluting, scripted "L" stands for lemon; and the raised "O" is for orange. Each piece is designated with its particular identifying mark.

Choosing one marked "L," I discover a perfect lemon cream. The tartness of the lemon merges with the cream, and the chocolate that embraces both creates a mutual fusion of good taste.

Paul's Truffles, which cannot be shipped because they are too delicate, are very close to the fabled Swiss version by the same name. Every piece he makes can be best described by one adjective—glorious. I include them all in that word. His confections are as lavish as they are large, and their size is an indication of how very special each is. Hand-made, hand-crafted, under the chocolate surface of each is the sweet craft of the candy maker at his finest. I cannot think of one you shouldn't have in triplicate. Starting with his Three-Color Opera Cream to any and all that he makes, each perfect pleasure bears repeating, and all of it in glorious chocolate.

Cummings Studio Candies
679 East Ninth South St.
Salt Lake City, Utah 84105
Tel. (801) 328–4858

He can't ship these during the summer months since the weather is too hot to guarantee their safe arrival, but during the rest of the year, they're all available, with the exception of the Truffles. When the temperature drops below 65 degrees, you should rush to your telephone or typewriter and order as many as you can.

Mrs. J. G. McDonald's Chocolate Company

At the very beginning stage of *The Chocolate Bible*, I was fortunate enough to meet the late L. Russell Cook, who wrote what many consider the essential book on chocolate production and use for the chocolate industry. His enthusiasm for my book manifested itself in his continued patience as he offered his help in explaining technical problems to me, and in sending me to others in the industry so I could understand exactly the way chocolate was made. His wife, VernaLee Cook, also contributed to this book in quite another way, for it was through her that I found out about McDonald's All Nut Chocolate Assortment. She sent me a box, saying it was one of her favorites, and it's thanks to her good taste that I can share it with you.

For four generations, Mrs. J. G. McDonald's Chocolate Company has been a family affair; it began April 12, 1862, and they've been making chocolate candies even since then. Mr. McDonald was one of the industry's more flamboyant candy manufacturers. In the early 1920s, he entered certain boxes of his candy into world competition, and they managed to win thirteen ribbon medals and forty-four solid gold ones. This was during the time candy manufacturers made their own chocolate coatings, as well as centers. In time this changed, and it became more expedient to buy the coatings for the centers. Today, their own special blends are still made for them, and arrive in tank cars, already melted, ready to be pumped into one or more of the huge liquid chocolate holding tanks which can contain as much as sixty-five thousand pounds of coating per tank.

Ambrosia and Boldemann's make the coatings McDonald's uses, and each makes theirs according to very exact specifications. Unlike most commercially produced chocolate candies, which have a thin coating of chocolate over their centers, McDonald's applies their chocolate lavishly over each piece. When you bite into a Brazil nut, you'll sink through a good quarter-inch of savory chocolate first.

I find McDonald's standard assortment of chocolate candies fairly ordinary, with the cream centers lacking much distinction, so I can't heartily recommend these as the best. But I can recommend their All Nut assortment, and I do. The peanut clusters contain enough peanuts to gladden the heart of a Georgia farmer, and the almonds, filberts, pecans, and walnuts are a virtual fall harvest of good taste and come in both light and dark chocolate coating.

My thanks to VernaLee Cook for sending me a box of chocolate covered nuts. I wasn't aware of this fine assortment, but I am now, and I suspect a great many other chocolate lovers will be more than happy to know about them.

Mrs. J. G. McDonald's Chocolate Company
2250 South Third East
Salt Lake City, Utah 84115
Tel. (801) 487–3201

Mrs. Thelma Lu White is the kind lady to whom you should write and ask prices and availability of various assortments. Since the box I enjoyed was mailed to me, I assume they'll be glad to make them available to others. They are available at any Gemco Department Store, should you happen to be near one, and I do strongly suggest you not pass up the All Nut selection.

VaLora's

VaLora's is quite a special place; it's small enough to assure personal attention to details, and just large enough to make great use of the fine products that arrive daily from the surrounding communities such as Cache Valley. After all, the dairy products for which Utah is justifiably famous are right at hand.

If you're lucky enough to get there at lunchtime, do. You've got a treat in store—Annie's homemade scones. They are delivered hot, tucked with butter, honey drizzled on the top. Each bite will confound you: the scones are a cross between a doughnut and puff paste. Once you've tasted one, you know the candy can't be less than remarkable.

Since I already started with the scones, let me go on to another gem that isn't chocolate, but worth a second piece anyhow. Alison Schanz, the owner, calls this one Pecan Log, and it doesn't appear to be all that unusual, since it looks just like its name: plump pecans on the top, a rich caramel holding them all in place, and inside, a fluffy moist divinity center. At least I thought it was divinity, until Alison said, "I'm really glad you like that. It's got forty percent of the sugar replaced by Swiss whey powder. I get it from a cheese company over in Logan, Utah."

I liked it even better when I heard that, so I brought one along to enjoy later. It's one of the ways small places manage to experiment and produce items with an inventiveness many of the larger companies can't afford. Alison is always open to new ideas and methods, and the Pecan Log is the result of one of those ideas. It's good, even if it isn't chocolate.

The Mint Squares *are* chocolate, and as Alison said, "One of the meanest pieces of candy to make." After watching them being made, I know why she says that. Salt Lake City is hot in summer, and in the cool back of her shop, where the candy is made, everything has to be in complete readiness for a batch of these to be created. An initial layer of chocolate is quickly spread as thinly as possible over an area as large as possible. It's allowed to cool just so long (each time the situation varies according to weather and temperature) before a mixture of pastel coating and mint is spread over the initial layer. That also has to be applied as thin as possible. When the two layers reach just the correct temperature, a final blanket of chocolate is poured on and spread rapidly. If it is all done correctly, at every stage, it is then cut into Mint Squares: a sandwich of mint between two layers of chocolate.

To do all of this requires speed, dexterity, and a fairly good idea of how your chocolate is going to set up. Misjudge, even by seconds, and what you get is not Mint Squares, but an unusable mess. They did it right.

All of the chocolate candies VaLora's makes are handmade and/or hand-dipped. No preservatives nor additives. As such, the shelf life is limited: buy and eat them fresh. What I'd recommend, if you can manage it, is to get to Salt Lake City. That way you can have her fine chocolates and Annie's outrageous scones.

VaLora's has three locations in Salt Lake City.
Main one: 2121 East 2100 South Salt Lake City, Utah 84109
Tel.: (801) 484-2532
Others: 7070 South State
        2001 West 3500 South

Mail orders will be accepted and shipped promptly, except during the summer, when it's really too hot in Salt Lake City to guarantee anything other than hot fudge arriving, no matter what's shipped.

Maxfield's Candy Company

For thirty years, Maxfield's has been a source of great pleasure to those in the Salt Lake area. I have friends there, and two of them told me how great these chocolate candies are. They also told me that Maxfield's made these great Logs—pecan, cashew, fudge, and assorted nut. The box I got didn't contain Logs, so I can't really tell you what they are like, but I can judge those items I did receive, which were chocolate-covered candies.

Perhaps I could judge my friends' tastes as well, for you really have to love sugar to love these. The assortment I tried was beyond mere sweet. There were pieces that had a sugar content high enough to serve as the model for the entire sugar industry. As such, I couldn't get through to the centers and find out what was beneath, beyond and above all the chocolate. What I discovered was the truth in the statement "a real sweet tooth." These are for those people. And the pieces I tried will answer their sweetest desires and then some.

Maxfield's Candy Company
1050 South 200 West, or
P.O. Box 554
Salt Lake City, Utah 84110
Tel.: (801) 355–5321

When the weather permits, these can be ordered and shipped to you. Write for prices and pieces available.

C. Kay Cummings Candies

Hand-dipped chocolates display a signature letter on the top of each piece. Not only as a decorative design, the signature indicates the flavor of the center hidden beneath. I was feeling quite confident when C. Kay Cummings held one of his beautiful chocolate candies out to me and asked if I knew which flavor this one was. I glanced at the top, which featured one perfect "L," scriped and flowing, and didn't hesitate as I answered, "Lemon cream."

Give me a few points for being half right. He gets 100 plus for being totally right with his Lemon Pecan. Chunks of pecans suspended in the thick center of a lemon cream, this piece is so lovely, so large, it takes three good bites to devour it all. Kay likes to make these large-centered pieces, he says, "You can get more chocolate around a big piece." I agree: Not only is each center superb, but the chocolate that encompasses it is as rich and smooth as a summer night's breeze in Salt Lake City.

Chocolate reaches its divine height with such pieces as the ones he calls Fuzzies, dusted with cocoa on the outside, containing buttercream and pecans inside. They look like tiny balls of earth: I can't imagine anything more sensual than plunging my hands into a whole box of them.

Chocolate liqueur is added to his smooth fudge; it gives it that deep, dark, rich taste that true chocolate lovers crave. And, of course, the pecans are there, right along with the chocolate. No one does a better job with pecans than he does and in more ways. There's the Rum Pecan and the Maple Pecan, any and all of which bring the rich blendings of his centers into counterpoint with the thick chocolate he uses to coat each and every delicious morsel. Kay makes a full range of candies in both light and dark chocolate. About the time I thought I had hit all the high points he makes, I encountered his Imperial, a vanilla pecan piece that zooms right off the point-counterpoint chart.

Two dippers work in the back room, coating Kay's centers, and they turn out these small works of art. They've been doing this work for years and their craft is exquisitely evident. This hand-dipping allows for a thicker coating of chocolate than most machines permit, and the flowing chocolate letter that tops each piece is a promise of all that lies rich and lurking beneath.

Aside from all those pecans, he makes a cream piece that contains black walnuts. It's a totally different taste, with a bite to it that's denied

C. Kay Cummings gift box. *(Warren Marcus)*

pecans. The walnuts add a sharper contrast to the smooth center. But I wouldn't pass up any of the pieces, from the subtlest to the most overt, each and every one is luscious.

People around Salt Lake City think of Kay Cummings' as "their" candy store. It's a compliment to him that they are also willing to suggest combinations they'd like to see made, and he's willing to listen and try some of their good ideas. He creates new flavors and combinations, while maintaining the old favorites. It's a very special candy store and one you should try. If you can't get to Salt Lake, he'll ship an assortment to you in his special mailing package, which he's developed. He's shipped me two so far, and every piece has arrived in the shape it ought to, suspended, coated, robed in rich chocolate, a wealth of treasures right down to the last lovely bite.

C. Kay Cummings Candies
1134 Herbert Ave.
Salt Lake City, Utah 84105
Tel. (801) 487–1031

Not only will he accept mail orders (except in the summer months), he'll package and send it to you to arrive in perfect shape. Write and ask for a price list and all of the chocolate candies he offers.

COLORADO

DENVER
Stephany's Candies, Inc.

With two stores at the Denver airport, Stephany's is as good a reason to change planes in Denver as any I've found. Be sure to land there during the day, since most of the airport shops close at nightfall. There's nothing

Stephany's Piece of the Block. (*Warren Marcus*)

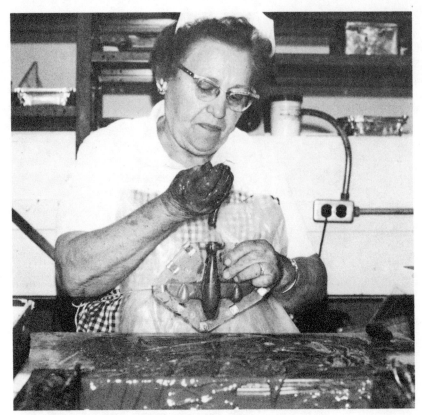

Dipper filling airplane mold at Stephany's. *(Warren Marcus)*

worse than standing with your nose pressed against the window of the shop, while just beyond reach all sorts of marvelous chocolate items are displayed.

It was the ten-pound chocolate bar wrapped in cellophane and appropriately beribboned that caught my eye. If the shop hadn't been closed, I'd have ended up bringing back ninety pounds of chocolate. If you've forgotten someone at home, in the way of a gift, this one would do nicely. It would also prove to be the conversation piece of your journey.

About a week after I stood in front of the closed shop, I returned to Denver, and this time I visited Stephany's, and the owner, John Poulos. He showed me around, and I could hardly resist his novelty items, such as his baseballs, tennis balls, or the solid chocolate piece which resembles a certain insurance company's trademark and is named "A Piece of the Block." Since I couldn't resist them, I didn't. He also makes a novelty item for the skier on your list; it's a chocolate ski boot (in miniature of course).

Although I'm not the world's greatest mint fancier, I was delighted with his thin Denver Mint. Stephany's has made quite a reputation on this piece alone, and I can see why: The mint doesn't override the taste of the chocolate, and it is neatly sandwiched between either light or dark chocolate so that its pale green center blends in perfectly, both in color and flavor. My mouth was aware of, rather than overcome by, the refreshing aftertaste of both chocolate and mint.

Speaking of aftertaste, try their fudge. The addition of chocolate liquor, which is the unsweetened chocolate mass, gives the finished product a deep, rich flavor. It takes at least five minutes for that velvet memory of chocolate, chocolate and more chocolate to wear off. By then, you're back, having a bit more.

With two shops in the airport, at two different locations, you can't really miss. Each one is bright and enticing, and both offer a full range of chocolate candies, from the boxed assortment, which is a splendid way to try the range of pieces he makes, to the specialty items. He makes them all, from the centers with fluffy marshmallow, to the dense rich chocolate fudge, and it's all ready to go.

What better way to travel than with chocolate? And what gift is more welcome than the one you pick out and present to the lucky chocolate recipient?

Stephany's Candies, Inc.
Denver Airport
Denver, Colo. 80207, or
3885 Newport St.
Denver
Tel.: (303) 355–1552

Mail orders are accepted when the weather permits safe shipping of chocolates. Write to them at the Newport Street address (which is the factory) for a price list and range of chocolate items.

Bernice's Fine Candies

Just a half-block off East Colfax Avenue, on a quiet side street in Denver, a small candy store caters to its customers' tastes, which do not follow the national trend toward lighter, milkier chocolate. Bernice's customers know what they want, and she knows exactly what makes them happy as she places another order for chocolate coating to be delivered from Nestlé in her usual proportion: two-thirds dark, one-third light milk chocolate.

"My customers want everything dark. Their preference is for chewy centers, anything crisp and crunchy," she says, and shows me her file cards on which she keeps customers' preferences handy. During the time I am there, the phone does not stop ringing. The calls are for particular assortments, already noted, so the callers identify themselves, and by the time they get there to pick up their assortments, Bernice has already filled out their order, thanks to her filing cards.

For twenty-four years, Bernice has had this shop. She doesn't just oversee it, she handles any and all of it, from the front counter, the telephone, all the way back to the dipping room. Whatever needs doing, she does it. That includes hand-dipping her own centers. After all, she began in this business when she was thirteen years old, at the side of an established candy maker in Denver.

"Take my Ting-a-Ling," she instructs me, holding out her piece of candy that consists of her own mixture—ground nuts, molasses chips, bits of honeycomb, rice crispies, all covered with chocolate. "What does *that* remind you of?" she insists. My mouth is too full to answer, so she answers for me. "Tastes a bit like a Crunch Bar, doesn't it?" I nod rapidly, remembering it is not polite to talk with your mouth full.

"I guess what we're really known for are our Truffles, we make all kinds of them: chocolate, mint, mocha, champagne, rum"—she pauses to catch her breath— "but the weather's been too hot and I don't have any here for you to try. So try this: I just made it." Before I can stop nodding, I'm mouth deep in marshmallow, which has just been dipped in caramel and nuts before it was coated in chocolate. I can't even say thank you before she's already motioning for me to join her in the back room, where a tray of centers waits to be dipped.

Watching Bernice work is a lot like trying to observe light in motion. Her velocity exceeds what the eye can see. Her quick hand whirls center after center into the chocolate mass, then flawlessly marks the design. It's all created by one swift motion of her fingers. It looks so effortless. I know perfectly well it isn't. Having attempted to hand-dip chocolates, I managed to produce pieces that could be labeled hand-dropped more than hand-dipped. Yet each piece Bernice does comes out swift and clean, from content to beautiful design on top.

What more can I say except voilà! Bernice's shop may be the place where the national trend stops, and if Bernice has anything to do about it, who knows, there is already a wave of dark chocolate, cresting, directed by her fast and determined hand.

Bernice's Fine Candies
1510 Locust St.
Denver, Colo. 80220
Tel.: (303) 388–3375

Write or call and she'll put your name in her files along with your favorite assortment. Her chocolates cannot be shipped during the summer.

Hammond's Candies

Most people in the Denver area have probably eaten Hammond's Candies for years without knowing them by that name, for the firm does a great deal of its business by wholesaling candies to department stores and other specialty shops. The chocolate candies they produce aren't unique, since they attempt to cover the widest spectrum of taste rather than cater to a very distinct market of discriminating chocolate buyers. Their milk chocolates are uniformly sweet. Even the darker ones lack a sense of definition that comes from a distinctive center that resists being overwhelmed by its coating. They aren't really terrible, but they aren't really that good, either.

I would be tempted to bypass the whole issue if it weren't for two items that Tom Hammond makes. These *are* unique and well worth buying. Years ago there used to be a candy store in Denver called Bauer's that made candies called Crystal Cuts. These small jewels came in a great many flavors—root beer, licorice, cherry, lemon, lime, and cinnamon, among others. I thought them lost, since the firm went out of business, but I was wrong. Hammond's continues to make them to the same recipe, and they are literally gems, hard candies of sparkling taste.

Hammond's has the corner on hard candies and not just for the Crystal Cuts. They produce those delightful Christmas sweets that have flowers or scenes embedded in their tiny centers. Hammond's assortment of designs and colors captures the sweet heart and eye of any child, and certainly the child in me. I respond completely to these tiny three- and four-color Cut Rocks with their patterns running through the centers. It's difficult to describe what Tom Hammond makes, but there, in the space of a circle no more than one-half inch across is a perfect, miniature Santa Claus. Or a house. Or a tree. He also makes large ribbon candies, and this factory in Denver is one of the last places that produces such intricate, special items, for they are hard to do, fragile to ship, and not mass-produced.

Since it is the handmade nature of this art which assures us of these rare treats, I hope this link to the past will not be broken. Last Christmas it was almost impossible to obtain anything more than lollipops with innocuous pictures forming their centers, and as for ribbon candy, well, I was told the candy maker who used to make it in California had died, and so there wasn't any. Hammond's is busy creating these items, and it is the only place in the world that makes those beautiful Crystal Cuts, a hard candy worth having. For that reason and the Cut Rocks, if not for the chocolates, I think Hammond's deserves to be noticed. After all, candy is an art that can take many forms.

Hammond's Candies
2550 W. 29th Ave.
Denver, Colo. 80211
Tel.: (303) 455–2320

I'd suggest writing Tom Hammond and asking if it's possible for him to ship these delights to you for the holidays. But order at least a month or more before Christmas to ensure your delivery of these brilliant treats.

MINNESOTA

BURNSVILLE
Abdallah's Candies

It was midnight in Burnsville, and there, in the icy Minnesota night, they huddled together for warmth, trapped as they were in the chocolate factory, one bare electric bulb beginning to flicker above them, threatening to go out. They would be plunged into entire darkness should it fail; the cold would seep in, for it had been snowing for a solid (as opposed to a liquid) week, and the drifts were so high it was impossible to escape. Even to nearby Minneapolis.

"What shall we do to keep warm?" one asked anxiously. "Let's make Oriental Mints," came the answer.

That's precisely the kind of fantasy Abdallah's Oriental Mints creates in my mind, as I look at their box. It displays two palm trees in mingled shades of orange and green which loom ominously in the foreground. Behind them appears to be some Oriental version of Howard Johnson's, done in these same shades, its domed curves squatting in a typical roadside attraction as if waiting to be come upon by the hapless traveler. Something must have possessed the folks in Minnesota who designed this strange box, but thankfully it didn't possess the mints, which maintain their rectangular and chocolate purity inside. They're good mints, fine meltaway mints, but it might take you a moment to try them, given the nature of the box.

Less exotic, at first appearance, is their next box—on a white background three yellow roses and one bud form the decor. That's fine, until I look on the side and discover what this assortment is called: Nut Kracker Sweets. What's going on up there in those blizzards? Really, this one deserves a better name. So, ignoring the humor, I decide to concentrate on what's inside. There are walnuts and filberts, Brazil nuts, cashews, and pecans, all pure and freshly coated with chocolate. I thoroughly admire the sweet cream and sweet cream butter used in creating their other pieces, but the nuts with their simple lavishment of chocolate are undoubtedly my favorites. The only adjectives I can use to describe them are snappy and crunchy. (That's the sound of two teeth enjoying.)

For those who prefer an extraordinarily sweet cream center coated with chocolate, Abdallah's makes a vanilla cream that lasts up to three months. These are a bit sweet for my taste, but the regular assortment is a good compromise, since it has some of everything for everybody. If I'm not taken by the creams, another would find them just right. Their English Toffee rectangles win my applause. They come wrapped in their own cellophane packages, two to each.

The people at Abdallah's have been making these chocolate candies for three generations, and the lucky folks around the Twin Cities have been buying and enjoying them as fast as they are made. Considering the cream marshmallow with pecans both unusual and spotlessly good, I can understand how they've done so well. Don't let the unusual packaging deter you. These candies are sweet jewels, and yours for the asking.

Abdallah's Candies
12220 12th Ave. S., or
P.O. Box 1126
Burnsville, Minn. 55367
Tel.: (612) 890–4470

They'll gladly mail-order if you specify what you desire from the various assortments they create—Almond Bark, Candle Light Creams—Butter Creams, Home Assortments, Nut Kracker Sweets, Milk Chocolates—Miniatures, Deluxe Assortment, Oriental Mints, or special pieces you want packed. Write or phone for their complete price list.

ST. PAUL

Regina's Candies

Two pieces Regina's Candies make deserve special attention. Their apricot fruit piece, half coated in chocolate, is a winner, as is their English Toffee, which is thick and crunchy, coated in fine chocolate, and then overwhelmed with fresh nuts. One of these could hold me for an entire evening, and two are sheer, delightful gluttony.

The assortment I enjoyed was their fruit and nuts. In both light and dark chocolate. The light chocolate is pleasant, but the dark is always my favorite, in any piece, since I feel it sets the centers off to best advantage.

Around holiday time, Regina's makes ribbon candy—large, multi-colored rainbows. Since they make these by hand, and the work involved in creating these fantasies of color is fast becoming a lost art, I'd suggest the ones they make should be on everyone's list. The colors shimmer in delicate sugary hues, and a box of them would be a visual as well as a gastronomic extravaganza. I am not sure if they ship them, since ribbon candy is incredibly fragile, but you can write to ask. With careful packing, they would be a touch of old-fashioned sweetness to grace any holiday.

Regina's Candies
248 S. Cleveland Ave.
St. Paul, Minn. 55105
Tel.: (623) 698–8603

You can mail-order their candies and they will be glad to ship you your favorites. Do ask them if they can ship their marvelous ribbon candies.

WISCONSIN

MILWAUKEE
Ambrosia Chocolate Company

What would you do with 150 pounds of chocolate? If you lived in Milwaukee County, that is the yearly amount Ambrosia Chocolate Company could supply every man, woman, and child who lives in their area. And they don't even make a candy bar. Ambrosia is not in the candy business; they are in the chocolate manufacturing business. The name Ambrosia was chosen by Mr. Otto Schoenleber to reflect how he felt about his product. Chocolate is the Food of the Gods; it is ambrosial. Mr. Schoenleber's company began business in May 1894 at the same Fifth Street location in Milwaukee that had previously housed his other business venture, office furniture.

In Ambrosia's early history, chocolate bars and other consumer-oriented treats like breakfast cocoa, semisweet chocolate nuggets, and Chocolate Logs were made. The public could buy this candy bar, which Ambrosia advertised as a "wonderful, mellow, honey-combed chocolate bar." There were also sweet chocolate cigars for consumers and, as business grew, so did the company and their chocolate products.

By 1916, what had started as a small venture was now large enough to warrant incorporation. In 1927 the daughter of the founder became the new president of Ambrosia. Under Miss Schoenleber's enthusiastic and firm leadership, Ambrosia survived the Depression and kept right on building. A new three-story plant and office building were added. Then, in 1953, L. Russell Cook took over as Ambrosia's third president, and brought his knowledge as a food chemist to the manufacturing business facets of the plant. Their laboratory facilities grew, and quality control became a key method, along with increased production. Cook would assure the consumer first-rate chocolate with each and every batch. The factory continued to expand: by 1926, three to six more floors had to be interlocked with the existing buildings.

There were huge silos for cocoa bean storage adjacent to the factory, plus additional space for holding tanks to store the liquid coating shipments. By now Ambrosia chocolate and cocoa products were being shipped in their company fleet of trailer trucks and stainless steel tank wagons. By the time the firm merged with W. R. Grace and Company, to become an international company, Ambrosia was one of the five largest chocolate manufacturers in America, supplying industrial bakers and users of chocolate. No more candy bars. Just chocolate in bulk. Mr. Cook remained as president of the chocolate and confectionary division of the Grace Company. Ambrosia's new president, Mr. Jarrold Tellier, brought his knowledge of food chemistry and chocolate manufacturing to the firm. The pattern stayed the same: growth and continued emphasis on quality coatings and cocoa.

As we now know, Ambrosia is not a candy company—it manufactures chocolate. Bulk chocolate is molded into ten-pound cakes, and liquid chocolate is poured, twenty-three tons at a time, into waiting tank trucks. You have had their product, anyway. Such items as Hostess Cupcakes, Dolly Madison Cupcakes, Heath Bars, and Eskimo Pies all use Ambrosia chocolate. Each of the three dozen different formulations Ambrosia makes is designed for a specific chocolate purpose. Some does become candies. Ambrosia supplies, for example, places such as Marshall Field's, which then makes Frangoes out of the chocolate. This meltaway chocolate rectangle comes in various flavors, such as mint and rum, and is available at better department stores all over America.

Stuckey's, in Eastman, Georgia, buys Ambrosia coating for their candies, as does Price's in Milwaukee. From the Deep South to the Midwest, East and the Far West, Ambrosia covers a great spectrum of the candy market.

One product they do make, Tixies, is not available to the general public, since they only produce a limited amount for special promotions and holiday giveaways. Having enjoyed Tixies, I cannot keep it a secret. The candy is a very special blend of light milk chocolate and dark, to which they have added four different kinds of nuts. Filberts, almonds, cashews, and Brazils in every bite make Tixies so good one wants to qualify as a special friend of the firm just to have a small bar or two when they make it available.

Ninety percent of Ambrosia's production is devoted to milk chocolate. This leaves only 10 percent for lovers of dark, but they do make a fondant type of chocolate coating worth savoring. They are one of the few firms that still produces this type of chocolate, since fondant requires very special care in both roasting and conching procedures. Ambrosia's fondant is the closest to the European taste in chocolate, which many of us prize.

Ambrosia's Food of the Gods is aptly named. From cocoa, which bakers buy, to coating, used by candy makers, any time you have Ambrosia, it is the right time.

Ambrosia Chocolate Company
Division of W. R. Grace and Company
1133 North Fifth St.
Milwaukee, Wis. 53203
Tel.: (414) 241–8572

Mr. Gene Hollenberger is the vice president and the man to whom my chocolate queries were directed. If enough of us wrote, perhaps we could convince Ambrosia to market Tixies for all chocolate lovers.

ILLINOIS

CHICAGO

Fannie May Candy Shops, Inc.

As long as I'm changing time zones—candy-time, that is—let's go back to 1920, when a man named H. Teller Archibald is busy making candy in his small shop on LaSalle Street in Chicago. He makes it in the back of the shop, and as fast as he can produce it, he sells it right out front. So he opens more shops, and these do well. It's almost as if everything he touches turns to success, and in the giddiness of the Twenties, what isn't possible? When 1929 arrives, and with it the stock market crash, his whole world begins to fall apart. He loses almost everything. His marriage fails.

But in the early 1930s, he gets another chance, another marriage. With his new young wife, he feels a sense of beginnings. He hires another young man, Harry H. Simpson, to help him in business, and this works. Just as everything is going as it should, tragedy strikes. In 1935, Archibald dies unexpectedly, leaving a new business and a new young wife as heir.

And that is how Harry H. Simpson stepped into the vacancy created by this loss to give Fannie May the direction it needed. His candy business thrived and built up a reputation for quality, freshness, and good taste that is maintained to this day. In 1969, Simpson handed over the presidency to the man who runs the company today, Denton Thorne. Having worked for Fannie May since 1947, Denton Thorne is no stranger to the Fannie May Candy Company. Every department, from kitchen, retail stores to accounting is familiar to him. He has worked in all of them. If Fannie May is synonymous with good fresh chocolate candies in the minds of many Midwestern customers who have never had a piece of Fannie May that wasn't fresh and top quality, part of the credit has to be given to this man who continues to make sure nothing is sacrificed to maintain the highest standards.

Freshness is assured through "control production," a process of daily inventory. On this basis, the company knows which pieces are selling, which must be made first, so the candy can be delivered to each shop twice a week on a regular schedule. Anything which is not sold in two weeks is removed from the shelves. It is a tight, exact schedule, and summer or winter, it must be met, so the butter creams for which they are famous taste exactly as fresh each time you buy them.

The firm uses Nestlé coating primarily, but what is most unusual, it is the only major candy firm I know of that uses straight chocolate liquor as a coating for some of its pieces. Chocolate liquor is straight chocolate—no sugar or milk has been added. It is unsweetened chocolate, like the best unsweetened chocolate one could use in a recipe. The combination of a sweet center with an unblended coating makes some of their most distinctive and lovely pieces of candy.

Take their fondant cream, which has black walnut kernels added and is coated in dark chocolate. It is sensational. I find that one excites my taste even more than the black walnut nougat, which is coated with a blended, sweeter coating. Fannie May makes a coconut cream coated in dark chocolate that plays off a creamy sweet center with the sharper coating taste in a way no sweet chocolate coating could begin to match. That is where taste comes in, when you know what you are attempting to contrast with your quality center. Each taste should complement and contrast with the other.

Their chocolate buttercream, coated in dark chocolate, is another contender for first place in the Fannie May taste category. When you find yourself overwhelmed with all that is dark and deliciously sweet, it is comparable to diving into a chocolate pool at night. Until you hit center, you can't even tell where one darkness ends and the other begins.

Their Trinidad has an equally rich chocolate center, but you couldn't tell it on first sight. It's covered with an ivory coating into which toasted coconut has been mixed. I was surprised to find I liked it enough to order a dozen more, since I'm not usually fond of pastel coatings, or "white chocolate," as it's sometimes incorrectly called. There is no such thing as "white chocolate." The coating has cocoa butter in it, but no chocolate. To get back to that lovely Trinidad, let me just say it's a smashing combination: The chocolate center maintains a darker, richer flavor while the coating with the coconut is just exotic enough to warrant going back again and again.

Their butter toffees are about equal to those See's makes. These two companies, large in the candy sense of the word, have the edge on making and selling the best butter toffee in their category. It's a difficult piece to make, and the smaller companies usually produce the best, but both Fannie May's and See's are a close match.

If you enjoy soft caramel, you'll love Fannie May's. And the nut pieces. There are always nut pieces. As Denton Thorne says, "Everyone can buy nuts the same place we buy nuts. Everyone can buy chocolate the same place we buy chocolate. If they buy good nuts and good chocolate and keep it all fresh, it ought to be good. Making good candy and selling good candy are two different things, however. You have to control the shelf life and the time it's exposed."

That's what makes them as good as they are; for in the Midwest and the East, when you ask what time it is, in candy, it's Fannie May time.

Fannie May Candy Shops, Inc.
1137 West Jackson Blvd.
Chicago, Ill. 60607
Tel.: (312) 243–2700

They are glad to ship their candies except when it's too warm to guarantee the chocolates arriving in any state but perfect. They use UPS exclusively. Write and ask for price list and assortments.

FOREST PARK

La Maison de Bon Bon

It took a trip to Europe and a box of French Crèmes made in America to make me realize what a nation of romantics we really are. Despite the fact that the French do things to their chocolate that would be punishable offenses anywhere else in the world, most of us have come to accept the terms "French chocolates" and "French candies" as something desirable. Our versions, thankfully, bear little resemblance to their namesakes. Having tasted more than my share of the real French chocolates, I can only think their appeal is limited to those with the taste buds of marmosets.

As I said, our own versions are infinitely better, in the wide world of chocolate, and that leads me to a place called La Maison de Bon Bon in the exotic town of Forest Park, Illinois. The label on the box states, "Home of 'French Crèmes' & Kitchen Fresh Candies since 1921." I'm glad I didn't let that frighten me off, for they make small squares of incomparable chocolate delicacy.

These "French Crèmes" reach their full bouquet and flavor when eaten a bit warmer than most chocolate candies should be. I tried them first after I brought them up from my chocolate cellar, when they were at about 60 degrees, and didn't think them extraordinary. But the room to which they were carried was much warmer, about 75 degrees, and at some moment just prior to stickiness, I picked one up and tried it. My, 15 degrees may not sound like much, but it made a spectacular difference in taste! They were good enough to be outrageous, and twice as rich.

I haven't had their other candies, but on the basis of this one, I'd be more than willing to try anything else they care to ship.

La Maison de Bon Bon
7353 Madison St.
Forest Park, Ill.
Tel.: (312) 366–0775

Since mine arrived by mail, I assume they will accept mail orders. Ask what else they'd recommend in the way of other candy pieces.

SPRINGFIELD

Pease's Candy Shop

It's great to be able to take time out to explore the chocolates of any region, and if you're really lucky, you could end up in Springfield, where Pease's holds forth a chocolate bonanza.

Plunge into the heart of their assortment and try to come up with the dark chocolate crunch. It is, as we casually say, divine.

I pass up the lemon and berry creams as too sweet for my taste, particularly when they're offered in light chocolate, but I never bypass their molasses chip. That's a piece guaranteed to improve anyone's disposition, and particularly good for the traveler, who needs a bit of energy and sweetness as a reward. Beyond chocolate (there are things, I am told, beyond chocolate) I also suggest their roasted nuts, the deluxe assortment which has all my favorites— almonds, pecans, and cashews. Pease's should be reported to the proper authorities for the fresh way they treat those nuts. Each one tastes separate; almonds are almonds, the pecans are pecans. Not what one usually gets in a "nut assortment" when the pieces all taste like salt. These are individual nuts. And proud of it.

Their old-fashioned chocolate creams, available with vanilla, buttercreams, and chocolate centers (in light and dark coating, also) are what Pease's is best known for. Since they've been in business for sixty years, I hear reports of faithful customers who have moved elsewhere but continue to write back and ask that these old-fashioned chocolate creams be shipped to their new addresses. The creams come wrapped in all shades of colorful waxed paper and look more like kisses. I suppose, in their own way, they are chocolate kisses, and I willingly and tastefully give them all the lip service they're due.

Pease's Candy Shop
State and Laurel St.
Springfield, Ill. 62704
Tel.: (217) 523–3721

Write to Robert G. Flesher and ask for a price list, which will include a complete list of all the assortments they make and their prices.

CHICAGO

Blommer Chocolate Company

In July 1939, three brothers joined together and named their new chocolate company. They weren't exactly strangers to the business, for their father, William, had been in the chocolate business most of his life as one of the original partners in the Milwaukee firm of Ambrosia. The sons had followed in their father's footsteps, first at Ambrosia, but they wanted their own business, and so Blommer Chocolate Company came into existence in Chicago.

It was both a daring and a correct move for the three sons, Henry, Al, and Bernard. By 1948, their business warranted further expansion. Instead of increasing the size locally, they branched out nationally with the addition of Blommer Chocolate Factory of California in Los Angeles.

It might have remained a southern California division of the firm if Dod Boldemann hadn't approached Henry Blommer, who was an old friend.

When the common stock of Boldemann's was bought in 1952, it became part of the Blommer firm, with Dod remaining as general manager. Today, Blommer is one of the five largest chocolate manufacturers in the United States. Its main plant is in Chicago, and Boldemann's is in Union City, California. Another factory somewhere on the East Coast is planned for the immediate future.

Their chocolate sales warrant the expansion, for they sell over one hundred million pounds of chocolate yearly. With over two dozen different types of milk chocolate alone, four different kinds of chocolate liquor, as well as a number of dark chocolate coatings, they offer the industry that uses chocolate coatings a wide choice. Add to that four other types of ice-cream coatings, plus eight different formulations of compound coatings, as well as candy bars, chocolate stars, cocoa and chocolate chips, not to mention the liquid chocolate, and you get some idea of the immense production and offerings which are available, all in the luscious name of chocolate, and all from Blommer Chocolate Company.

Primarily a manufacturer, Blommer's sells their coatings to others, and it becomes candy when firms such as Fannie May and Fanny Farmer place it over their particular centers. Even companies such as Nabisco buy chocolate from Blommer. This sounds strange when you realize Nabisco has its own chocolate division, Merckens, but Henry Blommer explains,

What makes Blommer a bit unusual in the chocolate industry is that it is independently owned, a family firm. Only a few others such as Guittard and Van Leer can claim this distinction, and they sell much less volume than Blommer, which is a giant, in every sense of the word, in an industry dominated by giants. "We all have our specialties, and I suppose we have certain items we're better known for. The largest part of our business is in the milk chocolate field. We're in the area of the largest milk chocolate supplier in the United States," Henry Blommer verifies.

For the retail consumer of candy, there is an item that Blommer makes that can be bought over the counter. It's their candy bars, and they come in almond, pecan, and plain milk chocolate. Each one is a treat, and the only grumble I can make is that they aren't widely available. "Our distribution is not large, even in the Chicago area," Henry Blommer says apologetically when asked why. Perhaps in time, that will be rectified, for these candy bars ought to go out to a wider, and waiting, public to enjoy. Meanwhile, you'll enjoy Blommer's coatings on some of your favorite candies. For those living in the Chicago area, you are the lucky ones. You have the privilege of enjoying a fine Blommer Pecan Bar. The rest of us have to write and wait until they're available in our area.

Blommer Chocolate Company
600 West Kinzie St.
Chicago, Ill. 60610
Tel.: (414) 226–7674

Henry Blommer is the man who is in charge of the fine products they make, and he's equally a marvelous consumer of good chocolates; write to him and ask when their candy bars will become available for you to enjoy—or if they'll ship you a few boxes to have and enjoy—and their price list.

MISSOURI

Russell Stover Candies, Inc.

Although I'm certain this company, having built their reputation on the firm basis of freshness as well as quality products, goes to great lengths to ensure all these things, I have had less than complete success at my end of the candy counter. The box I bought in Coronado, California, at a drugstore was more than a casual reminder of a previous box bought in the Midwest at a large department store.

Those large centers, which Russell Stover proudly pioneered, along with the two-handed method of dipping chocolates, left me totally unconvinced I ought to buy them a third time. The outside chocolate was fine, but the inside of a great many pieces bore a resemblance to a state just prior to the one that delights archaeologists. I'm exaggerating; these hadn't quite made it to the artifact stage, even if I felt they were well on their way.

So I did feel enough obligation to write directly to them and ask if they'd ship us some examples of what they considered their best chocolate assortments. We wanted to taste and to photograph them. The reply came back, and it was interesting to note the response. "I am enclosing several photographs of boxes of candy. Since candy is fragile, we thought this best. If we sent actual boxes of candy to you, they might arrive shaken or crushed." This presents a problem, granted, but the question remains, if they could not get here in perfect shape, how did they get to all those other places?

In all fairness, I do not think the fault was in the candy, but in my particular attempts to taste it. The manner in which the candy I tried was kept, and the conditions under which it resided may have subjected the boxes I bought to a life span that extended beyond what Russell Stover had intended. Or else they were two completely isolated examples of how slipups can occur in spite of attempts to avoid them by careful quality control. Since I didn't check the dates on the boxes, I've no one to blame but myself. Candy is fragile, and some places simply cannot give it the attention that a good candy store or a top-quality department store would.

The photographs were nice—the assortments looked delectable. If I hadn't struck out twice already, I might even have been tempted by the photographer's art to go back and try one more time. But I think not.

I'll stick with my other choices. Out of all the extraordinary chocolate candies available here in the United States, plus all the others available from all over the world (some of which are obtainable here in America in leading department stores), I don't think it is hard to do better than Russell Stover, though it's possible to do a lot worse.

My lot in life is to be a picky chocolate eater. I want to turn into salt all the candies that aren't what they should be. Since I don't buy my drugs at a chocolate store, I don't think I'm really persuaded to buy my chocolates at a drugstore.

Russell Stover Candies, Inc.
1004 Baltimore Ave.
Kansas City, Mo. 64105
Tel.: (816) 842–9240

I suppose if you are a great Russell Stover fan, you could write and ask them to suggest where you ought to purchase their candies.

COLUMBIA
The Candy Factory

Columbia is a university town, and most of Georgianna Lundgren's customers are young. Along with their courses in history, English and chemistry, they are receiving a great education in chocolate. Candies, that is, because it takes an educated palate and a fine sense of geography to bring together the various elements Georgianna does to create superb pieces of candy.

Take those staples of the West, fruit and nuts, and dip them in Van Leer's chocolate coating, which comes from New Jersey, and you've got the twain meeting. If there's anything as good as Georgianna's California almonds dipped in that Eastern chocolate, it has to be the pecan halves she's treated to exactly the same method.

Her sense of geography serves her well, for she's taken an old European favorite, marzipan, and translated this into American Midwestern taste, covering it with—what else?—chocolate. It travels well.

I feel no guilt as I pass up one of Georgianna's more exotic offerings, the goat milk fudge. My sense of adventure doesn't extend that far, but I will suggest you try her fresh strawberries, stemmed and hulled, which have been coated in a pure rain of chocolate. There is no doubt in my mind that fresh fruit and good chocolate coming together produces the best of all possible worlds.

But what then of the rest? Well, try her butter cream caramels. I think you'll be more than pleased at the way she's handled those. For people who want their chocolate but can't have sugar, she has produced a complete line of sugar-free chocolates.

Georgianna takes into account the tastes of her customers, and since their average age is twenty-one and a half this has led her to the kind of inventiveness that appeals more to them than it does to me. Frosted pretzels are a big item in her trade, as well as frozen bananas dipped in chocolate and then rolled in nuts. The last item will cross any age barrier.

I suggest you try a regular assortment of her chocolate candies. I ask her to omit the mint jellied ones. I'm not fond of these, but if your taste runs to strong mint, you will be delighted by hers. The rest of the assortment is quite good. She has a sense of adventure with chocolate that works for her more often than not. Only a stick in the mud wouldn't respond to The Candy Factory. As I say that, I can already see her taking a stick of butterscotch candy in hand and embedding it in that dark and luscious mount of Van Leer's chocolate. Go to it, Georgianna. It's worth a try.

The Candy Factory
117 North 9th St.
Columbia, Mo. 65201
Tel.: (314) 443–8212

Mail orders accepted, and around various holidays, special items are available. Write and ask.

ST. LOUIS
Mavrakos Candy Company

Melanie and I planned a leisurely drive from Chicago to St. Louis, arriving midday, just in time to see Tom Wotka's candy factory in full production. We left Chicago, where it was just beginning to rain, without planning to dodge tornados. But we did dodge them. Driving to

St. Louis under a sky black as the untapped heart of a cocoa bean, we encountered enough rain to cause us to pull off the highway and to wonder if our small car could be converted to a boat. When we finally arrived at our destination, we saw the parabolic arch that graces the city gleaming nicely under a clear sunset. But Mavrakos was closed.

Chocolate addicts are resourceful people. If one avenue of chocolate is blocked, they will find another that is open. We made our way to the shopping center, Plaza Frontenac, and procured our chocolates anyway. After a drive such as that, nothing, not even tornados, were an excuse not to have what we'd come this far to enjoy.

Rewarded by the Pecan Bark, we restored our flagging energy with a good half-pound of that dark delight before trying some of the miniatures Tom Wotka makes. He creates these chocolate dainties with lovely centers of cream and caramel. While Melanie lingered over these fine pieces, I was busy enjoying other fruits of his labor, the Pineapple Triangles. They were exactly what I had hoped for: tiny wedges coated in milk chocolate, bursting with flavor. We then went on to dessert: a few of the delicate chocolate-covered nuts.

I had tried a bit of the Molasses Puff on another occasion. It's nice, but I have to say I find Preston's Honeycomb more to my taste. Another molasses piece Tom makes isn't duplicated anywhere, and so I suggest this one: it is a chocolate-covered lollipop. Beneath the thin coating of chocolate is the merest resistance of thin, crunchy, perfect molasses. A whole box of these will bring a smile to anyone's face.

His tiny trufflelike candies, sometimes called French Chocolates, are worth the time and effort it takes to get them. Mavrakos makes a particularly exquisite version of this candy. You may find yourself eating an entire box on your very own. It would be wise to order at least two, that way, you'll have one to share with friends.

He makes other chocolate surprises that people in the St. Louis area look forward to. One is an unseasonal but a welcome addition to winter. Just after Christmas, Tom Wotka makes available to customers Mexican strawberries, dipped in fondant, then in chocolate. These fresh beauties won't hold up too long, so they can't be shipped, but the people around St. Louis buy them to enjoy immediately. So if you happen to be there at the right time, you can consume all you want on the spot.

The Nestlé coating Tom uses makes a perfect accompaniment to the berries, as it does to all his chocolates. If I am to be cast adrift on any strange freeway, under any weather conditions, I simply hope I have enough of his chocolates to see me through until an available exit comes along, or I have enjoyed the last chocolate crumb. Whichever comes first.

Mavrakos Candy Company
4711 Delmar Blvd.
St. Louis, Mo. 63108
Tel.: (314) 361–7000

He does accept mail orders, and you might begin with the regular assortment. Write for price list and available candies; don't forget the molasses lollipops, and be sure to have at least one box of the French Chocolates.

Karl Bissinger French Confections

Any city with two major candy stores is a city worth visiting. Karl Bissinger's, on McPherson Avenue, is one of the places you'll want to say you've been to. The window is a tour in itself, with French confections, exquisitely decorated candies, floating on their pedestals, as befits these tiny gems of royalty.

We had expected no less: St. Louis, after all, introduced three major pleasures into existence in 1904, when the great Louisiana Purchase Exposition was under way, gave the world its first taste of ice cream cones, hot dogs, and iced tea. It was inevitable that the city would move toward the more subtle delights of fine chocolate. And barely twenty-three years later, in 1927, the doors of Bissinger's opened, offering a host of candy and confections to the lucky people of St. Louis. Now the rest of us are equally fortunate, thanks to the magic of chocolate transportation.

Called "French Confections," these candies commemorate Karl Bissinger's move from France to this country. This candy store is one of two descended from his craft. Both use nothing but natural ingredients, and the candies are a tribute to their taste and skill. You can try (in either light or dark chocolate) over fifty different varieties at Bissinger's, and before you feel the least bit jaded, you can then enjoy the chocolate sculptures, choosing from such shapes as animals, vegetables, automobiles, cartoon characters, and famous people.

If ennui attempts to cast its shadow upon you at that point, let me suggest you renew yourself with Bissinger's chocolate-coated mints. The holiday assortments are unbelievable. If it's Christmas, each tiny surface (about an inch across) is decorated with such hand-crafted miniatures as Santa Claus, a white horn-of-plenty with its touch of green and red, or a wreath, a stocking, a Christmas cane or whatever else is appropriate and symbolic of the season. Each glimmering candy is decorated beautifully, and at Thanksgiving there is the tiny sugar turkey, and the Halloween season brought to its sweet conclusion with a petite pumpkin.

They also make fresh fruits coated in chocolate: I tried the strawberry, which had been first covered in fondant before receiving its blessing of chocolate. It lasts a bit longer this way, but it also tastes sweeter. What I did find unusual and able to last a bit longer were the chocolate-covered coffee beans. These are tiny candies which have freshly ground coffee reshaped into a coffee bean and then coated with chocolate—a welcome stimulant. You can indulge yourself with a good number of them.

The creams are also uncommonly good: Out of all Bissinger makes, I think the Lemon Spaded Cream and the Strawberry Cream are undeniably luscious. If you care for marshmallow, be sure to try their Marshmallow Gem, and the Raspberry Gum is one of the different treats they make in chocolate.

Their candies are lovely, and what's even nicer, they taste as good as they look: Bissinger is a feast for the eye as well as the tongue.

Karl Bissinger French Confections
4742 McPherson Ave.
St. Louis, Mo. 63108
Tel.: (314) 361–0647

Bud Kolbrener is the man to whom all thanks must be given, and to whom I suggest you address your queries. They have two other locations in St. Louis, at the Plaza Frontenac and Crestwood Plaza, but the store on McPherson Avenue is the one I enjoy most, with its marvelous old-fashioned exterior. Do write and let them know what you love most in chocolate, and they'll keep your personal assortment taste on file. Then all you have to do is call or write them to reorder, and it's yours. Mail orders accepted.

KENTUCKY

Rebecca-Ruth Candy, Inc.

Put me in the company of another Southerner, and there it is—my Southern accent is back, thick as ever. All the years I have lived in California slide right off as that nice gentleman from Kentucky and I talk, with not a single "g" at the end of a word still left intact. John Booe is his name, and gracious, he does make one fine kettle of candies after another.

Kentucky Colonels is what his firm is noted for. Where else in this whole wide country could you find anyone with the talent to combine chocolate of extraordinary taste with that bit of prime Kentucky, in the form of 100-proof J. W. Dant bourbon? Everyone for miles around is convinced Kentucky Colonels beat branch water by a long shot. The candy is a winner with its splendor of dark, rich chocolate coating a center to which bourbon has been added. Each piece is topped by an aristocratic pecan. I can go through an entire box faster than a Yankee's imagination.

That was the good news. Now, here's the bad. Unless you are in Kentucky, say Frankfort, Louisville, Lexington, or Woodford County, you are not going to be able to have these. They are legal in Kentucky, that remarkable state of good taste, but the backward rulings under which the rest of us must live make them unavailable to us. This also includes the rest of John Booe's 100-proof lovelies, as well as the crème de menthe–flavored chocolates. It breaks my heart to think I can't have the old-fashioned assortment he makes with this fine bourbon, or his Kentucky Irish Coffees, which contain that same unshippable substance added to pure coffee and creamy fondant coating.

But there are some things we can have. Just settle on down and let me tell you about some of the candies his family produces that make life worthwhile. Try the almond paste and fondant layers topped with a pecan half, or that coffee cream on which he has lovingly placed a sautéed salted pecan. Buttercreams? Of course he has them. The centers contain some of the freshest dairy cream, whole milk, and rich butter this side of Switzerland. The candies are pure flavor, and rich to the point of no return, all dipped in the most delicious, glossiest chocolate available. Rebecca-Ruth knows how to make candy, since they have been in the business for nigh on to fifty years. And what they don't know about making chocolates simply isn't worth knowing.

I might mention the raves the Kentucky Creamed Pull Candy has received. At my house, a few review and honors were available. I only tasted one or two pieces and loved them. When I went back for more, I discovered an empty box on which a note had been taped: "Hey, these creams are really out of sight." That simple statement was true, in every sense of the word, for there was nothing left of those creams that had been coated with unsweetened chocolate liquor. It was nice of the children to leave the note.

John oversees the production of all his candies from beginning to end. And he is truly a Southern gentleman. Tradition is admirable. I know he has never sacrificed quality or his own high standards by leaving a box of candy longer than two weeks on any shelf. I suspect it has never been a problem, anyway, since I imagine the turnover is rapid.

You can buy Rebecca-Ruth Candies at the Cincinnati airport if you happen to be there, since part of that airport happily resides in the fine state of Kentucky. There is not a candy he makes you won't want at least a box of to take along with you.

Rebecca-Ruth Candy, Inc.
112 East Second St.
Frankfort, Ky. 40601
Tel.: (502) 223–7465 or 223–8484

John has retail stores in the Lexington Civic Center Mall, Hurstbourne Park Plaza, Whittington Parkway, and 610 River City Mall in Louisville, as well as Woodford County, Kentucky, just off the U.S. 60 Interchange. If you are in Kentucky, or at the Cincinnati airport, you can buy any and all assortments. Try those containing bourbon because they're really something very special. You can order all the other assortments except those containing bourbon. He'll be glad to ship you an old-fashioned assortment or try the Opera Creams. Write and ask for a list. Incidentally, if you happen to be in Kentucky and buy some of these "forbidden" delights, get them to wrap them for you. John can't mail them for you, nor can the stores, but in my own devious mind I can manage to come up with a couple of slight questionable schemes to get them where I want to ship them, and I suppose you can also.

OHIO

Bissinger's

Bissinger's is to chocolate candy what Emperor Louis Napoleon III was to Karl Frederick Bissinger: royalty. It was that emperor's sweet loss when Bissinger took his leave of France to come to the United States, way back in 1863, and brought with him recipes he had perfected as the confectionist and candy maker to the emperor. France's loss was our gain: There's no way anyone will mistake these chocolates for anything but noble. They're done correctly, with impeccable taste, and that includes the box.

A candy box serves two functions: it not only keeps the chocolates fresh, it also tells you something about the way the candy maker feels the chocolates should be presented. Bissinger's feels quite imperial. From the rich-looking taupe box with its blue lettering and cord, to the seal it bears—"Confiseur Impérial by appointment to Emperor Louis Napoleon"—it's impressive. And the contents are equally so.

If I had world enough and time, I would wear you out with praises about their chocolate caramel creams. Smooth as silk sheets, and as voluptuous, the chocolate caramel cream could bring swooning back into style.

Each piece of candy in that box is perfect: From the fresh raspberry cream (identified by a pink rosette on top) down to the smallest nut piece, I can say I enjoyed each one and didn't find a single mistake in the entire selection.

Take the nut piece that has been surrounded by almonds, ground to a paste with more nut pieces added; dip it in fondant and apply a final coat of chocolate. That's an example of a good piece of candy, for each amazing texture complements the next. Layer by layer, this piece alone tells the story of fine candy making. The flavors melt, mingle, and merge: No two centers taste exactly alike. Each has its distinct, impressive taste to offer, and each is enhanced by its light or dark chocolate coating.

Their cherry cordials, a piece I usually pass up, are another example of how well they do things. Instead of one of those thick, fondant centers into which an impossible cherry has been mortared, Bissinger's has managed to make an incredible, edible piece. The liquid center is not excessively sweet, and it allows the cherry to have a flavor all its own. Coated in dark chocolate, the whole piece is a luxurious treat.

Although I strongly recommend you not attempt this, I found out how well their chocolates hold up. I tasted them first when they arrived (what else?) and placed the duplicate, surviving pieces down in the chocolate cellar where the temperature never gets above 65 degrees and there is almost no humidity. Three months later, when I brought the candies back upstairs, the centers were still moist, fresh, and blissfully good, with one exception—the Opera Cream. Although no one in his or her right mind could keep hands off the Opera Cream long enough to let this tragedy occur, it is made with pure cream and spoils quickly. You have to eat this piece within a few days.

Until I tasted their Peanut Butter Meltaway under chocolate, no one could have convinced me I would use these particular words about such a combination: "Try it." And then there is the French Mint, which melts so fast in your mouth it resembles a magical chocolate disappearing act. In fact, try all of them. I cannot think of a better present for anyone than a box of Bissinger's finest.

Bissinger's Inc.
205 West Fourth St.
Cincinnati, Ohio 45202
Tel.: (513) 241–8182

Will R. Gregg, Jr., makes these "Candy Creations for the Candy Trade," as he so aptly puts it, and he will be glad to include you, if you write for the price list and available assortments they make. Do not forget to order the cherry cordials.

LAKEWOOD
Malley's Candies, Inc.

There are many types of people in the candy business. What common denominator could possibly apply to all the different men and women I have met? Happy. I have yet to encounter someone who didn't enjoy being part of a business that brings so much pleasure to so many people.

Bill Malley is one of those happy people. If I ask him any question about candy, he is more than happy not only to answer me, but to provide a tangible example. His enthusiasm is as unlimited as the candy he makes, and reason enough for the broad, infectious grin he's never without.

"What do you think is the perfect combination for a buttercrunch?" I just happen to inquire. And there it is, in the gold box bearing his name: a square buttercrunch coated in chocolate, rich and creamy enough to bring a smile to anyone's face. My mouth is at full alert. Good? Not only is it good, it is astonishing. As it melts away in my mouth, the golden flavor lingers. I am content.

His chocolate cream comes as easily to hand as praises to my lips. Smooth, delicate, it eases the passage of time while one waits, turns a moment into casual sweetness, makes one feel as if the time spent idly contemplating chocolate delicacy after delicacy is of great importance. Before I lapse into the chaise-lounge, I revive myself with the crunchy free-form nut piece. Ah, that restores one. And then, another buttercrunch. It is circular, it is perfect.

Of all the assortments he offers, I find no piece that is not to my immediate liking. Each cream is a careful blend of thick richness and tangy flavor, each has a coat of chocolate thick enough to offer just the right amount of resistance before its heart of cream is revealed.

There is only one thing to do when the box is empty. I must take pen in hand and write to Bill Malley, telling him that since I cannot come to Ohio, would he please send Ohio to me?

In a few days, the candy drop will be made: No matter what color the sky is on that afternoon, no matter what catastrophe might appear imminent, it will be a glorious day. The gold box shimmers in its own brightness, and beneath the protective covers, I will unwrap piece after piece to bring a smile to my face. Chocolate and nuts, smooth creams and buttercrunch, these are chocolate candies worth traveling for.

Malley's Candies, Inc.
14822 Madison Ave.
Lakewood, Ohio 44107
Tel.: (216) 226–8300

Bill Malley will send you a box or two of his delectable candies if you write or call him. Send or ask about assortments and pieces he offers, and you too can smile. The only time he will not ship is when the weather becomes too hot: At that time, only the lucky people who live in the vicinity of Lakewood, Ohio, can enjoy his marvelous creations.

VERMILION
The Candy Shop

Never having given Vermilion, Ohio, all the justice it deserves, I find myself speechless, almost overwhelmed, as I sit here eating these chocolate candies that have just arrived from Ohio. If I had known what The Candy Shop was up to, I would have made straight for their doors years ago.

With ease I pluck a caramel from its brown crinkly paper and taste the goodness it provides. The candy doesn't even resist as, buttery and smooth, it slowly dissolves into submission. Gently, my hand flutters back down into the box and comes up with a thick coconut cluster. Two flavors united in mutual harmony, the coconut texture combines with the milk chocolate to be all one could wish in a perfect blend. Done in milk chocolate, as all of these pieces are, each is a delight, from the French Whipped Chocolates right on through to the fruits and nuts, down to the very last jelly.

If I have any regrets, it is that there aren't any dark chocolates in my selection with which I might further be tempted. My consolation is that these are not just plain milk chocolate, but pieces that have been bathed in the luxury of Ambrosia chocolate, the coating Thomas Zahar has always used. His customers in Vermilion prefer milk chocolate, and The Candy Shop obliges by making 97 percent of its production to suit their tastes. Ambrosia, after all, was and is the Food of the Gods. And now, as I sit here poised over the last one of these dainties (the jelly), I can say, even for a discriminating mortal, these candies are divinely decadent.

The Candy Shop
South Shore Shopping Center
Vermilion, Ohio 44089
Tel.: (216) 967–6318

Although The Candy Shop is not in the mail-order business, Thomas Zahar assures me he will accept your order and ship candies to you. Write and ask.

NORTH CANTON
Harry London's Candies, Inc.

Someone has finally done it: come up with the perfect gift. What I need now is the occasion to present it, for it more than fulfills all the criteria implicit in that phrase, the perfect gift, and might even be said to go beyond that. Taking the form of chocolate, Harry London's has placed this consummate item in a large polka dot box, then bound the package with a gold cord and given it the name The Ultimate Pacifier.

I'm sure it's a natural for baby showers, pediatricians, new mothers and fathers, all of whom London's suggests as recipients, but I'm taken by the other, more subtle, ramifications that include those occasions in life which need an appropriate gift as the answer beyond speech. Think of all the people to whom you could send it as an expression of your sentiment. Think of all the greetings you could inscribe on the card to accompany it. Doesn't it make the hand tingle, just considering it?

It almost makes me willing to relinquish another marvelous item that they suggest for someone quite special—their huge Sugar Kiss, wrapped in foil, all chocolate beneath. Why, London's has answered the chocolate lovers of the world with every possible chocolate ultimatum!

Harry London's also makes more conventional chocolate candies that are likely to please anyone. They are masters in packaging: Their regular box is gold paisley on a white background. Inside, the milk chocolate cup is graced by a single almond, but it holds a double surprise in its depths—two more almonds. Their dark nut cluster is a virtual collection of peanuts, and equally surprising, for they have used Spanish peanuts, complete with skins, and it adds a sparkling note of saltiness that blends with the sweetness of the chocolate.

These all come in their London's Gourmet Candies assortment. The only piece that might be questionable is the vanilla cream, which is too sweet for my taste. I prefer their other cream, the one with the same Spanish peanuts riding chocolate tandem on top. Its interior is the color of maple cream and tastes exactly as I wish the vanilla did. Another piece worthy of attention is the square caramel. It's coated in milk chocolate, and should only be attempted by those with a firm bite and well-anchored fillings. I loved it, but I love a good, chewy caramel. It has one further feature I liked: a hint of cinnamon as an aftertaste.

They have one other box that might entice you. It looks, at first glance, like an oversize counterfeit bill. When you look closely, you'll see its name, The London Mint. It's a mint meltaway, and a good one, even though the box declares, right on top, "This is not legal tender of all debts, public and private."

The Ultimate Pacifier is the chocolate gift I plan on ordering first. It satisfies me on any number of counts. I cannot help but think it delightful to be pacified by good chocolate humor.

Harry London's Candies, Inc.
1281 South Main St.
North Canton, Ohio 44720
Tel.: (216) 494–2757

Write and ask them to send you a catalog, which has all kinds of candies and gifts displayed on its pages; then write for the ones you want.

YOUNGSTOWN
Gorant Candies

With these two boxes of chocolates here at my side, I am reminded periodically that my desires in chocolate are not necessarily the same as those in a given region. For the region from whence cometh milk chocolate and sugar in great quantities has called these forth. Youngstown, Ohio, is the place, and for those who love the sweet flow of light, milk chocolate, combined with a goodly sugar content, Gorant candies are the answer. There is not a single piece resembling anything bittersweet or tart in the entire box.

Gorant has a new, spectacular factory and outlet which they've just completed in Youngstown. This indicates the taste of that area demands lighter, sweeter chocolates, since the candy maker provides the type of candy his or her customers prefer. Old fussbudget that I am, I can't get through them, since sugar is not one of my favorite flavors. But Gorant will please people who take lots of sugar in their coffee, or demand endless candy bars of what I consider indeterminate substance but sugar-compelling aftertaste. And there are lots of people who insist that chocolate be that sweet: So you could send them a box of this assortment, or the nut, caramel, and chocolate pieces that go under various names, such as Turtles and Paddies. For the true milk chocolate fancier, this is a giant improvement over anything those chocolate bars have offered.

Gorant Candies
6999 Market St.
Youngstown, Ohio 44512
Tel.: (216) 758–5701

They'll be glad to fill your mail-order requests; write and ask.

)

MICHIGAN

DETROIT

Sydney Bogg Chocolates

When Sydney and Dorothy Bogg decided to retire, sell their factory and candy store they had opened during the Depression, they looked to the past to find new owners. Ralph and Doris Skidmore were offered the chance to buy the business, for Sydney Bogg had trained Ralph in the candy trade years before. Ralph and Doris had left Michigan to pursue other careers. They were in Florida, where Ralph was working for a newspaper, when the offer came. It was an offer they did not refuse; they returned to Michigan and bought the factory and candy store. In the following years, the Skidmores opened new stores, in Royal Oak and Birmingham as well as in Rochester, Michigan, all needed to handle expansion.

When you taste the chocolates they create, you can understand why they have continued to do so well. They do an incredible job of producing an entire range of fine chocolate candies. Not only do they offer a choice of hundreds of chocolate-covered candies, but they make custom party favors for every occasion as well. Should the celebration command champagne, a chocolate champagne bottle with foil-wrapped cherry cordials hidden inside can be ordered. This moment of giddiness is captured in Nestlé chocolate: Broc and Burgandy coatings are used for all their pieces, from the largest fantasy down to the tiny chocolate leaves.

What I love are their specialties, which capture the holiday flavor in chocolate, from the Irish potatoes and green snakes done for St. Patrick's Day to the chocolate and caramel apples that are the treats of choice at Halloween. Whatever the holiday demands, Doris and Ralph will meet it, from Christmas to Mother's Day, right on through to Valentine's Day, a wedding, a birthday, a new arrival in the family. It will come right and in chocolate, with all the appropriate decorations lovingly done by hand.

Don't neglect their regular assortments, by any means. One box I recommend highly is the Miniatures, which features over ninety pieces of delicate persuasion per pound—and it is a true miniature offering. Look for the lemon cream, with bits of real lemon peel in its tiny but tart interior, and taste how it melts perfectly in your mouth along with the chocolate coating.

The Sweetheart Assortment is a larger version of some of these same pieces; you get twice the flavor in each piece with this one, and each assortment is made just as carefully as the next, as they use fresh dairy butter and 40 percent whipping cream in making the centers for their chocolates. Chocolate bark, brittles, and fudges are all available for the asking, as well as their extensive and luscious variety of nut rolls, pralines, chews, fruits, and crisps. If that doesn't fulfill your fantasies, you can ask for some special treat you would like them to make in chocolate, for as Doris says, "Whatever turns someone on, if we can, we make it!"

I think it would be difficult to come up with new requests, considering all the Skidmores offer already. I am partial to their whole apricot halves dipped in chocolate and to their prune nut rings covered with dark Nestlé coating. Among the cream offerings, maple and lemon are my favorites, and their nutty marshmallows are hard to pass up, unless I come upon the Butter Toffee Crunch first.

No preservatives are used in their candies, but the Skidmores would not have to use them anyway; their customers never let these lovely chocolates stay around long enough to require preservatives. The special party trays Doris presides over, hand-decorating each tiny circle of chocolate, are works of art that must be seen to be believed (then eaten).

I try not to be envious of the people who live in Detroit and enjoy so many of the delicacies Sydney Bogg Chocolates makes to order, from the tiny chocolate leaves to the decorated chocolate logs, and the special party trays with their fragile motifs. After all, I tell myself, there is more than enough to satisfy even this chocolate addict, as I see these four boxes waiting to be plundered. Four boxes of assorted chocolate goodness ought to keep anyone happy and willing to share her good fortune in chocolate with others.

Sydney Bogg Chocolates
18932 Woodward Ave.
Detroit, Mich. 48203
Tel.: (313) 368–2470

Be sure to ask Doris and Ralph Skidmore to make all these goodies available to you by writing and asking what they will ship you during the cooler months, when their chocolates can arrive safely. There are Sydney Bogg shops in Royal Oak, Mich., at 1205 South Main St., and in Birmingham, at 3584 West Maple Rd., and a new one has just opened in Rochester, Mich. As busy as they are with these shops, the Skidmores will take time to fulfill your chocolate fantasies (try their chocolate match books, for instance) if you write and ask for a list of their assortments. Don't hesitate to order a special item you'd like them to make.

Ricelli Candies and Chocolates

I opened the rich, glossy brown box and discovered that between the moment these were shipped and the moment they arrived, the beautiful chocolates had come into full contact with their hated enemy—heat!

What can I say? They licked quite nicely right off the bubble wrap inside, and in all flavors: strawberry, vanilla, chocolate cream, to mention a few. And I guess I came into my own as far as suggesting possible combinations of flavors in a single experience, but it does leave me unable to tell you which individual pieces you might like best. I have a conglomerate view of the situation.

My friends in Michigan tell me that this is a true loss, for they find Ricelli very much to their liking. I'm going to pass their words along. They say, try the standard assortment. The box bears the legend, "A little different . . . a lot better."

The box I received, alas, is a testimony to that, but in no way anyone intended.

Ricelli Candies and Chocolates
N.A.I.C. Building, 1515 East 11 Mile Rd.
Royal Oak, Mich. 48067
Tel.: (313) 542–3200

Leon Ricelli also makes available to you, by mail order (and be sure it is *cool* when you order) his famous 3-Footer box of chocolates.

PETOSKEY
Kilwin's Candy Kitchen

About the time I think I've seen everything that can be made out of chocolate, something will turn up to prove me wrong. People who work in chocolate love to make sculptures, molds, unusual designs—and that brings me to Kilwin's, where they make a chocolate calling card. It's a chocolate block five by seven inches (or thirteen by eighteen centimeters for the purists among us), with whatever design you send them reproduced on its surface.

I've seen some of their productions. One is a tiered birthday cake with a delicate design surrounding it; there's the legend beneath that says "Happy Birthday." For the sailing enthusiast, they've created an afternoon of pure chocolate, fluffy clouds and sailboats bending forever fixed on this chocolate body of water and sky. That one is inscribed "Greetings from Petoskey, Michigan," but I'm sure they can put your harbor as easily into view.

These are only two examples of the cards they produce, and although I'm not sure what the minimum order is, they'll be glad to let you know. Just send them the card you wished reproduced, or suggest what it is you wish on the surface of that chocolate block, and they'll be glad to make it up, just for you.

Kilwin's Candy Kitchen
316 Howard St.
Petoskey, Mich. 49770
Tel.: (616) 621–2354

Mail orders are gleefully accepted and created; just send your specifications and requests; they have assortments of candies also available.

PENNSYLVANIA

Hershey Food Corporation

A deprived childhood, for me, would have been one in which there were no Hershey Bars. If you had been really good, you went over and asked your folks for a nickel to buy some chocolate. The phrase "some chocolate" was understood. It meant Hershey's. You didn't even have to say the name. Clutching the nickel in one tight paw, you headed up to the grocery store and waited your turn in line, faced with the most difficult decision childhood provided: Almond or Plain?

I ran out of that store, tucking the bar into my back pocket, and it was only a matter of minutes before the heat of running child and the Southern sun combined. I can remember to this day that feeling of hopelessness as I extracted what had been a perfectly shaped chocolate bar. It resembled a doubled over, limp facsimile. But desperation is equal in force to a child's perseverance. I peeled off that brown cover, unglued the white inner wrapper, and began to lick away at the molten chocolate. It may not have been the way nature or Hershey's intended, but I enjoyed that bar lick by lick with more pleasure than anyone has a right to know. And that's where it starts: the reward, the chocolate, and how I came to associate Hershey's with all the good things of life.

I approach the town of Hershey, Pennsylvania, with all of these thoughts, not really knowing what I am going to find, or even if I will like it, but as a kind of homage, a journey to the place where my chocolate memories begin.

I enter the town of Hershey knowing it began as a company town. A planned community. Even the street lights on the main street are replicas of Hershey Kisses. Milton Snavely Hershey built all this, just as he built the chocolate factory and the Milton Hershey School for orphaned boys.

Driving through the town, I think how much it looks as one wishes a hometown to look. As if in 1945, when the rest of America swerved off into the future, Hershey decided that no, we'll stay right here. And it is a childhood from some storybook, the neat frame houses, the perfectly manicured lawns, and even a postman walking his rounds to deliver the mail by knocking at each door and talking to the person who answers.

It is a perfect June day. There is the sun at midheaven, the postman at midrounds, a grandmother rocking on her front porch chair. And everywhere there is the smell of chocolate—chocolate beans being roasted, chocolate being made. It hangs in the air, making the mouth water.

After all, this is the main reason for Hershey, the chocolate place. I walk in and talk with the people in the main office. They, too, find the town perfect, a place they wish to live and raise their children in, a reflection of Milton S. Hershey's original dream.

To bring Milton Hershey back down to life size, one only has to note how many times he managed to fail before he succeeded. Apprenticed for four years to a candy maker in the town of Lancaster, Pennsylvania, Hershey had already served an earlier apprenticeship as a printer in the same town. Candy making seemed to be a second career choice. At the age of nineteen, Hershey left Lancaster to start his own candy business in

Early 1920s train station running behind the Hershey Chocolate Factory. (*Hershey Foods Corporation*)

Philadelphia. That was in 1876. And that didn't work either. So he went to Denver and worked for a candy maker who taught him a new recipe for caramels that made the candy even tastier, and best of all, longer lasting. Then there was Chicago, New Orleans, even New York; each place another attempt by Hershey to make a living in the candy trade. None worked out. He returned to Lancaster, Pennsylvania, penniless but still determined to succeed.

There was, after all, that fine Pennsylvania milk and cream available all around the area, so he began to make caramels. Again. This time, he and his market coincided. The caramels sold as fast as he could supply them. By the time he was thirty-five, he was prosperous. By the time he was forty-two, Hershey sold his caramel business for a million dollars.

Money was not his criterion for success. If it had been, he could have retired at this point and lived quite handsomely. He had a persistent, nagging feeling that there was something still bigger he wanted to do. So he went into the chocolate business. He experimented and came up with his own formula for making a milk chocolate bar. By 1911, just four years after the town of Derry Church had honored him by changing its name to Hershey, the sales of chocolate from Milton Hershey's factory had reached five million dollars.

Milton and Catherine Hershey had no children. In 1918, the business he founded was donated to a trust for the Milton Hershey School, which he had established nine years before. The school still exists, with one change: now it also takes in girls. Children who do not have adequate parental care can live there and receive their education.

Milton Hershey died in 1945 at the age of eighty-eight. What he started continues to grow, and with it, other monuments to his name. The Milton S. Hershey Medical Center is one. Just on the outskirts of Hershey, a fifty-million-dollar medical center was built, thanks to money made available by the Hershey Chocolate Corporation in 1963. It proves the Hershey touch is still sure. For today, it is a seventy-five-million-dollar University Medical Center, part of the Pennsylvania State University, and at least one of the students from the Hershey School has already completed a medical education there.

There is too much to see and do to spend only one day in Hershey. I admitted as much to the man who took me around the factory. Jim Edris is the third generation of his family to live and work in Hershey. He started out as a caddy in the country club there, worked for ten years for

1920s shot of Chocolate Avenue. *(Hershey Foods Corporation)*

the U.S. Information Agency, living in Pakistan and Ecuador, based out of Washington, D.C., before he decided to return to his hometown. As he put it, "I figure my kids can enjoy the advantages I had as a child." He talks of stability and tradition, two things that are more than words in Hershey, with its rural atmosphere and outdoor activities. There is also something any kid would love in Hershey: Hersheypark.

That and Hershey's Chocolate World are two very impressive reasons to bring the whole family for a day or so to Hershey, Pennsylvania. Chocolate World accommodates up to sixteen thousand people daily. With a few modifications, they expect to accommodate more than thirty thousand people a day in the near future. Chocolate World was built to allow the public to enjoy the process by which chocolate is made. Automated cars take the family through scene after scene. Each one is a facet of the chocolate adventure—cocoa beans being harvested, the roasting procedure—and it ends with chocolate being made into the shape we all know: the Hershey Bar. The tour is free, but I don't think

Filling Hershey's cocoa cans in mid-1920s. *(Hershey Foods Corporation)*

Late 1930s wrapping room. *(Hershey Foods Corporation)*

you will leave without buying a few mementos to take home with you. After all, how could you pass up the golden box of Hershey with almonds? And this one is literally half almonds. The other half is, naturally, chocolate, and the whole thing is called Golden Almond. There are T-shirts, playing cards, belt buckles—all bear some resemblance to the products they depict. There are also desserts to enjoy, and the chocolate soda is very, very good on a warm June day.

I may confess to other, more sophisticated chocolate needs at times, but I also confess that I have eaten my share of Hershey's. For a moderately priced bar of milk chocolate, smooth and creamy, with just the right snap to it (if not left in a back pocket too long) it is a good buy. The company's standards are high, and all the chocolate they make is used by them. They do not wholesale to other manufacturers as they once did. At Hershey, all their products are available for you to buy—the bars, the chocolate chips, the milk chocolate Kisses, and the Hershey-ets, as well as the Golden Almond.

The simulated trip from cocoa plantation to final processing permits you to see how chocolate is made, since visitors aren't allowed to tour the factory. But if you were, you would see the large granite rollers going back and forth, conching the chocolate for seventy-two hours. This process is what gives Hershey milk chocolate its distinctive taste. As it is conched, heat is generated by agitation, and the molecules get rubbed smaller and smaller while combining the chocolate with the other elements, such as milk and sugar, until what is produced is smooth and ready to be molded into bars. This is the old way of doing it; many factories now use high-speed, high-production conches. I think the old way has a number of benefits. Not only does it make a fine milk chocolate, but you can stand there, enjoying wave after wave of chocolate as it advances and recedes, the rollers pushing it back and forth.

The factory is, in its way, old-fashioned, but spotlessly clean. The wooden floors shine with the patina of years of walking. New equipment is used. Nothing could be more fun than watching the wrapping machines spew out miles of glittering Hershey Kisses in their foil.

If you have children, there's no way you'll be able to leave without visiting Hersheypark. It wasn't open when I was there, so all I can tell you is that it's popular and has lots of rides as well as a great emphasis on the cultural heritage of central Pennsylvania. There is music, dancing, and even variety shows when it's in full swing, and a seventeenth-century English setting called Tudor Square. And, of course, everywhere you go, there's chocolate in the air.

Milton S. Hershey in Egypt. *(Hershey Foods Corporation)*

It's the storybook town, and like all good stories, someplace we can visit and remember. It exists today as the perfect testament to a dream that Milton S. Hershey had—to create a town where things are done for the people who choose to live there, and for the rest of us, those who come as visitors, to enjoy.

Hershey Food Corporation
Chocolate Ave.
Hershey, Pa. 17033
Tel.: (717) 534–4200

You can buy their products anywhere. It is worth touring Hershey just to spend your day as a child, enjoying and tasting everything. They have convention facilities and their own hotel which is a Moorish rococo structure translated into the language of Pennsylvania. I found the food

Packing Hershey Milk Chocolate Bars in boxes. *(Hershey Foods Corporation)*

One of Hershey's many milk chocolate specialties. This one is the lavish Golden Almond box. *(Warren Marcus)*

Women sorting through candy kisses. *(Hershey Foods Corporation)*

Modern-day Hershey Foods Corporation.
(Hershey Foods Corporation)

at the hotel did not put Hershey's products to best use, but if you skip the meals there, at least look at the dining room. It is a room without corners. The hotel itself is an expensive, expansive structure and its walls look as if they have huge almonds embedded in them.

PITTSBURGH

Bolan's Candies

Although Peter Bolanis insists he makes quite ordinary candies, I suggest you try his caramel piece. It is a cut above any ordinary caramel, and his toasted coconut candy is also worth trying. They both have the high sheen of Merckens chocolate about them, and they are class all the way.

He also makes strawberries coated in fondant and then dipped in chocolate available only to those in the Pittsburgh area; those of us living farther away will have to settle for other pieces that can be shipped, such as his unique and tasty chocolate-covered almonds.

Bolan's Candies
6018 Penn Ave., Penn Mall
Pittsburgh, Pa. 15206
Tel.: (412) 441–1220

You might be able to convince Peter Bolanis to ship you his chocolates, but he is not exactly overjoyed about shipping perishables such as his creams. During the summer months, he declines to ship anything.

ERIE

Pulakos 926 Candies, Inc.

Would you believe a chocolate version of Versailles? How about the Warner Theatre? Or the Supreme Court? All of these sculptures, which surpass description, and many more have taken shape under the talented hands of Gus Pulakos, who created them out of the element in which he works so well—chocolate.

Even though most of us will never own our own monument in chocolate, the care he lavishes on his sculptures must be reflected in the candies Pulakos makes. They are reticent about shipping candies out of Erie, so I can only tell you about them via their hosts of admirers. I am told these chocolate candies are models for the entire chocolate industry. Gus Pulakos and his son Achilles offer their facilities and run a candy school for members of the industry, making their knowledge and premises available to the people in the chocolate industry to exchange methods and learn new ones.

Some of our finest candy makers have gone to the Pulakos school to learn their trade. Tom Kron was a participant years ago, as were many others.

So I have to support the Pulakos candies, even though I haven't tasted them, on the recommendations of those who are as finicky about chocolates as I am. On the say-so of many others, I pass along my own praise, and suggest if enough of us write, perhaps they will make their chocolate candies available to a wider public.

Pulakos 926 Candies, Inc.
2530 Parade St.
Erie, Pa. 16503
Tel.: (814) 455–5995

The firm has been in business since 1904, and the folks around Erie are lucky enough to enjoy all the chocolate treats Pulakos makes. Write and ask how you can join this select group.

LITITZ
Wilbur Chocolate Company, Inc.

With names such as New Holland and Gap, you're in the heart of the Amish countryside. Civilization slows down to permit looking, and there's a great deal to see. The sculptured farms, the rolling green wilderness of Pennsylvania are graceful reminders of what lies just off the Pennsylvania Turnpike's frenzy, a slower route, something to restore the senses.

You can plan your day to arrive at Lititz, a small town near Lancaster, Pennsylvania. After you've seen the eighteenth-century buildings still in use on East Main Street, walk over to the Wilbur Chocolate Factory, and there you can discover the Candy Americana Museum. It's exactly as promised in the brochure—informative, historical, and fun for the whole family—and it's free. You can't tour the chocolate factory, but you can

A five-pound milk chocolate extravaganza with almonds is made by Wilbur's Chocolate Factory. *(Warren Marcus)*

tour the past. There are rooms that re-create a candy kitchen at the turn of the century. The old-time equipment and molds, and especially the display of fragile chocolate pots from firms such as Limoges, Bavaria, and Haviland, are a reminder of how valuable chocolate was, and how it was served in the finest china made. It's all on display.

Started in 1972 by Penny Buzzard, the woman who saw the need to gather the artifacts that are part of our history, the museum resembles a country store, with room after room devoted to our candy heritage. As the wife of Wilbur Chocolate Company's president, John Buzzard, Penny has spent six years devoting her considerable energy to this museum. And it shows, for where else could you see an old-time taffy and caramel cutting machine, or a collection of chocolate molds that were used to create chocolate fantasies for children of a bygone era?

What could be more pleasing than a chocolate and candy museum as part of a chocolate factory? Wilbur Chocolate Company, Inc., a subsidiary of MacAndrews and Forbes Company, has been a part of the candy heritage for almost a hundred years. Established in Philadelphia in 1884 as H. O. Wilbur and Sons, the company has gone through various name changes. It was Ideal Chocolate Company at one time, then, after joining with Suchard Société Anonyme of Switzerland, it became Wilbur-Suchard. Not only has its name changed, but also its location.

From its origins in Philadelphia, it became part of a three-factory production that included Newark, Lititz, and Philadelphia, until 1930, when the Philadelphia operation was joined with the Lititz one. Then the Newark plant was sold back to Mr. Brewster, and for a while the Wilbur people were busily producing Suchard items, selling them directly to the public via vending machines. That went on until 1958. Now the corporate name seems to reflect a turn back to the original, where it all began: Wilbur Chocolate Company.

Chances are if you live beyond their immediate area, you may not have had their product under its own name, Wilbur, although they are beginning to introduce their complete line of candy bars to a wider, eager public. You may have eaten their chocolate, not knowing it was theirs, in other chocolate forms. They produce and sell chocolate to other companies, and food manufacturers use Wilbur's coatings, as do bakeries

Old boxes and chocolate artifacts. *(Candy Americana Museum: Wilbur Chocolate Company)*

Replica of old-time candy kitchen. *(Candy Americana Museum; Wilbur Chocolate Company)*

and dairies. More than twenty-nine million pounds of cocoa beans are brought to Lititz from all over the world. Seven different types of beans are used in their blends. The beans are processed here in Lititz, along with thirty million pounds of sugar, an enormous quantity of milk, and substantial amounts of butter and flavors. What finally comes of all this is one of the best chocolate coatings and candies anywhere. You have enjoyed it on Godiva candies as the coating which Godiva has made to order just for them.

Now Wilbur Chocolate Company has come out with a new package and distribution system which makes The Wilbur Bar Collection more readily available in this country. Up until this year, I couldn't find their products unless I ordered them directly from the company. Our small but select local food specialty store, Torn Ranch in San Rafael, found out about Wilbur and carries at least three types of their chocolate bars. I would think that if I can enjoy them here in California, the rest of the country is being equally well treated, thanks to Wilbur's new advertising and distribution campaign to introduce their products to a wider audience. The Ideal Company (one of the many names Wilbur's has enjoyed over the years) has been credited with having originated the popular chocolate bar containing almonds. You can have this one, the Wilbur Milk Chocolate and Almond Bar, or enjoy any one of their other marvelous, naturally flavored chocolate bars. They make a large selection—Orange Milk Chocolate, Chocolate Almond Toffee Crunch, Dark Sweet Chocolate, Mint Chocolate Crunch, Milk Chocolate Crunch, Coffee Milk Chocolate, as well as a Sugar-Free Milk Chocolate with Whole Almonds. My favorite is the Milk Chocolate with Almonds, although I am equally partial to the Dark Sweet Chocolate.

Wilbur makes one other item, and that was the initial reason I found myself on the road to the factory long before I knew anything about them or their museum. When I started doing research on chocolate, I asked people in the chocolate business who they felt was the leading authority in the field. They recommended L. Russell Cook, a man who was greatly respected and probably knew more about cocoa and cocoa production in this country than anyone else. He had written the book that everyone continues to refer to as the "Bible for the chocolate industry"—*Chocolate Production and Use*. I pestered Russ with questions, and he always took the time to answer me or to refer me to someone who could give me answers firsthand. I was lucky enough to meet him in person a year before he died. I remember that meeting, and I remember asking him what his first pleasant memory of chocolate was. His reply, "Wilbur's Buds," led me to Wilbur. After tasting them, I can understand why, if that was my first experience with chocolate, I might have gone into the industry myself. Each of these rich chocolate candy drops swirls up into a point. There is no way to eat only one or two. Buy a few boxes. My favorite is, of course, the Dark Milk Buds.

Wilbur operates a candy store outlet right there. You can purchase all the Buds you want, and even one that they make with mint. I am not as fond of that one. I do suggest you take home their old-fashioned can of Wilbur's Ideal Cocoa. Wilbur's is about the best cocoa powder for that hot cup of chocolate (always with milk, never with water, please) that I have found to soothe the morning into a contented state.

In addition to the complete museum of chocolate artifacts, there is a candy kitchen where someone is busy demonstrating how to use chocolate, and makes hand-dipped candies right on the spot. Every day you can choose from a selection of Penny's fudge, which is available there. I did not try the fudge since I was much too busy with my own box of Buds, plus a few chocolate bars. The others buying and eating the fudge had happy looks on their faces, just like mine.

However you manage to get there, by America's first turnpike, the Pennsylvania (and I leave that one for hardier souls) or by driving through the back roads of the Amish country, plan on a family outing and a whole day in Lititz. You can't miss the factory, since the road takes you there, and you don't want to miss the museum and the candy kitchen. It is all courtesy of Penny and John Buzzard and all of the good folks at Wilbur Chocolate Factory. I am thankful that our heritage has been preserved. Visiting Lititz was one of the nicest days I have ever enjoyed.

Wilbur Chocolate Company and The Candy Americana Museum
48 North Broad St.
Lititz, Pa. 17543
Tel.: (717) 626–1131

The museum is open Monday through Saturday, starting at ten in the morning until five in the afternoon. The admission is free, and all the exhibits are well worth seeing. You can buy candy there. I do not know if Wilbur takes mail orders, but you could write and ask. If you do, don't forget the Wilbur Buds.

DOWNINGTOWN
Godiva Chocolatier

Godiva makes some of the most beautiful molded chocolate candies in the world. They are exquisite to look at. The gold "Ballotin" in which they are packed and the lavish gift boxes in which you can purchase these chocolates are always presented to display each and every piece of candy to its best advantage. Godiva was already known in Belgium as a fine chocolate, but Americans had had little experience with shell-molded chocolates unless they had purchased them in Europe. For shell-molding is a process by which few chocolate candies in this country are made, since it is expensive, time-consuming, and requires a great deal of knowledge to do correctly. Putting the centers through an enrobing machine is simpler, but no less an art, when done properly. That is the way most of our chocolate candies are made.

Godiva chocolates are shell-molded chocolates. To shell-mold, you have to be sure the chocolate has been tempered properly, reached the right viscosity, and is ready to be placed in the mold. Once the mold has been filled, it is turned upside down, so the excess chocolate runs out, and what is left is a small hollow chocolate shell, which is then filled. Another chocolate shell must then be placed to complete the candy, and if you have done it all correctly, you have now managed to produce one single piece of shell-molded chocolate.

With over thirty years experience in all the problems that chocolate can present, John Moon is in charge of this intricate process for Godiva in Downingtown. He'd been with Pepperidge Farm, which is owned by Campbell Soup, the parent firm that owns both the Belgian and the American Godiva firms, for over seven years. His responsibility is to see that everything, from coating right through to centers and the finished products, is done correctly.

I visited John at the plant in June, when the factory was on vacation, so production was not going on at that time. We talked about Godiva, some of the problems and pleasures involved in making these candies, which many people regard as the most luxurious treats they can purchase in America. Godiva chocolate candies are readily available in most cities, in the fine food or candy section of leading department stores. Godiva also has its own boutique on Fifth Avenue in New York.

When the original Belgian formulations were brought over to America, the first candies produced utilized Belgian chocolate coating. The unpredictable problems of delivery and varying conditions which existed then began to pose problems. Godiva had to look for an American firm that could produce the same coating they needed in sufficient quantities to assure them it would always be available. Wilbur and Van Leer, two of America's finest chocolate companies, were selected. They could make Godiva's coatings to the exact specifications required. Pure vanilla, not vanillin, had to be used in the blending of the chocolate. Various formulations of beans would be maintained to produce the flavor desired. As much attention would be paid to the ingredients for that coating as to the centers they would embrace.

Anything as expensive as a shell mold should never be filled with less than the best, and Godiva's Grande Mint is a splendid example of how perfectly this precise attention to every detail results in an unusual and correct merging of ingredients. The dark chocolate on the outside contrasts vividly with the mint and alcohol interior of the candy. Godiva prefers liquid, flowing centers, and their Grande Mint meets every requirement. Their Caramel Shield is equally responsive to this treatment, with its delicate caramel suspended in chocolate.

A piece such as their strawberry-molded chocolate has puréed strawberries in fondant locked inside a firm, sweet chocolate. The Comtesse is a square piece, dark or light, which features Lady Godiva as its emblem. To bite into that is to enter a heaven of dairy cream, cognac, and chocolate.

Special attention to details is the key to Godiva's success. Some pieces are handmade, since the two shells that form top and bottom are put together by hand; such a piece is the ground hazelnut (praline) center, surrounded by chocolate.

My own preferences are always toward their darker pieces; I find the light ones a bit blander than I prefer, but again, that's more a taste preference than a criticism. Godiva is constantly making new pieces and trying out new recipes. Two I'm looking forward to enjoying are their new liquid marzipan and a pineapple molded chocolate that will contain pineapple and kirsch in its center.

What I admire is the risk Godiva took in coming into the American market with a product they felt warranted the best packaging and attention to details. If their primary appeal was to an upper echelon in both market and price, they did prove that chocolate lovers were willing to spend money for chocolates that are beautiful to look at and unusual in taste. They insist on quality, from coating to center, and have introduced a great many of us to our initial pleasures of Belgian chocolates. Show me someone who isn't excited by a box of Godiva as a gift, and I'll show you someone who doesn't deserve your special attention.

Godiva Chocolatier
Chestnut St.
Downingtown, Pa.
Tel.: (215) 269–2500

Their head office is in Norwalk, Connecticut, but the candies are made in Downingtown, Pennsylvania. Address inquiries to John Moon, General Manager, Godiva, at the address above, and I'm sure he'll forward them to the proper person; or write to the president of Godiva, Mr. John Griggs, P.O. Box 5500, Norwalk, Connecticut 06856. You will find a selection of Godiva products in almost any good-sized city at the leading department stores.

SHARON
Philadelphia Candies, Inc.
Using Nestlé's fine coating, Philadelphia Candies has made a whole range of my favorite pets, from chocolate chickens and eggs to puppies and ducks. They even make a pet they call Peeps, which I assume corresponds to chicken puberty. At the other end of the scale, they create chocolate roosters. These pets show up every Easter, and for the traditionalists, yes, there is the chocolate Easter Bunny. Last year alone they made over 409,165 of those bunnies. That's sort of a tribute, since it was the Easter Bunny who rescued Philadelphia Candies from the giant floods of 1959.

I assure you that's true. The Macris family lost five thousand pounds of chocolate that had just been delivered the day prior to the flood. What kept them afloat were those bunnies, who had escaped the watery depths.

So I have to give credit to the bunnies, even as I enjoy my box of fruit and nut assortment, and with each and every Pecanette I eat, from the other box, I realize what a shame it would have been, had these candies been lost to us. At holiday time, as well as other times, you can fill your fantasies with all of the chocolates they make (most of which are created in milk chocolate) and enjoy a parade of Easter ducks, puppies, rabbits, chickens, and bunnies. It's good to indulge the child in all of us.

Philadelphia Candies, Inc.
P.O. Box 808
1534 East State St.
Sharon, Pa.
Tel.: (412) 981–6341

If you write to Spyros Macris, he'll be glad to advise you on which particular fantasy fits your needs, and then ship it to you. Philadelphia Candies also makes a wide range of assortments in their inimitable chocolate manner; be sure to order a box of Pecanettes.

BUTLER
Peter's Chocolate Shoppe
The early 1900s brought wave after wave of immigrants to America. Whatever fears they may have had arriving at a place so far from home, so huge, so foreign to them, it was no bigger than their determination to

succeed. The myth of America tells us it is possible to find the definition of oneself, to find success, as long as you are hungry enough to take risks. In just such a way a young Greek boy arrived from the island of Chios and apprenticed himself to a master candy maker to learn his trade.

Years later, it was time to take another risk—he wanted his own business. Butler, Pennsylvania, was about as far away from that Greek island as the imagination allows, but it was and is the place he chose to open his candy factory. With his new wife, Mary, he began to work, and in thirty years the small factory became a larger one, until today, Peter's Chocolate Shoppe is living proof of Peter Meliotes' dream.

Even nicer, he and Mary share that dream with all of us, for inside the gold box are some of the fine examples of his craft: the notable chocolate candies they create. Milk chocolates are a good way to test the art of any candy maker. If he can take that blander coating and add to it a touch all his own, produce chocolate candies that are distinctive in flavor and texture, then you know you have come upon a master candy maker.

Each of these candies in the all-nut assortment is splendid; from the almond island, with its rocky protuberances, to the other select nut pieces. You can chart your way easily from one to the other, never tasting the same flavors twice. The legend on the box says it all, and as well as anything I could, "Buy where it's made . . . it's fresher!"

Peter's Chocolate Shoppe
326 West Jefferson St.
Butler, Pa. 16001
Tel.: (412) 187–5096

Peter and Mary Meliotes will gladly fill your chocolate order if you specify what you want, in light or dark chocolate. Be sure to enjoy the nut assortment promptly: fresh natural ingredients taste best when consumed in prime condition, and chocolates with nuts should not go uneaten for longer than a week or two.

PHILADELPHIA
Whitman's Chocolates

Stephen F. Whitman's decision to open his confectionary shop on Market Street in Philadelphia must have been considered quite daring in 1842. The location was near the waterfront, and hardly one that

Early Whitman's packaging. *(Whitman Candy Corporation)*

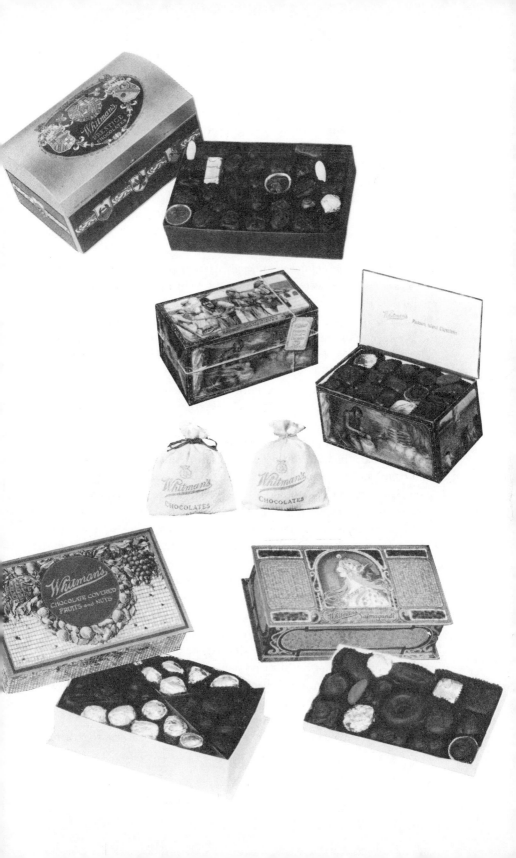

guaranteed a wealthy clientele that provided much foot traffic. Whitman took advantage of this location to buy the rare ingredients for his candies direct from the ships that arrived in port. Rare fruits, nuts, and spices were readily obtained this way. As his reputation grew, so did his need for a larger, more central location.

In 1868, he relocated closer to downtown Philadelphia. His confections sold to the carriage trade, Philadelphia's Main Line. As more people bought his candies, he kept their individual preferences on file cards. When a customer asked for "my assortment," it was filled promptly.

Whitman's son, Horace, joined his father in the business in 1869. The next few years were busy ones, and Whitman's introduced a new product to the market—Instantaneous Chocolate. This instant mix for chocolate drinks was offered for sale in tins. Horace Whitman assumed the presidency of the company when his father died in 1888, and the following year, the factory relocated once more. This time it moved to Cherry Street, where it would remain for seventeen years. By now, the firm was large enough to have its own salesmen and dealers, who sold Whitman's candies in nearby New York, Baltimore, Washington, and parts of the South.

By the time Walter P. Sharp became a partner with Horace Whitman in 1904, Sharp had already been in the firm since 1873. They made a good team, and the firm continued to expand its business, until it moved again, this time to Fourth and Race streets, where it would remain for more than half a century. Sharp saw the advantages in advertising, and with a large sales force ready to place the products in selected stores throughout the country, Whitman's became more than a local or regional candy. During Sharp's presidency the best-known Whitman package came into being. The Whitman's Sampler was Sharp's idea. The box, which made its first appearance in 1912, was lithographed from an available, anonymous sampler. Its success was due not only to its old-fashioned and appropriate exterior design, but also to a novel idea which appeared inside, an "index" which showed the consumer which candy was in which compartment. Whitman's Sampler still accounts for a great deal of the firm's success. And it is hard to quarrel with success, for the box is a familiar one to most Americans who have bought candy, and most have had at least one Whitman's Sampler of their own.

Whitman's makes all its own coatings, and still gathers together all the ingredients from the various centers. Nut meats from every source, pineapple from Hawaii, and mint from Michigan are brought to the factory. The firm roasts and blends the cocoa beans according to their secret recipe, and when the coating is made, the cream, milk, and butter can be added to the centers, along with the other ingredients that complete the candies. Just as they have always made their candies, in Philadelphia, the process continues.

I find a difference between what I remember as a good, moderately priced assortment of chocolate candies and what I have bought recently. The cherry, still wrapped in the gold foil, was as good as I remembered, but the creams taste different. Perhaps it is their new process, which produces an aereated center, though this is a drier center to my taste. The nut pieces are fine, but the pineapple piece is more a pineapple jelly than a chunk of fruit.

The two pieces I prefer out of the Sampler are the Caramel Cordial, which is moist and delectable, a rectangle of dark chocolate coating the center, and another dark chocolate piece, the Mocha Cream. This last-mentioned is shaped like a seashell, and I like the flavors, which contrast mocha with chocolate.

Whitman's distributes their candies through their own national sales organization. Theoretically, this permits the firm to keep a close check on what is where and how long it has been there. Department stores, drugstores, airports, specialty shops, grocery stores, and gift shops are equally adept at carrying Whitman's products.

The new Whitman plant is located on thirty-seven acres, right on the outskirts of Philadelphia. This move toward expansion has also been reflected in ownership, as Whitman's is now part of Pet, Inc., and has been since 1963.

Whitman's remains a moderately priced assortment of chocolate candies, available in almost any town. I prefer Whitman's or Pangburn's over Russell Stover if a local candy outlet is simply not available. But I always choose See's when I can. My tastes are conditioned to the more lavish See's assortments, and the cost is about the same.

Not everyone is lucky enough to have their own candy store down the street, so out of the various offerings Whitman's makes available, the one I suggest is still the Sampler or the new Sampler Favorite in the all-nut assortment. And out of the Whitman's Sampler, I reach for the Caramel Cordial and the Mocha Cream.

Whitman's Chocolates
Division of Pet, Inc.
P.O. Box 6070
Philadelphia, Pa. 19114
Tel.: (215) 464–6000

James Nixon is the president of Whitman's Chocolates, and he works closely with the people in production to ensure freshness and top quality are maintained. Whitman's welcomes customer comments and suggestions.

NEW JERSEY

TENAFLY
Critchley's Candies

Politics and chocolates make strange bedfellows, although candy has never been accused of partisanship. Democrats and Republicans enjoy it equally, and it has graced as many conservative parties as it has liberal. Chocolate candies go well at state dinners, which brings me to Critchley's Mint Oritani and the precedent they have set by appearing at many of those state dinners.

That thin mint with the green center travels in the best circles, and is at home in Paris, where it is sold, or here in the United States. If you happened to be at Lyndon Johnson's Inaugural Ball at the Sheraton Hotel in Washington, D.C., you might have enjoyed it there. For that is where President Johnson first tasted it. When it was time to plan exactly what was going to be served at his daughter's wedding, he remembered those mint candies and called up the maître d'hôtel at the Sheraton to inquire about them. He wanted to know who made them and what were they called. And that is how Nick Phillips' Mint Oritani came to grace that sweet event.

Since I don't move in those political or social circles, but in the widest chocolate circles, I happened upon these by receiving them as a gift. They resolved a number of misconceptions I had held for years.

With the first taste, I overcame my previous prejudice about mint and chocolate being uneasy allies, for Nick has made them inseparable friends. Taking the thinnest layers of chocolate imaginable, he has placed a light and lovely mint center in between. The two flavors merge perfectly. Of all the mint and chocolate candies I have attempted to try, only five or six have proved good enough to warrant a second piece. Nick's creations provide another kind of proof: it is hard not to devour the entire box. The mint never overrides the good taste of chocolate, and both flavors linger in the mouth for minutes afterward.

As a diplomatic courier, these mints could be sent to say "Thank you," and are appropriate for any occasion, state or otherwise. I would make them mandatory at every table, from high level to family dinner. Many a tense moment would be resolved by these delightful Mint Oritanis, since attention would focus on what is in hand. From the first taste to the last thin square in the box, they are to be shared. Critchley's Mint Oritanis are a candy worth talking about.

Critchley's Candies
145 Piermont Rd.
Tenafly, N.J. 07670
Tel.: (201) 567–5050

Mint Oritanis can be ordered by mail and will arrive in perfect shape, if the weather is agreeable and not too warm. I find them a lovely gift to send as well as to receive. Write and ask Nick Phillips to share these with you.

WEST NEW YORK
Harry C. Nagel and Son
With my usual talent regarding geography, I came upon West New York, New Jersey, in Chicago. It is the luck of the chocolate traveler. Such discoveries reaffirm my belief that wherever you came into the presence of good chocolates, it has to be the right place.

For three generations, Nagel's has been the right place for a great many chocolate lovers. Beyond their usual assortment, which always pleases, Nagel's makes some items that can only be said to astound. Anyone can find chocolate bunnies at Easter, and Christmas means there will be chocolate Santas, but how many have ever confronted a two-foot chocolate-molded airplane, complete with pilot? I did, and Nagel's made it. They make other molded novelties, each decorated for specific occasions and concepts, and all in chocolate.

Their large box of miniature chocolates has about two hundred pieces and just about as many flavors to enjoy. If your taste is for larger chocolate candies, you should consider Nagel's Raspberry Jellies. Everyone else seems to—they sold some fifteen thousand pounds of that one fruit flavor alone just last year.

It all travels well and under the best coatings of chocolate. Merckens and Nestlé provide the coatings for these pieces. Sixty percent of all the candies Nagel's make are done in light milk chocolate.

One other item should be on your list of treats—their French Chocolates. Pure pleasure, these candies are still made with heavy cream, just as the original recipe required. From marzipan to marshmallow, you can name and claim any number of chocolate candies as your own. Nagel's makes a tremendous assortment. But for something a bit out of this world, I suggest you ask Nagel's to make you one of their hollow-mold chocolate fantasies. If you feel the airplane is a bit much, they will furnish you with other forms of transportation. They have trains and cars, even Volkswagens. Whatever travels best, travels in chocolate as well. Nagel's chocolates take one someplace worth going to.

Harry C. Nagel and Son
580-82 67 St.
West New York, N.J. 07093
Tel.: (201) 868–6661

Mail orders are promptly filled, but the hollow molds won't survive shipment unless they are specially packed. You might write and ask if these will arrive safely, but I'd suggest carrying these beauties by hand. The regular assortments come through in perfect condition, as long as the weather is cool.

JERSEY CITY
Lee Sims Candies

What has four sides, is based on an ancient design in which height was increased by building rectangular additions of diminishing sizes, one on top of the other, and usually comes complete with a treasure hidden

Lee Sims gift packaging. *(Adrianne Marcus)*

inside? One further clue: this item is guaranteed to bring any and all chocolate archaeologists to a state of pure excitement. The answer? The great pyramid of New Jersey.

That's what Lee Sims Candies provides. It isn't your standard assembly of monumental blocks, but three layers of pure, sweet discovery, piled one on top of the other, all waiting to be plundered. These particular pyramids come wrapped in lavish paper with a giant bow to complete their assembly.

Unwrapped, the fun begins. At ground level, in the dark recesses of the largest box are some of the deep and sweet secrets they make, lying side by side. Fruit centers, prune and apricot under chocolate—each is a discovery and a taste reward. Try the nut and caramel piece. As you bite through the bittersweet Nestlé coating, there is the fine balance of nuts in proportion to caramel, entirely covered in thick chocolate.

The box is divided into two sections: dark chocolates on one side and lighter milk chocolates on the other. The gold piece marked with the firm's name features an interior of solid milk chocolate. I always return to the bittersweet, and Lee Sims is master of those. Their creams are of less interest to me than the roasted nuts. All their nut pieces are splendid, and each is treated to a cape of chocolate, lavishly applied. The large Brazil nut is one of those particular treasures. It's coated and gleaming, and you break through to taste the ivory-colored freshness of the subtle center. One piece is bound to lead to another. One piece of candy, as perfect as the divisions of the box, unlocks and unites the entire selection. It's a completely delicious square of pure whipped chocolate, half light and half dark.

By the time you get to the second level, the box containing their French Style Butter Cookies, you are prepared for the treats they have in store. These are another treasure, of different but equal delight. The colorful leaves of infinite lightness, held together by a thin layer of chocolate, are one flawless example of confectionary art. The long, buttery finger cookies are another. These are dipped at one end in chocolate, with a sweet center of jam. At the point where self-restraint would be foolish, take a rolled chocolate cookie with its crumbly nut coating and enjoy it. This cookie is overwhelming. I wish there were more of these beauties in the box. Consolation comes quickly to hand, however, with the fluted, layered cookie with its shimmer of apricot perfectly centered in the delicate circle.

As I ascend to the final box, the one containing their freshly roasted nuts, I must report euphoria. I can also report a good nut assortment with pecans and cashews in abundance.

Having explored the great pyramid of New Jersey, I bring back into the light one last treasure that Lee Sims makes, separate from all those others—a Gold Bar can be yours in ten-pound size, and is available down to a quarter of a pound. But for all chocolate intents and purposes, New Jersey has the pyramid to visit. Lee Sims is the only place I know where you can have a pyramid shipped to you with its wealth of chocolates and confectionary treasures intact.

Lee Sims Candies
743 Bergen Ave.
Jersey City, N.J. 07306
Tel.: (201) 433–1305

Nick Vlahakis, the owner of Lee Sims, will be glad to create a pyramid to your exact specifications. Three different assortments are available, and all are shipped by UPS. They'll be rushed to your eager hands, once he knows exactly what special tastes you have. He keeps his customers' preferences on file, and considering that some of them have been steady consumers of his candies and confections for over a quarter of a century, you'll be glad to be placed in such good company. Write and ask, or call, or just go over and get some.

Van Leer Chocolate Corporation

There are individuals in this world who habitually ignore all the good advice and warnings given to them, to follow their own direction. The chance of failure is disregarded, the sensible course left unpursued. How else could you describe a person who decides to give up a secure future in the bank, leaves his homeland, Holland, to begin a trip around the world? What could you say to him when he gets only as far as the United States, meets and marries a woman from Mobile, Alabama, and takes up residence in America? There are few words that could serve to describe such an individual, but determined is one of them. It is the word which characterizes L.K. Van Leer.

In 1930, in spite of the Depression that was gripping this country, Van Leer once again disregarded all the good advice of his peers, and decided it was time to go into business for himself. He began importing Holland Dutch Cocoa Powders. Not only was he successful, but he became prosperous.

So it was no use telling him, in 1950, that he couldn't become a chocolate manufacturer. People tried to do just that, pointing out that it was a field dominated by giants in the industry. But he decided that was what he was going to do and he began his own firm, Van Leer. Again, history proves him right: the chocolate products Van Leer makes are a success, both financially and gastronomically. Van Leer is well known to confectioners, bakers, and people in the dairy business. He supplies coating and cocoa to a great many of them, as well as coating to some of the best candy makers in the United States.

One of my favorite chocolate cakes made by Colette's, Le Trianon, uses Van Leer chocolate, and achieves a deep rich taste unmatched by any other chocolate cake in the world. Of course, it is easy to obtain chocolate from New Jersey if you are located in New York, but more and more places, geographically removed, go to the extra shipping costs to have their chocolate made by Van Leer. Candy makers have turned to Van Leer since he tailors his production to the special needs of his clients. Godiva Chocolatiers is another buyer of Van Leer coatings, as well as Bailey's in Boston. Each has its particular blend of chocolate made to exact specifications by the folks at Van Leer.

This is a family business. Mr. Van Leer works with his son, Ted, and his brother-in-law, Malcolm Campbell, to produce these continuous chocolate bonanzas. The firm makes high quality, made-to-order coatings, and a full range of them, from light to dark. They are also the leading manufacturer of dietetic chocolate coatings.

The firm is not giant size. They are small, but they are giants in every other department. I received a ten-pound bar of their Alkmaar chocolate coating, the dark, delicious kind. It arrived broken. Rather than let it fall into the hands of those hopefuls who stood around, anxious to eat it all up, I remained my firm, disciplined self while we photographed it. Then we all tasted what was before us. The consensus from both chocolate devotees and casual chocolate consumers was unanimous: "Fantastic!" "The best I ever had." "I want to go wherever they make this and stay there (sigh)." And my own—"I'd better get the rest of this gathered up, just in case the pictures have to be retaken."

This fine rationalization shows my streak of determination, which Mr. Van Leer would understand. He insists, after all, on using real vanilla in a great many of his blends, and the best of all cocoa beans. He produces eighty different formulations, from sixteen milk chocolate coatings to one hundred dark ones, plus pastels and other products. Each and every one is exciting and luscious. I have just tried their Van Aarden, a medium-light chocolate with an unbeatable taste.

It takes a stubborn, determined individual to go against the odds, and Mr. Van Leer has done just that. The evidence, these marvelous chocolate coatings, shows he is a winner in every category.

Van Leer Chocolate Corporation
110 Hoboken Ave.
Jersey City, N.J. 07302
Tel.: (201) 789–8080

If your chocolate needs approach twenty pounds or more of their fabulous products, you might prevail upon Malcolm Campbell or the Van Leers (father and son) and persuade them of your good taste and intentions.

From the fruit of the gods, the cocoa pod, comes the bean out of which cocoa powder and ten-pound chocolate bars are made. Milk and dark chocolates are molded in singular pans. *(Fred Lyon Pictures)*

The Bolton strawberries begin their march on the conveyor belt to be coated by a rain of Nestlé milk chocolate. Once they are completely covered, Munson's Candy Kitchen makes these seasonal confections available to the fortunate chocolate lovers in the area. (*Melanie Annin*)

A fantasy of chocolates, created by candy makers and manufacturers. (*Fred Lyon Pictures*)

From all over the world, a wheel of chocolate candy bars spins out individual flavors. Some are solid, others contain centers of contrasting flavor. All offer their individual regional delights. (*Fred Lyon Pictures*)

A shell mold from Corné with two molded chocolate coatings from Callebaut books an
array of Belgian chocolate candies from such firms as Godiva, Neuhaus, Wittamer,
Manon, Corné, and a few Côte d'Or chocolate bars. (*Fred Lyon Pictures*)

Demel's fabulous Annatorte.
(*Adrianne Marcus*)

Chocolate in Switzerland is featured in this solid milk cow made by Nestlé in Broc, Switzerland. It weighs over thirty pounds, and the white markings are Snowcap coating. (*Adrianne Marcus*)

Art Preston's delicious Honeycomb and other chocolate candies. (*Adrianne Marcus*)

The blessing of Vienna, all in chocolate, and most of all, by Demel's. (*Fred Lyon Pictures*)

Out of Guittard's copper kettle, ten-pound bars from Ambrosia, Van Leer, and Hershey are surrounded by some of the finest chocolate candies created. (*Fred Lyon Pictures*)

Orders for less than one hundred pounds, add twenty cents per pound. But it's worth it at any cost.

CONNECTICUT

HARTFORD AND BOLTON

Munson's Candy Kitchen, Inc.

Would you believe a three-thousand-mile drive just to watch Bob Munson make his chocolate-covered strawberries? We did just that, but I don't blame anyone for being skeptical. Bob didn't quite believe me when I called him up a week earlier to announce I was going to drive across the country with my friend just to see the strawberries being made into a chocolate treat. He responded quite courteously, but I could detect a small note of incredulity in his voice. When I walked in his door to the shop, precisely one week later, the first thing he greeted me with was, "I can't get over this. You really did drive here!" It was more a question I heard than a verification of my presence.

It was worth the entire drive. And that is an understatement. These treats are only available three weeks out of the entire year, when June and the Bolton strawberries come due, around Father's Day. They are that special.

These perfect, tart strawberries can't be praised enough, but let me try. Somewhere in childhood flavors happen, and you can spend a great deal of your life measuring one flavor against one you enjoyed way back when. The taste of strawberries is one of those measuring devices. Although I've nothing but awe for the strawberries grown in California, those huge, meal-in-themselves extravaganzas, the Bolton variety makes any others tasteless and a bit vulgar by comparison. These small burgundy explosions of taste are perfect captives in the Nestlé milk chocolate coating Bob Munson uses. Once you've released all that taste, savored even one of them, you'll spend the rest of your year wishing it were June again.

There are many other kinds of chocolates for sale in Bob Munson's shop. They range from a chocolate pizza (a chocolate base with cherries on top, a throw of walnuts here and there, all drizzled over with white chocolate, and looking, at first glance, like a pizza) to a golf club with accompanying golf balls in chocolate. One novelty I respectfully declined: a chocolate-covered gherkin seemed more an adventure than I cared to see myself trying.

For those of you who are devoted to chocolate, however, I'll heartily recommend my other favorites, even though they sound conservative. Bob Munson's blend of flavors and top-quality ingredients is liberally applied to such pieces as the chocolate-covered creams. There is not a one I would call less than perfect—all of his creams are worth lingering over. I tried to taste as many as I could, and had more than my share of doubles when no one was looking.

Try his buttercrunch, coated in chocolate, the caramels, any and all of the pieces, including the whipped chocolates, which are light as clouds and twice blessed with a rain of chocolate. Then, back to the strawberries; always, back to those strawberries.

If he has them, you will want as many as you can hold, plus a few blueberries, also coated in chocolate. He makes them every other day. Come next June, I'll be camping on his doorstep. Even though I am fully aware the shelf life of these blueberries and strawberries is about a day and a half, I plan on procuring at least ten pounds of them. I have many friends who would love to share them, and I feel it's my duty to bring them these treasures back by plane, hand-carried, of course. They are the kind of gift for which you will be remembered always. And favorably. Everyone who tasted them immediately wanted to know where to get them. You can torture your enemies by not telling them, or casually mention to dear friends Bob Munson's other two outlets in Hartford, Connecticut: the West Farms Mall and the Civic Center.

As I said, it was worth the drive to have those strawberries, if nothing else had been available. There are so many reasons at Munson's Candy Kitchen to visit that lovely area with its rolling green hills, that I plan to get to Route 6 by any means possible. Good chocolate candies are worth traveling for.

Munson's Candy Kitchen, Inc.
P.O. Box 224
Bolton, Conn. 06040
Tel.: (203) 649–4332

Write and ask Bob and Marie Munson to send you a list of their chocolate assortments that can be shipped. The fresh fruits, in chocolate, cannot be shipped since they wouldn't survive transit. But if the weather is cool, a great many of his other sweet treats can be yours for the asking.

MASSACHUSETTS

SHREWSBURY

Herbert Candy Mansion

Somewhere beyond Bolton, Connecticut, and long before you reach Boston, is the town of Shrewsbury, Massachusetts. The map shows it, but I didn't find it. Instead, I settled for Sturbridge. That is right off the Massachusetts Turnpike, where one of Hebert's candy stores is readily available. Even if it had been the Hebert Candy Mansion in that mythical place called Shrewsbury, I could not have been any happier than I was with this one. Since it took me some thirty years to get here.

The whole thing started, as they say, a long time ago. Before air conditioning. It was impossible to keep chocolates in the Eastern summers way back then because they melted. My father, who has always had a sweet tooth and a way around problems, discovered what he called "White Chocolate." It came from someplace near Boston. What he didn't tell me created two problems. The name of the place where it came from, and what it actually is.

Well, it is not "White Chocolate." No such thing exists. What people mistakenly refer to as "chocolate" in such cases does not have a drop of that marvelous substance in it. It is white candy made with cocoa butter, and no chocolate flavor survives the processing of cocoa butter, nor can be detected. It does melt nicely on the tongue, but it is made of confectioner's sugar, flavorings, and cocoa butter. But no chocolate. Ever.

As for the source of the candy, the ivory milk coating my father used to give us was from Hebert. You see, Hebert invented this ivory candy and started the whole trend toward summer coatings. We used to enjoy that candy on our long rides, and it did hold up very well, since white, pastel, or ivory coatings survive in extremes of heat that would turn chocolate to syrup.

Nowadays, with newfangled inventions such as air conditioning, a huge choice is available—you can have your candies in either ivory or actual chocolate coating. Or both. In the case of Nut Patties, a triple-decker assortment of buttery caramel and pecans (also comes with toasted cashews and almonds), they will gladly top the whole lovely piece in Hebert's ivory milk coating and alternate rows of chocolate.

Two generations of the Hebert family still preside over the kettles. Their skill is most evident in one piece I like, the maple flavor cream, domed with chocolate. Although I find their Fudge and Penuche too sweet for my taste, they are favorites with many New Englanders. The Genevas, tiny cups of solid Hebert chocolate, are equally beloved. These come plain and with crispy nuts tucked inside.

There are days when I wish I could enjoy the ivory coating with the same pleasure I used to. For a change of pace, or for those who want to delight a child, I look on the novelty pops such as the bears and the elephants with a certain nostalgia. But I have grown up and into the taste of good old chocolate, nostalgia and family notwithstanding. Still, I do send a selection to the folks at home. They'll take the light road. I always take the dark.

Hebert Candy Mansion
575 Hartford Pike
Shrewsbury, Mass. 01545
Tel.: (617) 844–8051

Ask for their brochure which lists all six locations of Hebert's, plus all the candies which they can make available to you by mail order, when the weather permits shipping.

BEDFORD
Fanny Farmer Candy Shops, Inc.
Eastern chocolate time begins with Fanny Farmer. As one of the first candy shops in the New England area, and now with over 350 shops in some twenty-two states, Fanny Farmer is synonymous with chocolate

Fanny Farmer antique candy boxes. *(Design Studio, Bedford, Mass.)*

candies. My own taste for their confections goes back a long time, also. You might say I have a certain personal involvement, although no vested interests in their products, since my mother adored them. She kept a constant supply of their Nut Rolls around. No matter how well she hid them, I always managed to find them. I learned quite early exactly how many slices I could enjoy before it became apparent the roll had diminished in size.

I still enjoy those Nut Rolls, and I am delighted Fanny Farmer is still making them. I am sure my mother is delighted that her own supply lasts much longer than it used to.

From the first shop Frank O'Connor opened in Rochester, New York, back in May 1919, his decision to take the name Fanny Farmer was a stroke of genius and good taste. He wanted that name because it was one that had merited the public's attention and trust. Fanny Farmer was the first American to set her recipes into a cookbook and use level measurements such as teaspoons, tablespoons, and cups to indicate the exact quantities a recipe needed. She thought of food as "anything which nourishes the body," and included all types of edibles in her gastronomic survey, from jelly sandwiches to quenelles. Of course, she also included recipes for candy. Her cooking school made excellence and quality its standards, just as they were hers. She was a tireless worker, and continued to pursue her career until almost the end of her life. In fact, she gave a lecture only ten days prior to her death.

When Frank O'Connor wanted a name for his new candy stores, her name quickly came to mind. The integrity and quality associated with Fanny Farmer were precisely the aims Frank O'Connor had for his own products. These new candy stores were to be a direct outgrowth of the Canadian company, Laura Secord Candy Shops, which he had founded. It was natural for him to adopt the same black and white simplicity that had proved successful in the Secord shops for his new candy stores. His initial goal was to stay in the United States until he had exhausted his capital of $50,000 or become successful. By 1969, the assets of Fanny Farmer exceeded $26 million.

Fanny Farmer does most of their business in their own shops, but their products are also available in department stores and drugstores. Whenever I am in Boston, I head for their familiar black and white shops, such as the one on Tremont Street, even though I know these stores extend to the Great Plains. Somehow my childhood insists in thinking of them as primarily Eastern, and so I stand outside the familiar glass window and enjoy my bit of nostalgia before entering.

Of course, once inside, I begin with my all-time favorite, Nut Rolls, with their chocolate centers tucked away under the nut and caramel exteriors. For the sake of freshness, I think these should be eaten promptly. I say "for the sake of freshness," but that is a virtuous rationalization for my own lovely lack of willpower, since I am busy trying one as I walk out of the store. And yes, it is fresh, crunchy, and meltingly good.

Their bark is always as good as the bite. Fine chocolate and wholesome almonds make this special item another favorite of mine. Their creams are lovely, with moist centers, but they have to wait until I have finished with the buttercrunch.

The chocolate Fanny Farmer uses to coat all these lovelies comes primarily from three sources: Merckens, Nestlé, and Blommer. Each firm makes a fine, distinctive range of chocolate coatings, and Fanny Farmer selects the right center to be coated with just the right chocolate. This shows the entire candy piece to its best advantage, since the center and coating must add to one another to produce a unique flavor.

For the past few years Frank Benson has been president of Fanny Farmer. His background is not so much candy maker as candy consumer. Arriving there at an auspicious time, he decided to move back toward the old-time candy image, and to the ingredients and conditions that had made Fanny Farmer so much a part of America these past fifty years. For just prior to the time he joined them, my Boston friends were telling me, with regret intended, that the candy just wasn't what it used to be. Frank Benson changed all that. He put back into the firm what was needed and his direction was a return to the old-fashioned idea in both concept and tradition. "We use premium, fresh-from-the-dairy-four-times-a-week, the freshest butter," he told me, and then went on to say the same kind of care had been extended into every area of production.

He talked about preservatives in candy, and the reasons for their use. To keep his candy in prime condition, a few preservatives must be added, since Fanny Farmer is sold in a great many places other than their own shops. This gives their candy a little longer shelf life than their Western or Midwestern counterparts, See's and Fannie May.

For a firm of their size, with products sold in as many places as theirs are, Fanny Farmer does a good job in providing a moderately priced, consistently good selection and range of chocolate candies. I still recommend, however, purchasing their candies at their own stores. Call it nostalgia on my part, but I think they taste best fresh from the counter, purchased directly. That is the way I always buy it, or I order it, direct.

Fanny Farmer Candy Shops, Inc.
4 Preston Court
Bedford, Mass. 01730
Tel.: (617) 275–1300

Ms. Carol Gamache is the person in charge of customer relations and a fine knowledgeable candy consumer herself. She will be glad to answer your questions about their fine products.

DANVERS
Putnam Pantry

Just to confound me, the Massachusetts highway system has placed a new bypass in front of Putnam Pantry. This bit of cloverleaf madness is impossible to figure out logically and improbable to come upon. It gives you many views of the place you are trying to reach from any number of inappropriate angles. I kept seeing Putnam Pantry just across the way as I trundled down one incorrect frontage approach after another, until finally, in desperation, I pulled up at a firehouse and asked specific directions.

You would think, having once gone through that series of maneuvers, I would know how to manage it the next time. No. I finally had a police escort, who laughingly led me to the front door. When I managed to get there, Galo Putnam Emerson, the owner, took one look at my distraught countenance and insisted that I go over to his ice-cream counter. "Make a sundae," he instructed. As I stared down at the incredible choice of homemade toppings, I must have been reeling from the drive. Which one—or better yet, which ones? I couldn't decide, so I asked for two helpings of his freshly made ice cream, and began. Start with the Hawaiian pineapple, and then you can proceed right through the hot penuche sauce, chocolate, hot fudge, butterscotch, and marshmallow toppings. There are other toppings as well, but that should indicate the heaping conglomerate I brought back to the table.

When I felt restored, I went on to the chocolate candies. Galo is reticent about lauding one over another. "I don't think there's an awful lot unusual about *our* candy relative to other retail confectioners', our candy is about the same," he modestly said. It's a good thing his candy isn't as modest as he is, for it only takes a few moments of careful snooping to discover the tangerine jelly, coated in chocolate. It literally bursts into flavor on the tongue.

Another bit of exotica is his wild assortment of chocolate lollipops. It isn't often you can have a chocolate pony, bear, or an insoucient duck for your very own. He makes these to delight children, but I imagine there are adults who are equally fond of them.

His Snowflake, which has coconut in it, rises above his modest claims by a mile, as does his Buttercrunch, with its unusual coat of Brazil nuts. With the wide assortment of chocolates he makes available, the summer favorites (coated in pastels) are big sellers with New Englanders who stop to buy a box of candy. But I'd hate to have to pass up the creams or the

enormous Snowballs, those giant marshmallows dipped in dark chocolate, just on the basis of a warm summer day.

If it is one of those hot, sticky days, I'd suggest one item that met all
the prerequisites chocolate lovers want, plus its own bit of cooling taste.
The water fondant mints, resting on chocolate wafer bases, are refreshing
and guaranteed to banish any heated thoughts. Then you can go ahead
and enjoy his nut-encrusted centers, those crunchy marvels hidden away
as they are beneath hand-dipped chocolate coating.

Try a few Frappes, also. And while you are there, do look around,
because the history of Putnam Pantry is unique. Galo's ancestor was
General Israel Putnam, second in command to George Washington. The
house next to the store is the original house in which the general lived. If
all history lessons had been in as interesting surroundings as this one
proved to be, and had been as tastefully presented, I might have managed
to equate history with less than stale books and dry dates.

Putnam Pantry
Route One
Danvers, Mass. 01923
Tel.: (617) 774–4484

Mail orders are accepted and shipped when weather permits. Do ask for
the Homestyle Assortment.

BOSTON
Bailey's

As we grow older, memory has a kind way of editing rich moments so
they become even better. Of all the summer weeks I spent visiting my
grandparents, who lived just outside of Boston, one particular evening
still comes to mind. It was one of those New England summer evenings
when even the breeze off the ocean has ceased to move. The air was heavy,
and all my cousins were gathered on the front steps of the house, arguing
listlessly about some trivia. Uncle Archie came outside and watched us
for a few minutes, then took out his keys and announced we were all
going for a ride.

I remember we squeezed into the Mercury and headed toward
Boston. Endless questions of where are we going and when will we get
there were met with complete silence. He simply lit another cigar and

Old-time photograph of Bailey's. *(Bailey's—Franklin Wyman, president)*

continued to drive until he reached his destination. Then he led us inside what I remember as an ice-cream parlor, sat us down at a marble-topped table, and ordered hot fudge sundaes for all of us.

"These aren't just ordinary hot fudge sundaes," I remember him saying, and a few minutes later they arrived. I would like to believe it was my shorter point of view that convinced me we had each been served a mountain of ice cream, for the tall silvery goblets were Everests of ice cream, over whose chilled surface flowed a swiftly hardening hot fudge mingled with marshmallow river. The rim was already a pool of chocolate, as we reached for the long spoons, ready to climb into the whipped cream, nuts, saving the inevitable maraschino cherry for last.

I doubt we ever got around to the cherry. As a child, it was a prodigious feat of gluttony to attempt to eat it all. Now, years later, more or less an adult, I find it still takes no small effort, as I introduce my daughter to Bailey's, using the same phrase my uncle used: "This isn't just an ordinary hot fudge sundae." Oh, understatement!

When it arrives, her face mirrors what mine must have years ago: delight, pleasure, all this along with disbelief. The moment in which one

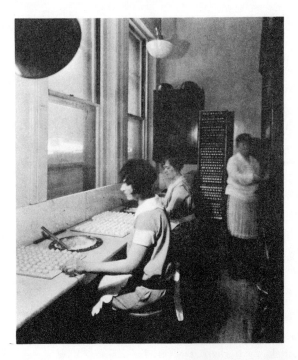

Old-time photographs of
Bailey's. *(Bailey's—*
Franklin Wyman, president)

is overwhelmed. For once, nostalgia has not betrayed me. Before us stands the Mount Fuji of sundaes, and not only is it as I remember it, but the taste is the same, luscious. I knew Bailey's would not fail me; how could I have held the slightest doubt?

For over a hundred years, Bailey's has served chocolate to a discriminating Boston public. File cards, with the customer's preferred assortment, are still kept up to date for those good patrons who have bought candies there time and time again. If your name is on record, you can simply phone up to ask that an assortment be sent. Bailey's will know exactly what you want.

Downstairs, where the chocolates are made (and most are still hand-dipped), a fine English candy maker, John Lewis, instructs. The formulas have been altered very little from the original ones: Bailey's still insists that vanilla be used in their chocolate coating, instead of the more usual and less expensive vanillin. Van Leer Chocolate Corporation makes Bailey's special blend to the specifications required.

We taste and define the various chocolate-covered nuts. Then we pay homage to a few caramels with their dark, rich coatings. The marshmallow, domed with chocolate, is a special piece. In the hands of a less competent candy master, it would be a treacled disaster, but no, this one is bouncy, light, and just this side of gratification.

"These are marvelous," I say, by way of understatement, as I try a few more pieces. Then even I must give up, and admit I am chocolated out.

On the way toward the door, the thought of chocolates should be beyond me. My body and tastes are full, satisfied, complete, but for old time's sake, I detour, pause at the candy counter, and buy a small assortment: a few whole-stem cherries dipped in dark chocolate, one or two pieces of solid chocolate wrapped in Bailey's gold foil, their name scripted in red over and over.

Only then can I walk out. Into the streets of Boston. I feel both familiar and unfamiliar, in this city in which I am walking. These are the streets I remember as a child, and now I am tracing old paths with my own daughter. The least I could do was to buy these, then give them to her as we part, sharing one more of my sweeter memories of childhood.

Bailey's
26 Temple Pl.
Boston, Mass. 02111
Tel.: (617) 426–4560

They will accept mail orders and will ship your favorite assortment to you when the weather is cool enough to guarantee their chocolate candies can arrive in as lovely shape as when they were packed.

MARBLEHEAD
Harbor Sweets

For those of us who love to sail, few things can match the excitement of being on a small sailboat as the land slips away, the nylon flutters, then catches a full breeze. The tide running with us, our landlocked selves shed their cumbersome, slow movements. It is as if we take on those elements of which we are now part: water and air.

When winter comes, you can re-create these moments, thanks to my friends in Marblehead, Massachusetts, who understand these yearnings and make Harbor Sweets. When you unwrap the classic red box, the fabric ribbons fall away to reveal chocolates as adventurous and beautiful as a regatta.

Ben Strohecker's Sweet Sloops are guaranteed to please any sailor. Wrapped in gold foil, each takes the shape of a sailboat (all are done by hand), and you can see the outline of the sloop, as it rises from its base of crushed spindrift (bits of pecans, in actuality) to float on a perfect wave of Nestlé dark chocolate. The mainsail and jib are covered with Wilbur's white coating. But the real treasure lies just beneath the surface as you taste the finest almond buttercrunch anywhere. The rich butter mingles with nuts, and dissolves with chocolate into a moment of complete pleasure.

There are other pleasures to be had at Harbor Sweets, as well. All have a nautical theme. Marblehead Mints features a rounded sea and sky of bittersweet chocolate, embossed with a sailboat. As if that weren't enough, this night sail into a sea of savory chocolate has tiny peppermint "starlights" hidden away in the depths. These, too, are hand-wrapped in foil, and each is as lovely to look at as it is delectable to devour.

Recently, they've come up with a new candy piece called Sand Dollars. It features bittersweet chocolate as the coating, with a buttery crunch sandwiched midway through. The top looks like a sand dollar; hence, the name.

Ben and Connie Strohecker make all of these lovely candies available in beautiful gift packages. Old-fashioned glasses, with hand-cut sailboats, are filled to overflowing with these gleaming jewels. The

Harbor Sweets Candies—Sweet Sloops.
(Harbor Sweets: Ben Strohecker)

Harbor Sweets Candies—Marblehead Mints.
(Harbor Sweets: Ben Strohecker)

Stroheckers expect their candies to be sold in places that feature rare items: good crystal and china, gifts for the particular people. The candies are deserving of such magnificent displays, for each is a work of a master in taste and in concept. Each is hand-created, and the people who work in the factory with Ben Strohecker are interested in producing the unusual in candy, the best that can be had.

Harbor Sweets is anyone's delight; and certainly a sailor's, with a clear sky and a delicious chocolate night.

Harbor Sweets
P.O. Box 150
Marblehead, Mass. 01945
Tel.: (617) 745–7648

Connie and Ben Strohecker, who are responsible for these giddy treasures, will be glad to accept mail orders and ship a catalog to you of all the different ways you can send them as gifts. Write and ask. You'll be as happy as I am to know about them.

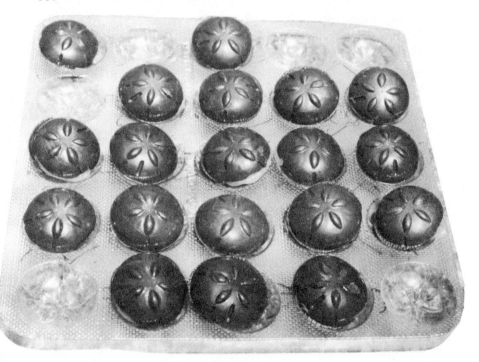

HYANNIS
Cape Cod Candies, Inc.

If it's fudge you want, you will have to be a lot more specific than that one word. Cape Cod Candies has lots of fudge—fourteen different kinds of it to choose from. I chose the dark chocolate with walnuts as my selection, but that was because they had made it easy for me, by only shipping me two of the fourteen they make. I can imagine if I were to go into their shop on Main Street in Hyannis and ask for fudge, I would be there for the better part of an hour trying to decide which one I wished to try first.

The Cranberry Fruit Drops, which contain pure cranberry juice, are one of the ways Cape Cod Candies has devised to allow the chocolate devotee to cleanse the palate between chocolate tastings, and then go on to try some of their Almond Bark offerings. All are made with Nestlé coatings. I am particularly fond of the Monogram coating, although I do not pass up the Broc chocolate with almonds, if it comes my way.

I did not care for their Dream Cups, which are cupcakes of Broc chocolate, marshmallows, crisp rice, and coconut sprinkles, but my friend Julia Poppy was more than delighted to take one home for herself. She loved it. I contented myself with their Buttercrunch, which is a butter brittle, covered with chocolate and then liberally rolled in a cashew, almond, and macaroon mixture. I ate all of that myself. Try it. You'll like it.

Cape Cod Candies, Inc.
550 Main St.
Hyannis, Mass. 02601
Tel.: (617) 775–0297

Michael E. DeBenedictis makes these fudges, hand-dipped chocolates, and homemade candies available to us. Write and request a list from which to choose what you want sent. He will ship you your favorite assortment whenever the weather makes it possible to guarantee safe delivery.

MANSFIELD
Merckens Chocolate Company

Merckens Chocolate Company is a subsidiary of Nabisco. They do make things other than the cocoa for Oreo cookies, although that is one product for which they are famous. They make the chocolate drops for Chips Ahoy, as well as chocolate coatings and candies. Nabisco isn't in the boxed chocolate business, and Merckens supplies coatings to retail candy manufacturers. The high-grade, quality chocolate they make can be found in the nicest places. One such place is on top of Paul Cummings' Three Color Opera Cream, as well as on his other chocolate extravagances I dearly love. Paul's coating is made just for him, to his recipe, and its taste is unlike any other, with just the slightest hint of smokiness to it, and a texture as smooth as the trade winds.

I'm getting carried away just thinking about it, but it's easy to when you taste a chocolate that has been conched for seventy-two hours until it reaches that correct stage called perfection. Merckens doesn't discriminate—big customers as well as smaller ones enjoy their coatings. Fanny Farmer uses Merckens.

Merckens moved to Mansfield only a few years ago, but they didn't alter a long-standing tradition, since the building in which their factory is located has been used for manufacturing chocolate since the turn of the century. The date on the building's front is 1903. It may not be altogether unusual in New England for a factory to remain in use seventy-five years, for New Englanders are rather traditional, after all. But this is one of the few chocolate factories that employs gravity to work for it. The beans are delivered to the top floor, where they begin the long process, floor by floor, down, until they become chocolate. The taste, however, goes up, and that's thanks to the craft and knowledge of John Unger, their head chocolate chemist. He knows chocolate, how it should taste. "Remember, for every unwanted flavor you drive off, Adrianne, you also drive off a wanted flavor," he reminds me.

The skill involves knowing what you are gaining, along with what you are willing to give up, and John *does* know, since he is responsible for all the chocolate, plus developing new flavors and blends, as well as for keeping the formulations of customers exactly the same year after year.

"We have," John tells me, "an American taste, as opposed to a European taste. The Europeans feel we overroast, and we feel they underroast, which produces what we consider a raw bean taste. We like to have a fuller roast. Most manufacturers roast a bit fuller here in America.

"When you get out into the Midwest, they prefer the blander blend. If you have a European dark and an American dark, you would find you don't get as much 'bean' taste in that as you would in the European."

This is reflected in Merckens's customers' continued preference for the milkier chocolate. Sixty-five percent of the chocolate Merckens produces is milk. They ship all over the United States, but a few candies are made here in the Mansfield plant.

I watched them make chocolate-covered cherries, which was the first time I had ever had the chance to see cornstarch molds. Large sheets are filled with cornstarch, which is then indented. The mold will be filled with fondant, containing a cherry. The cornstarch is shaken off, the chocolate coating is applied, a bottom added. At this point, the cherries are still in their fondant stage; firm, white fondant surrounds them. They are put away in a cool place and allowed to "ripen"—that is, given time for the fondant to blend, liquefy. By the time the chocolate-covered cherries are ready to be sold, the fondant has turned to its familiar liquid state.

Merckens is the sole supplier (and owner of the equipment) that makes the Dutch Process Powder for Nabisco, which is very special and is sold only to Nabisco and no one else. When you get to taste it, it is already named Oreo. I admit to eating more than my share of Oreos at one time or another.

I also admit to being more than casually fond of a great many of the Merckens chocolate coatings. Their bittersweet coatings are examples of laudable virtue and impeccable chocolate taste. My very favorite is the one they ship only to Paul Cummings, their Tehauntepec Vanilla, and it is worth a trip to Salt Lake City to enjoy it.

But if I cannot get there, I will settle for a consolation prize—the Nantucket chocolate coating. It's no less a treat, and closer at hand.

Merckens Chocolate Company
P.O. Box 434
Cambridge, Mass. 02139
Tel.: (617) 491–2508

H. J. "Hank" Bornhofft, Jr., is the president of Merckens, and under his fine hand come all these chocolates. If you can use some ten-pound bars to amaze and delight your favorite chocolate consumer, he's probably the one to whom you should write and direct your inquiries. They also provide the coating for Sugar Daddies and other products. Their bittersweet coatings are my favorites.

FLORIDA

DUNEDIN

Harvey Merckens

This chocolate bar comes complete with "Greetings from Florida" scripted along the bottom, right under the picture, which features oranges and orange blossoms in full sunshine. The title is to the left: "Orange Milk Chocolate Crunch," but that seems to me not a full enough description to suggest the combination of fine chocolate with crisped rice, orange oil, sugar, and concentrated whole milk, which is held together just under the gold foil wrapping. It's good enough to brighten the dullest, dreariest day with its flavors. Bring a bit of Florida into your life at any season. This sunshine is delivered to you, direct, courtesy of Harvey Merckens, that little old sunshine and chocolate maker.

Harvey Merckens
Distributed by Florida Chocolate Specialties
P.O. Box 251
Dunedin, Fla. 33528

NEW YORK

NEW YORK CITY

How to Get Through an Entire Day
on Chocolate Alone

Some of these places are more than mere chocolate moments in time, and carry a great many things other than chocolate. Chocolate-minded as I am, even I have to admit there are other things besides chocolate. On the supposition that I had a whole day to spend, with nothing better to do than gather fine chocolates morning, noon, and night, aside from the strict chocolate places, here's how I might spend my time.

I would start off at Bloomingdale's—the chocolate division, of course. You enter right off the street, and there before you are endless counters of chocolate candies gleaming and waiting. Since they carry a considerable number of fine chocolates, you can spend an hour or so choosing from all of them. I suggest Corné and Godiva, two fine Belgian chocolate candies. Just take your time and ask questions. The person behind the counter can tell you all about a particular chocolate, where it is from and what makes it so great. Do try a box of the Corné, since these are special favorites.

Then jaunt on over to Macy's Cellar. The rest of the morning can be spent deciding which of the Côte d'Or chocolate bars you want. Their bittersweet fondant is luscious, as well as some of the other Belgian bars made by Côte d'Or. I would pass up the boxed assortments for the bars.

If Macy's is out of any, there is Simon's Pure Food on Fifty-seventh Street. This shop carries the complete range of Côte d'Or bars as well, and some other chocolate products.

By now, it is lunchtime. I would head over to one of three places. Since I'm inclined to think Swiss food is about the best of all possible taste worlds, thanks to the Italian, French, and other interests which make it as marvelous as it is, I would choose Dézaley, on East Fifty-fourth Street. Not only are the meals here outstanding, but the head chef, Hans, makes some spectacular chocolate desserts. I will even recommend their "white chocolate" Mousse d'Hiver, made with that fine Swiss coating that Tobler produces. There's one other dessert that features melted Toblerone, poured liberally over a meringue shell. It is sensational. All utilize the products of Tobler's, and to their tasty advantage.

In the event Dézaley is closed, I go over to the Swiss Pavillion, where there is no slouching in the way of chocolate desserts, either. If you think you are beyond being impressed, just order the chocolate fondue. It's delivered to your table, chocolate bubbling in a fondue pot, surrounded by fresh fruits and cake, plus the other extravagances they create to go with it. You can have the exciting pleasure of drowning each and every piece in warm, thick chocolate. Toblerone again. One other dessert that lends itself delightfully to their chocolate touch is pedestrian sounding but uncommonly good: the cream puffs.

Périgord Park, over on Park Avenue, makes a perfectly acceptable chocolate cake for dessert. It is the house specialty, and my only niggling with them is that they claim the top has bittersweet shavings gracing it. They tasted more like dark milk chocolate shavings to me, but I didn't pass it up in any case.

By now, it is afternoon. I think you will want to rest a bit. So just have the taxi driver stop for a moment at Colette's so you can pick up one or two of the chocolate cakes, Le Trianon. It never hurts to lay in a supply of these cakes. They freeze well, so you can always have them for company that way. Since you are in the neighborhood, you will also want to take home the bittersweet chocolate cake from William Greenberg's Bakery.

After teatime, with chocolate delights, you can go out to supper at your favorite New York restaurant. But no evening should end without a late evening snack, and since the Plaza doesn't offer their Sacher Torte until very late evening, you should end your day with a bit of that and a

Hotel Plaza's Sacher Torte. *(Adrianne Marcus)*

cup of espresso in the Palm Court. You will find Gale O'Malley's Sacher Torte just right, and a bit different from its European counterparts. The chef uses almond flour and gives the cake a proper rum soaking, prior to putting the layers together with lovely apricot jam. It is the best Sacher Torte I have found in this country. In fact, it surpasses the original from the Hotel Sacher.

That will take you through an entire day. Since I only visit New York on occasions, I suppose there are natives who know of other places that produce other ultimate chocolate trophies that deserve mention. As a visitor to that marvelous, exciting city, I have found my share of chocolate treasures to tell you about. And these should get you started on the chocolate path. Each treasure is worth the time it takes to get there, worth the trip to New York—one of the best of all chocolate worlds.

Vermonti

I responded to this advertisement by Vermonti which promised me "Three of the world's richest chocolates—all melded together into a chocolate dessert." So I walked over to Jane Street and bought one. After all, the rest of the ad stated, "foods that go beyond the ordinary."

Yes, it did precisely that, but in no direction I found favorable. I tried it and disliked it. I thought maybe it was just me, so I attempted a simple test using a native New Yorker, a rather unsuspecting friend. I asked her to taste this new dessert without looking at it prior to trying it. She tasted and said, "That's an unusual pumpkin pie. Thick. Dense." Then I let her look at it. Unless you actually see it, there is no way you will be able to say it is chocolate. Vermonti has gone to some lengths to circumvent any chocolate taste, with heavy spices and a rather gummy texture.

At $5.95 per half pound, plus $2.25 for shipping charges, my only consolation is that I did not pay to have it delivered. I went and got it myself. I threw the rest away, and tried not to think of the great many other places I could put my chocolate dollars and feel they had been better spent. This is not one of them.

Vermonti Enterprises, Inc.
35A Jane St. Department CG-1
New York, N.Y. 10014
Tel.: (212) 924-1572

If you are feeling particularly treacherous, mail someone a two-pound version for only $22.05 plus shipping and handling of $2.95. That'll fix them.

Barton's Bonbonniere

These candies, made in New York, use a Swiss chocolate coating. Since the candies are also kosher, I remember having them around the Jewish holidays, as they were shipped down from New York to those of us in North Carolina who did not have access to a delicatessen. I had not tried them in years until recently, and I now think the only way I could consider consuming them is with a hot cup of chicken soup. Nothing else seems to dissolve them.

One of my tests for chocolate is to hold it in my hand. If it begins to melt promptly, there is enough cocoa butter in the coating to ensure it will also dissolve nicely on my tongue. With Barton's, my palm remained spotless for quite a long time. The candy did not want to give up its shape, which led me to believe that it had absolutely no intention of being consumed and was perfectly content simply to look like a piece of candy.

If all you desire is to have something that looks like candy, you will find Barton's meets that requirement. The taste is not exceptional, the flavor mediocre, and four out of five who tasted it here did not go back for seconds.

Barton's owns fifteen to twenty stores of their own. Their candy is sold in stores throughout the United States (including Hawaii and Puerto Rico) at over twenty-five hundred places. But I do not feel obligated to seek it out again. I consider giving a box of Barton's to any chocolate lover as the ultimate in insults.

Barton's Bonbonniere
80 DeKalb Ave.
Brooklyn, N.Y. 11201
Tel.: (212) 858–5000

Barricini

I could be mistaken, but I find Barricini to be a close tie or a second only in taste to Barton's in the wide world of chocolate candies. As the wide world of candy goes, you couldn't go much further and find less flavor or taste than these.

After the first bite, there is no other. To make me eat a whole box would be both a cruel and unusual punishment.

Barricini
22-19 41st Ave.
Long Island City, N.Y. 11101
Tel.: (212) 786–2200

They own two stores, one of which is located in Brooklyn, the other in Long Island, New York. They also have hundreds of franchises which buy and sell their candy throughout the United States and in Canada and Puerto Rico.

Sweet Temptation

It was not virtue that allowed me to resist Sweet Temptation. It was the box I bought, which two of us tried and had to discard. From the chocolate-covered nuts, which, at best, weren't lethal but genuine geriatric problems, to the rest of whatever those other things were which they sold me as candies, I am now certain they have reached a low point in alchemy. They managed to turn chocolate into lead and me against chocolate for an entire day. I consider that covers a multitude of sins.

Sweet Temptation
Madison Ave., between 34th and 35th Sts.
New York, N.Y. 10016
Tel.: (212) 532–3741

Madison Ave., between 80th and 81st Sts.
New York, N.Y. 10021
Tel.: (212) 734–6082

My suggestions involve alternate routes: anywhere.

Li-Lac Chocolates

When you enter Greenwich Village, there is no immediate feeling of dislocation, no sense that you are leaving the twentieth century.

Everything appears as it should, at first, until you become aware of all the individual presences. What is really good about the Village is how little technology and mass production are apparent. I had a dislocated sense of myself as I stood in front of a shop on Christopher Street, thinking "This place is not of this time." And I was glad it isn't.

Inside Li-Lac's, this feeling does not diminish, but increases, as Margaret Watt, the pleasant and responsive lady behind the counter, takes time to show me pieces of handmade, hand-dipped candy she feels, quite proudly, evidence her craft. If I were allowed to have only one piece, I would not hesitate to choose her Lemon Chiffon. It tastes of sunlight and exotic lemons, under a bittersweet chocolate midnight.

Thankfully, I am permitted more; so I recommend La Petite, their milk French assortment that is not all light chocolate by any means. Tiny chocolate morsels are arranged in eight rows of perfect formation. The third row in, a bit colorful with green marzipan, is a piece half-dipped in chocolate. Try that one, or the square-shouldered brown chocolate piece that stars in the second row: bits of nuts and cherries cresting like tiny plumes on top. A few pieces are rolled in chocolate bits, which add to their beauty and texture.

Half the pleasure in this beautiful assortment occurs before you taste it. It looks exotic and inviting. Each piece seems to have been created with a special effect in mind. Extraordinary care is lavished on the production of these pieces. The hand lettering on each is an individual, proud signature of what is inside.

When I leave the Village, it is with one of these boxes wrapped in its colorful paper. Somehow it makes the transition back to the "real" world all the easier—to know that a place exists where you find the measure of an art such as candy making, and carry it back with you, back to your own particular place and time. I unwrap a box and enjoy it, as it should be enjoyed, leisurely. One more reason to support your local candy maker: It is the past to which you are entitled, and with any luck, it will follow you into the future.

Li-Lac Chocolates
120 Christopher St.
New York City, N.Y.
Tel.: (212) CH. 2–7374

Ask Margaret Watt for her recommendations. She will probably accept mail orders if the weather is good and she can be sure her chocolates will reach you in as good a condition as the day they were made.

Prince Street Bar

Though I like to think of my friends as people of good taste, sometimes their chocolate fantasies have led me astray. I followed directions which stated: "You have to go here and have this incredible cake they make." I did. It's called the Tunnel of Fudge Cake. Among the better qualities it exhibited, I note the following: raw, heavy, moist, and wet. Surrounded by tasteless chocolate, the center resembles an under-done brownie in which stale nuts have been embedded. According to the bartender, "It's very popular."

Arghhhhh.

Prince Street Bar and Restaurant
125 Prince St.
New York, N.Y. 10012
Tel.: (212) 228–8130

Colette's French Pastry

Colette's calls this cake Le Trianon. I call it the best chocolate cake in the world. That sounds excessive, I know, but how else could I possibly describe what appears to be a modest, plain chocolate loaf with its few shaved chocolate curls on top? This one cake could teach me the best lesson ever: never judge a chocolate cake by its appearance.

That plain exterior hides an interior of such lavish proportions, it makes all other chocolate cakes seem dull, fading examples of taste by comparison. Colette's makes these cakes daily. Wrapped in aluminum foil, they travel easily. I brought four home with me, froze two, served the others for dessert. My guests were overwhelmed and asked where they could obtain a dessert this spectacular in flavor. The raves on this cake proved to me chocolate lovers were deserving of this secret, and so I pass it along to other chocolate lovers.

Le Trianon is rich, ravishing, and renews my faith in chocolate cakes. Van Leer supplies the chocolate that goes into this superb production of Colette's. Mouth open, hands down, this is a cake you can't match at any price. It deserves all the good adjectives in this book, and more. The best anywhere.

Colette's French Pastry Shop
1136 Third Ave.
New York, N.Y. 10021
Tel.: (212) YU. 8–2605

Colette's Le Trianon. *(Adrianne Marcus)*

They're closed for a great deal of the summer, but when the weather is cool, cake is obtainable and they will ship it. *Be sure to specify* you must have it *airmailed*. Parcel post destroys it, and leaves you with no cake worth eating. They'll bill you extra for airmail and packing, but it's essential that it be shipped by air, *no other way*. It's $5.00 for the small size (about half a pound) and $7.50 for the larger, plus shipping and handling.

Kron's Chocolatiers

My first encounter with Kron's was less than auspicious. They had just opened their shop on Madison Avenue. I placed my order for chocolate candies via the phone, as a friend had told me to, since I planned to take them back to San Francisco that afternoon on the plane. When I got there, at eleven-thirty, they had already sold out of the particular assortment I thought I had ordered. Fuming, I yelled at Tom Kron, "What did you do with my chocolates?" He attempted to placate me with offerings of chocolate-covered strawberries.

Kron's Candies. *(Richard Steinheimer)*

Since it was December and the strawberries were freshly dipped in chocolate, I was restored to a calmer state, until I attempted to purchase some of these and was told, "I can't sell you these to take across the country. They don't travel well." Despite him, I bought some and took not only these, but chocolate-covered naval orange sections with me. They didn't have time not to travel well. I ate them immediately.

What Tom does with chocolate, he does well. He makes items that are unusual, and run the gamut from A to Z. Yes, an entire alphabet in chocolate, your choice of letters. I chose four of them: LOVE, and brought them home in their wooden crate. They're quite popular for Valentine's Day and other sentimental occasions.

For the feminist on your chocolate list, I'd bypass that hollow mold chocolate leg (complete with garter) he makes. But if you have a tennis friend, Tom has the racquet. Done in chocolate. He makes a chocolate ruler, which I brought back for a teacher friend who found it amusing and tasty.

His freshly dipped fruits are marvelous, as is their price. No one, least of all me, will accuse Kron's of being inexpensive. After all, why should one expect a good piece of chocolate, done artistically, to be priced at less than the maker feels it deserves?

Tom Kron has claimed his chocolate is made right there on the spot out of cocoa butter and cocoa powder. Aside from being a bit fanciful and not unreasonable sounding if the person asking does not know that Federal Drug Administration rulings do not really permit this, this claim has made Tom the *enfant terrible* of other candy makers. While they openly give credit to the manufacturers who produce their slabs of coating in ten-pound blocks, Kron has bypassed this question when asked. But credit ought to go where credit is due, and I think it is due to Nestlé. Perhaps one other manufacturer also is responsible for Kron's coatings, but there is no reason that anyone could call Nestlé's coating anything but uncommonly good, and Kron puts it to good use.

Tom Kron is a showman, and that has to be taken into account, since he finds no chocolates but his own meet his standards. Kron makes good chocolate candies, and I enjoy them tremendously, as I do most carefully produced quality chocolates.

There is nothing wrong with his packaging, either. The items you choose can be packed in his distinctive wooden boxes and shipped anywhere in the country. He makes no cream centers, nor pieces that will not keep for a bit, with the exception of the fresh fruit.

Tom's wife, Diane, deserves a great deal of the credit for such items as the ruler, which was her idea. She works right alongside Tom, and both provide chocolate assortments to gladden the heart, eye, and tongue of all of us.

Try the seashells, tiny chocolate shells of solid chocolate. Dark or light, they are sensational. The dried apricots are also fine, dipped as they are in dark, glossy chocolate.

My advice is to order early in the day and pick up your order early. Tom Kron has outlets in other cities, such as Washington and Beverly

Hills. His chocolate candies go fast anywhere. Not bad for a firm that started business with a total capital of two hundred dollars in the basement of a building in New York, and called its first candies Hello Candies.

Not bad at all. As chocolate reputations go, Kron's became known to a discriminating chocolate public which passed his name along, word of mouth, one to another. It was worth trying then, and it still is.

Kron's Chocolatier, Inc.
764 Madison Ave.
New York City, N.Y.
Tel.: (212) 288–9259

They will accept mail orders and ship their chocolate candies (except the fresh fruits, which cannot be shipped) when the weather is suitable and candies can arrive in good shape. The milk chocolates should be enjoyed promptly, although the solid dark pieces (bittersweet) hold up a bit longer. Write and ask Tom and Diane for your special assortment. Prices are expensive, compared to some other chocolate firms, but packaging is splendid, as are the contents. Price list supplied upon request.

William Greenberg Jr. Desserts, Inc.

In their Madison Avenue store, Greenberg's has a bittersweet-coated chocolate cake which is quite good. It has a fine, dense, good chocolate taste throughout, and the glossy frosting is a bittersweet chocolate lover's dream. Imagine a shiny, rich frosting with just enough sweetness, that pulls away as you slice it, suspended on the top and sides of the cake. Hot, one would almost be tempted to think of it as the hot fudge that covers the best sundaes, but cool, as it is on the cake, it has that same thick and sensual consistency over the heavier, dense layer of chocolate cake. The two textures go together perfectly, and it is a marvelous conclusion to any meal.

I find it travels well when carried by hand to its proper destination: a dessert plate. And it is rich, so a small slice is ample. I've hand-carried this one on a plane, and it came through in perfect shape, to be enjoyed the following evening at dinner. Chocolate lovers in New York told me about it, and my chocolate contact, Sheila, made it available to me the first time. We now present it to you, as another chocolate gift from the Big Apple.

William Greenberg Jr. Desserts, Inc.
817 Madison Ave.
New York, N.Y. 10021
Tel.: (212) Le. 5–7118

William Greenberg Jr. Desserts, Inc.
1100 Madison Ave.
New York, N.Y. 10028
Tel.: (212) 744–0304

W. Greenberg Jr. Desserts, Inc.
17 East 8th St.
New York, N.Y. 10003
Tel.: (212) 674–6657

William Greenberg Jr. Desserts, Inc.
1377 Third Ave.
New York, N.Y. 10021
Tel.: (212) Un. 1–1340, or 876–2255

I don't think they can ship this one, but you can pick it up in New York if you order it early in the day.

Cella's Confections, Inc.

This 114-year-old firm is devoted to only one thing: chocolate-covered cherries. What makes this firm unusual is the fact that it is the only manufacturer in the country that makes these chocolate-covered cherries in a liquid center. Other firms produce chocolate-covered cherries, but the cherry is suspended in fondant, which must ripen and liquefy before the candies are sold. In some cases, the fondant never completely dissolves, or leaves a sugary residue on the chocolate shell's bottom.

Cella's makes this candy differently. In 1929, when they introduced this item into their varied line of candies, they hadn't intended to gear all their production to this one item. By 1941, the demand for the cherries was so strong, the other candies were discontinued. Their attention was devoted to making and selling chocolate-covered cherries.

In 1972, the company found itself in financial difficulties. Hy Becker, a career candy man, stepped in, and under his guidance the firm began moving forward again to financial and confectionary stability.

New packaging and new methods replaced old ones. Now, liquid chocolate arrives at the forty-thousand-square-foot multi-level plant and is piped into holding tanks, while corn syrup is received in fifteen-thousand-pound tanks, and sugar is stored in a tank that holds forty thousand pounds. From Michigan, pitted cherries arrive in 275-pound drums. They are processed for over two weeks, and only then can all these ingredients come together in the making of chocolate cherries.

The chocolate is fed into metal molds, which are dome-shaped. Once the chocolate is deposited, the molds are inverted so that the excess is removed, leaving a thick outer shell for what comes next: liquid filling and a cherry. The bottom goes on last. Now the candies are cooled, then fed into other machines. Some pack them into boxes, others wrap individual candies in foil (three hundred pieces per minute can be foil-wrapped).

The candies come in light and dark chocolate coating. I find the milk chocolate is a bit sweet for my taste. The milk chocolate itself is sweet, the liquid center a second sweetness, and the cherry adds a touch of its own. So I leave that box for those who prefer the sweetest touch. I prefer the darker chocolate-covered cherries. There is a good contrast between the coating, which has a deeper chocolate taste as it gives way to the sweeter liquid center, and the cherry seems to be outstanding in those surroundings. They are rich and full-bodied cherries, and about three pieces is my limit at a time.

The chocolate they use is top-quality coating. In light or dark chocolate, Cella cherries are easy to obtain in most places that carry good candies. I wish they made a bittersweet one. I would love to taste that cherry suspended in liquid inside a bittersweet shell. But for now, I content myself with the dark chocolate-covered cherries. Try them. See if these please you as much as they surprised and pleased me, accustomed as I was to the more ordinary fondant ones.

Cella's Confections, Inc.
327 West Broadway
New York, N.Y. 10007
Tel.: (212) 925–3260

Hy Becker, the president of Cella's, will be glad to let you know where you can find these cherry candies. They are available in a great many places, and the foil-wrapped individual ones and the three-packs are usually sold in grocery stores. I've spotted them at the checkout counter of my own supermarket. You'll know them by the phrase on the package: "Chocolate-Covered Cherries with 100% Liquid Center."

WHITE PLAINS

The Nestlé Company, Inc.

Although the first Nestlé product, Henri Nestlé's Instant Milk Food, was introduced into the United States over a hundred years ago, it was imported from Switzerland, where Nestlé began. The history of Nestlé in America dates from 1900, the year they opened their first American manufacturing facility in Fulton, New York, with a total staff of eighty employees.

The Fulton plant produced baby foods, condensed milk, and cans in which to pack Nestlé products, such as cheese. The cheese was an example of typical Swiss ingenuity, since it was a summertime by-product of all the milk Nestlé used. Within seven years, these items were no longer being made in Fulton, with the exception of the infant milk food, since the plant was busy producing chocolate. The parent chocolate firm in Switzerland had agreed to allow Nestlé in America to produce their own chocolate, using the Swiss-formula chocolate method under an agreement with Peter Kohler Chocolate Suisse, S.A.

In 1912, Thomas L. Leeming became the first president of Nestlé's American operations, and within seven years, another brand came onto the market here: Nestlé Milk Chocolate, made in Fulton. It wasn't until 1938 that Americans got their first taste of an item that would become one of the top five chocolate bars sold in retail outlets: the Nestlé Crunch Bar.

Chocolate isn't the only thing Nestlé produces. The American consumer buys many of the firm's products, such as Nescafe, Nestlé Tollhouse Morsels, Maggi and Crosse and Blackwell products, Taster's Choice freeze-dried coffee, and goods that bear the label Libby, McNeill, and Libby. Nestlé is the largest food corporation in the world.

By 1976, Nestlé Alimentana, S.A., the parent organization in Switzerland, established a wholly-owned U.S. holding company, Nestlé Enterprises, Inc. Worldwide; the entire organization operates 297 facilities in 52 countries and provides jobs for over 140,000 employees.

With all this expansion, the company has made provisions for administering and coordinating its world wide activities. In 1957, it established a Management Development Institute in Switzerland in cooperation with the School of Business Administration of Harvard University. The school's purpose is to train global executives.

This was and is necessary, considering the rate of growth and expansion Nestlé has undergone. By 1972, Nestlé Alimentana and allied companies had 100 administrative centers and offices, 297 factories, and 697 sales branches and depots in 51 countries. With sales of $4.2 billion, Nestlé is the largest industrial Swiss company as well as the world's largest food corporation. In an effort to bypass the problems that have plagued some multinational corporations, particularly those in the developing countries, the 81 manufacturing plants Nestlé operates in 27 developing countries provide more than just jobs for 27,000 employees. They provide the necessary training for local people at all levels of the operation, from factory jobs to the highest management level. The plants, after all, are considered long-term facilities. After an initial stage, the "foreign" people are usually replaced with local management. Today in Africa, Latin America, and Asia, less than 2 percent of Nestlé employees are foreign-born.

Every Nestlé subsidiary has a high degree of autonomy from the parent organization, and its products, such as chocolate, are manufactured for the people of the area in which they are made. They are usually not for export. That's why the Nestlé Crunch Bar you adore in Switzerland tastes different from the one you buy in Germany or Belgium or England. They all bear the same name, but each is directed toward the particular taste of the region in which it is made.

In the United States, the Nestlé Crunch Bar, Milk Chocolate Bar, and Choco'Lite are well known to the public. On every supermarket shelf, other Nestlé products from Hot Cocoa Mix to cookie mixes use the famous Nestlé chocolate.

Home base in America for Nestlé's is White Plains, New York. From here, operations are directed to the fourteen Nestlé plants. Not all are busy making chocolate. In Hilbert, Wisconsin, the plant produces cheese and Wispride Cheese Spread. The instant tea plant is located in Granite City, Illinois. New Milford, Connecticut, produces Maggi seasonings and bouillon, regular and Toll House cookie mixes, vending soups, protein hydrolysates and natural citrus flavors.

You have to go back to Fulton to return to the thought of chocolate,

Nestlé is another name synonymous with American chocolate.
(*Nestlé Company, Inc.*)

for it is still being made, right there, with items such as Crunch, Choco'Lite, Quik, Hot Chocolate Mix, and chocolate coatings. Heading west, the next chocolate plant is in Burlington, Wisconsin, where Morsels, Quik, Nestlé's Milk Chocolate bars, the $100,000 enrobed bar, and chocolate coatings are made. And at the edge of the continent, in Salinas, California, a new plant is totally devoted to chocolate. Quik, chocolate bars, and coatings are produced on the West Coast.

The bulk chocolate division of Nestlé is responsible for the coatings. Milk and ice-cream companies, bakeries, and candy makers buy their coatings in great quantity from Nestlé. Two superb milk chocolate coatings, Ultra and Broc, are favorites of a great many candy makers, for these products are as close to Swiss milk chocolate as anything made in this country. Used correctly, the coatings set off contrasting centers with such success that they put a candy a degree above perfection.

Nestlé products. *(Nestlé Company, Inc.)*

Having tasted both, I can see why candy makers insist that these milk chocolates are the best. I have melted about two pounds of their milk chocolate in a crock pot—for it must be melted slowly and at a low temperature to avoid burning—and then invited my guests to a chocolate fondue. Fresh slices of peaches, apricots (pitted), and whole strawberries are dipped. When the warm chocolate hits the cold fruit, it begins to harden. You have instant candy. Guests adore dipping their own fruit-ka-bobs—various fruits on long skewers, ready to be plunged into the crockpot which is half full of warm, aromatic milk chocolate. I have never managed to convince them to take the fruit after it is dipped and place it in the refrigerator to finish hardening. No one wants to wait that long.

Some of my favorite chocolate candies use Nestlé to achieve star status; Edelweiss in Los Angeles coats its wide range of confections in Nestlé, and on the East Coast, Bob Munson of Munson's Candy Kitchen in Hartford, Connecticut, runs the Bolton strawberries through Nestlé chocolate. He's a master of fruit and chocolate confections as far as I'm concerned. I've also spotted ten-pound Nestlé coating bars at Kron's factory on Park Avenue. And Nestlé supplies See's with coating. The same care is given to the big and the small consumer, and the coatings Nestlé makes are available to anyone in the candy business. Each is marked "Peter's" with the legend "High as the Alps in quality," as per terms of the original agreement. Only the compound bars, those that replace part of the cocoa butter with another vegetable oil, are marked "Nestlé." These hold up a bit better in extremes of hot weather, and to most people, taste the same as chocolate. But I prefer the "Peter's" bars. I'm old-fashioned enough to think I can taste the difference. Since Ultra and Broc are exceptionally smooth and creamy, I gravitate to those two coatings.

Hershey and Nestlé are the two biggest chocolate manufacturers in America, but only Nestlé makes coatings available to others. The boxed chocolates you enjoy are likely to have Nestlé coating on them. In the hands of a master candy maker, the candies I have tasted, using Nestlé coating, are extraordinary in flavor and a pleasure to enjoy.

Nestlé Company, Inc.
100 Bloomingdale Rd.
White Plains, N.Y. 10605
Tel.: (914) 682–6206

Malcolm Blue is the man I spoke with at Nestlé. He knows all the subtleties of taste, from the lightest milk chocolate coating, Ultra, to the lowest-viscosity milk chocolate coating, Glenmere. If you like fondant-type bittersweets, Zenda and Newport are great, but Burgundy is the one I find lingers on the tongue the longest. If you can use one hundred or so pounds, I'd recommend asking Malcolm if Nestlé can ship to you. I think the Fulton plant makes the best coatings. If you're going to nibble away at that much chocolate, it's worth the extra mileage charge. William Savel is the vice president in charge of all this, and a fine consumer of candy himself.

SYRACUSE

Ronsvalle's Candies

Gladys Ronsvalle's energy is extraordinary, and she applies it in every way possible. If you can name it, she's probably made it, and that includes what I'm beginning to think of as common—chocolate-covered pretzels (I still won't eat them, no matter how many firms make them) and chocolate-covered potato chips, right on through a miniature assortment of your more usual centers coated in chocolate, to an item which people ask her to ship everywhere in the world: her handmade, hand-created, boxes of chocolate. These are *not* chocolates in a box, as you usually think of them. This item is a chocolate box, created for a special occasion, per your request. It can be as creative as you can come close to finding anywhere. One box has sides of chocolate and nuts, then a plain chocolate top. All sorts of decorations are available to grace the lid: flowers, "Happy Birthday," "You Are a Jewel," or whatever the customer desires.

As a true candy maker, there's little left that Gladys hasn't attempted in Nestlé's coating, from a Wedgwood design on a chocolate box to the simplest thirty-cent piece of candy. So you can imagine the range and diversity of her products; if they start at thirty cents, they go all the way up to very special boxes which can cost, say, thirty dollars, but if the person to whom the gift is being sent is worth his or her weight in chocolate, this seems a small price to pay.

Ronsvalle's Candies
205 Cannon St.
Syracuse, N.Y. 13205
Tel.: (315) 478–0089

Just write and ask Gladys or give her your idea and she'll fill it to fit the occasion. She ships just about anywhere.

BUFFALO
New Garden of Sweets
The New Garden of Sweets is a family business. It's owned and operated by the Tassy family, father, mother, and son. All their recipes are the original ones with which they began making and offering candies to the people of Buffalo back in 1944. That was the year they opened their first shop and made their hand-dipped and handmade chocolates available to customers.

While other stores began as they did, hand-dipping chocolates, then gradually turned production over to machines to enrobe and coat centers, the Tassys have remained firmly and chocolately committed to having hand dippers make their pieces. With 176 years of combined experience behind those chocolate kettles, the hand dippers can produce candies with a speed that makes some enrobing machines look slightly slow by comparison.

Nestlé coatings are always used in the various chocolate creations. I adore the little flowers they make in chocolate, as well as the colored marzipan pieces. There is, of course, a complete variety of chocolate-covered creams, nuts, and chews, which they make right there. Each box is unique, for the Tassys allow their packers to arrange the assortments according to the individual packer's personal selections. It makes the box of chocolates you get that much more distinctive and original.

During the months candies can be shipped safely, I am sure one of these luscious displays can be yours. Just write and ask E. Dean Tassy what is available.

New Garden of Sweets
3180 Bailey Ave.
Buffalo, N.Y. 14215
Tel.: (716) 836–9625

They operate three retail outlets in and around the Buffalo area, but are happy to answer mail-order requests and ship chocolates to you.

5
THE GREAT EUROPEAN CHOCOLATE CHASE

By the time Melanie and I returned to California, I felt we had a chocolate overview of America. Having visited factories that manufacture coatings, we saw these same coatings take on every shape possible, over as many candy centers as possible. From the hands of dippers to the belts of giant enrobing machines carrying their chocolate treasures through a rain of chocolate, we had tasted every conceivable combination. I had lost eight pounds, despite the fact I had consumed chocolate daily, sometimes as much as a pound of candy in a single twenty-four-hour period. A few months before, when Pat Tellier had told me she lost thirty pounds by eating chocolate before meals, I had nodded politely. Now I knew exactly how that happens. Chocolate before meals depresses the appetite, satiates the hunger. We always ate chocolate early in the day. Doing so gave us unbounded energy.

Now we were preparing to depart for Europe to broaden our chocolate horizons. We were afflicted with the joyous chocolate travel syndrome. In America, people would mention a particular chocolate candy that was obtainable only in Belgium, or Switzerland, but alas, not here. We were beholden, in this pursuit of goodness, to make an attempt to discover what Europeans enjoyed in the way of chocolate that we had not tasted yet. After all, it was their gift to us, I reminded myself, and good chocolate candies are worth traveling for.

Six thousand miles of America behind us, we boarded our transatlantic flight. What could be nicer than September in chocolate? We anticipated a great deal, and we were not disappointed. No matter which country we visited, each had its own kind of chocolate.

We began in Belgium. We could not have made a more fortunate choice, for Belgian chocolates are a rare treat. In Brussels, candy stores seemed to be on every corner. It was hard to choose which shop to enter first. We visited Belgian chocolate manufacturers, as well as tiny retailers. The candies were so incredibly good that we made a special trip back to Brussels, just prior to departing on our homeward flight. We wanted to buy some of these chocolate Belgian creams and bring them back here. Aside from simple, enjoyable gluttony, it was a true scientific test. Would these delicate Belgian creams take to freezing? And what would happen to them in the process? We knew that under ordinary circumstances, their life span was approximately four days. Then the whipped cream centers under the chocolate turned to cheese. Could we stop that process? Would the chocolate hold up? The answer is *yes*. They can be frozen, if certain precautions are taken, and they will last for months. Or until eaten.

In Switzerland, we had the pleasure of all the Swiss milk chocolates we could hold, plus chocolate desserts that defy comparison. Two of my favorite places, the Tobler factory and the Nestlé factory, opened their doors and their chocolates to us. There is nothing more pleasurable than wandering through a chocolate factory that is in full production. It is hard not to want one of everything. There were also small confectioners in each town. We did not pass up these sources of delight. Each place had an array of chocolate candies to be found nowhere else.

Only in France were we disappointed, but Italy more than made up for that. Pernigotti, Perugina, and Ferrero provided us with some of the darkest, creamiest candies imaginable. Liquor-filled chocolates, hazelnuts suspended in chocolate, creamed hazelnut centers under chocolate—all were suddenly within reach. And we took them.

Denmark's chocolates were a treat in themselves; Anthon Berg made them. We ate them. England and Cadbury were next. We compared Danish to English chocolates before going back to Belgium and on to Germany.

Join the adventure. Here is what is in store for you in some of the chocolate moments of Europe. Chocolates can cross any language barriers; their pleasure is universal. When the language of a place was foreign to us, the custom of chocolates wasn't. Here are the special places we found and I now share with you. Each was and is very special.

BELGIUM

BRUSSELS
Godiva Chocolatier

Before I left America, a friend called me up to express her mixed feelings about Godiva. She demanded to know why I had not told her that Godiva chocolates in America were owned by Pepperidge Farm. "After all," she said, "I bought them as Belgian chocolates." I agreed that Godiva chocolates had come from Belgium originally, but they, as a Belgian firm, and their American counterpart happened to be owned by yet another company. While she enjoyed her moment's relief at that news, I am afraid I did not alleviate her next question, "Well, who does own them?" with my answer, "Campbell's Soup." The silence which greeted my announcement indicated her suspicion of treachery on my part. She kept repeating the name as if this sudden revelation had invalidated all those gold Ballotins of chocolates she dearly loves to give and to receive. I finally had to remark, perhaps tactlessly, that I didn't think it affected them, did it? After all, she had never eaten a single one with a chicken noodle center as yet.

What I did not tell her was that the Godiva chocolates she buys in America are not the same as those in Belgium. Yes, they do look the same, but no, they do not taste the same.

Americans are not permitted to bring chocolates with liquor in them into this country. About 80 percent of the chocolates made by Godiva in Belgium contain enough liquor in their making to deny them import into this country. You can use a certain percentage of liquor with chocolate, and the American ones do contain the permitted percentage, but it is a great deal less than their European counterparts. Not chocolate-liquor—that is just chocolate mass plus cocoa butter—but liquor-liquor: booze. That is forbidden in the United States because of old rulings and the idea that children might buy them.

Godiva's original recipes called for liquor to be added to the chocolate mixture itself. The amount required in the formulation of these candies means that they cannot enter this country. Legally. They can't be shipped from Godiva to America. In order for the American firm to import the Belgian candies, the formulations would have to be altered to conform to our American laws.

Godiva was planning to ship some at the time I visited their factory in Brussels, but they were careful to point out that the chocolate would meet our qualifications. Unless these qualifications are changed, we will continue to be denied a whole range of lovely and tasty European chocolates.

Aside from that, there is another factor involved that may or may not limit our imports. Europeans, we were told, tend to prefer these darker, heavier chocolates. The American version is much lighter, and to my taste, blander. The standard operating reason is an old one: Americans want a milkier, blander-tasting chocolate. On behalf of chocolate lovers everywhere, I wish to announce publicly: No we don't! Given a chance at anything else, one's taste graduates to prefer the innocuous less and the extraordinary more. And Godiva-Belgium is, front and center, extraordinary.

After having these chocolates for a week, I would be willing to bet if they were available on a full-time basis, we would eat them at a faster rate than we now consume our own lovely, but somewhat pallid-by-comparison beauties. For as beautiful, exquisite, expensive, and above all, lavish as Godiva candies are reputed to be, the Belgian version is even more so. Their packaging is as luxurious as any, anywhere else in the world. Each box is designed by an artist. Velvet, feathers, rich brocades with art reproductions serve as the top of the box and these elements are only the beginning.

Each season is complete with its own color schemes. For fall, the time of year in which I was in Belgium, the boxes came in autumnal shades, moss green and light gold, decorated with tufts of pheasant feathers. One brown velvet sported a bit of plumage arching up and over the top of the gift box. There was a celadon velvet that looked as rare as imperial Chinese celadon, cold as the Snow Queen, as ornate as a winter palace. To receive any of these with their nestled contents of chocolates would be a rare treat. The chocolates themselves are as ornate as the boxes.

Belgian candy makers specialize in shell molding their chocolate candies. This permits those tiny sculpturelike pieces to be created in likenesses of bunches of grapes, pineapples, crowns, hearts, and other forms. Each is visually different from the next, and all are a gift. Godiva, a master of this art, is aware of the presentation and display of its products and equally proud of what goes inside those thin shells of molded chocolate. They use creamy-textured centers—pralines, as they are called—and the headiest mocha, along with the best-quality ingredients.

Godiva has come out with new pieces. At the time I was there they were introducing the top of their new line. Candies, almost tiny pastries in looks, were each individually crafted. Cherries in marzipan, a cream with nougatine—these were two of the ten offered. All have liquor in them, and alas, will only be available in Europe. When I was there, the production was still so limited that these pieces were only obtainable at Godiva's own stores in Brussels.

Godiva is responsible for what happened to chocolates when the American public was given a chance to buy more expensive chocolates than ever before. First, they broke the three-dollar barrier, the price at which chocolates were not supposed to go above, because no one, it was said, would ever pay more than that for chocolate candies. With a risk that was revolutionary, they took the Belgian ideas, translated them to American tastes, and announced the most expensive, elegant, and snobbish idea in chocolate ever presented: the instantly recognizable, European look-alikes at a price that appeared astronomical at that time.

Europeans are accustomed to paying a considerable price for the chocolates they love. Americans responded exactly as their European

Godiva shop in Belgium. *(Adrianne Marcus)*

counterparts had—they bought them. Now that our willingness to spend money is sweetly and clearly a matter of record, I wish we could have the chance to taste both Godivas. It would be nice to have the European chocolates alongside our own. The American Godiva is good, but the Belgian Godiva is darker, stronger, with more distinctive centers, and yes, uncommonly great.

Godiva Chocolatier
Rue de l'Armistice 5
Wapenstilstandstraat-B-Brussels
Tel.: 428–00–80

No; they can't ship these to you, but you can also buy them in Paris and a great many major European cities. I like to have them in Brussels, and no one should pass up a chance to visit their chocolate boutique; it is like walking into Wonderland.

Here is a list of Godiva shops in Belgium:

BRUSSELS:
Ch. de Charleroi 11
Tel.: 538–13–50

Rue Grétry 27
Tel.: 217–90–31

Bd. A. Max 87
Tel.: 217–35–14

Gd. Place 22
Tel.: 511–25–37

Bd. Léopold II
Tel.: 426–93–65

Ch. de Waterloo 1312
Tel.: 374–84–03

Manhattan Center
Tel.: 217–47–41

ANTWERP:
De Kzyerlei 31 031
Tel.: 33–43–67

Mair 95
Tel.: 32–36–82

LIÈGE:
Rue Pont d'Avroy 34 041
Tel.: 32–10–64

Baeyens' department stores in Bruges carry Godiva products:
Knokke Lippenslaan 269
Tel.: 60–22–18

Zoute Av. du Littoral 173
Tel.: 60–40–31

Oostende Kapellestraat 33
Tel.: 70–85–57

Manon Chocolatier-Confiseur

It isn't difficult locating a chocolate shop in Brussels: every corner seems to have one, so the question I asked the Belgian Trade Commissioners was, "Where do you buy your own chocolates?" Mr. De Ridder graciously directed me to Manon's, and gave me the address. Finding it was another matter. Brussels is one of those cities in which it is possible to take one wrong turn and wander, delightfully, for hours. I suggest you find a cab driver with a fluent knowledge of English, or patience, but however you get there, do, for this tiny shop on Chaussée de Louvain makes some of the best Belgian creams.

One you'll identify immediately is the Sputnik, a tiny dot of gold topping its projectile of chocolate. Beneath that clever bit of rocketry lurks a payload of delicate cream. Another of my favorite pieces is called Pineapple Cream. It is puréed pineapple, exquisitely blended with light whipped cream in proportions so subtle and exact it will take you a moment to distinguish all the tastes that are there.

I praise both the Coffee Cream and the small candy named for the firm, Manon. These candies are carefully made by hand, just as their marzipan is.

Again, I urge the American consumer to remember: these delicate morsels will not last over four to five days. Either get them at the last moment and rush them home to the freezer, or enjoy them there. It is worth the effort to locate Manon.

Manon Chocolatier-Confiseur
#9-A Chaussée de Louvain
Brussels 1030
Tel.: 217–64–09

No mail order, but you can buy them there. They wouldn't hold up in shipping. If you bring them home on the plane, be sure to hand-carry them with you.

Those handmade Manon Belgian creams. *(Adrianne Marcus)*

Côte d'Or

A college education is worth its weight in chocolate bars, particularly when it took my eldest daughter to Europe for a semester of study. She was kind enough to bring me back all sorts of chocolate bars I'd never had. That's how I happened to first taste Côte d'Or, the best of all her offerings.

With the singular determination of one convinced disciple seeking to procure the chocolate grail, I made arrangements with the Belgian consulate in San Francisco for a letter of introduction that would permit me to visit Côte d'Or. Until recently, Côte d'Or was unobtainable in the United States, and it is still difficult to buy anywhere but in New York.

Only 30 percent of their production is exported. The rest still goes to those fortunate and happy Belgians who are busily consuming most of Côte d'Or's output. And I can taste why. If you think that I went to a lot of trouble for a plain old chocolate bar, you have another think coming. Their taste is so distinctive that having once had a Côte d'Or bittersweet fondant bar, you can recognize and distinguish its taste from any made anywhere else in the world.

Côte d'Or makes a full-flavored and luscious milk chocolate bar, which would be my first choice if it weren't for that bittersweet, with its pure, dark overtones of intense chocolate that remain on the tongue long after eating. You might try an unusual bar called Panache, a chocolate in whose center resides a cream-filled raisin mixture. It's surprising, but quite good.

The Mokkabitter is a deep sharp chocolate with a hint of coffee lurking in the aftertaste, and Double Diable is a heavy, chewy caramel-filled chocolate bar that can occupy you for a half-hour. For an unusually refreshing delight, I suggest their Peach Apricot Bar, with its cream-filled center encased in bittersweet chocolate. The interior is pale, but lavishly fruited. It has no food coloring added, so each bite is pure, if not simple, pleasure. The only bar that failed to please me was the Pistachio. I do not like its cream filling. The rest are fine, and there is a great variety from which to choose.

I do not find their boxed assortments to be as interesting as their bars. The boxed chocolates are not nearly as tasty. That may be because the boxes' shelf life and cost do not guarantee they last as long as the bars'. However, I have had the boxed assortment only in America, where I bought it. I did not see it in Belgium, but I was too busy enjoying the chocolate bars.

The good news I was saving for last: you can buy them in Belgium or in New York. Simon's Pure Foods on Fifty-seventh Street carries a large assortment (and the boxed chocolates as well), and The Cellar at Macy's in New York carries the Côte d'Or products.

Of course, they are available everywhere in Brussels at almost every grocery store. When you are there, be sure and enjoy them daily.

Côte d'Or Société Anonyme
Rue Bara 40
Brussels 1070
Tel.: 02–523–20–00

Mr. K. Ossieur, assistant manager of Côte d'Or, will be glad to advise you on the possibility of shipment in case you cannot find them here in your area. All that were shipped to me arrived in perfect condition. They had to be airmailed, and it is costly. But worth it.

Chocolaterie H. Corné de la Toison d'Or

These gorgeous shell-molded chocolates are as exquisite to look at as they are divine to eat. The rum and praline cream fillings are decoratively captured in individual chocolate designs. Corné creates as choice an assortment as can be found anywhere. Their elegant chocolates come in the shapes of tiny ears of corn, clusters of grapes, walnuts, leaf-hearts, and squares with raised designs on the chocolate surface. The surface is only the beginning of Corné's pleasurable attributes, for inside there are those lavish centers. And what amazes me is how Corné has managed to take a piece as small as their heart-shaped leaf and put as much ambrosial flavor into it as that center contains. A great many of the Belgian molded chocolates use the same forms to make their thin, hollow chocolate shells. Corné's tiny clusters of grapes may resemble another firm's exterior design, but the interior, the center, is where Corné makes a definitive statement. Corné's centers speak of the richness of creams blended with savory flavors, fresh nuts ground to a fine paste, and each is a rapture of chocolate.

Of the eleven shops in Belgium Corné operates, my favorite is the one at 21 Chaussée de Louvain. It carries all of the pieces they make, including some that are not exported elsewhere. The firm is a family one. Madame Henriette Girardi-Corné greeted me with the story of how the firm got its name. "Chocolate Corné of the Order of the Golden Fleece."

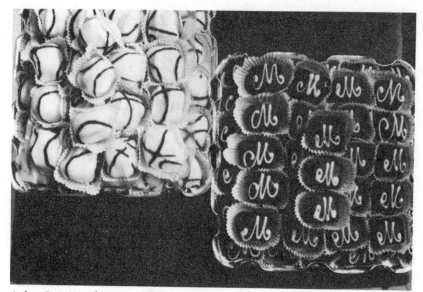

A few Corné confections. *(Melanie Annin)*

This was inspired by a fifteenth-century story. It seems that King Philip the Good of France created an order of chivalry, and he bestowed membership in this coveted order only to a select circle. Emperors and kings who had displayed outstanding merit and valor were among the few recipients. Virtue was necessary to Philip's creed, and he had taken as his motto, "Aultre Nauray," which meant "No other shall I have" in reference to the high regard he placed on virtue and faithfulness to his own queen, Isabeau. He had sworn faithfulness to her.

When King Philip was struck down by an illness, his court doctors prescribed as the necessary means to save his life the services of a young virgin. King Philip refused, and would not break his vow. Whether it was this determination to be true to his creed, or a disease which had run its course, the king recovered, and managed to regain his health and his full strength, as well as to keep his vow to Isabeau and chivalry.

Inspired by this authentic and charming story, Chocolaterie Corné chose Philip's motto as their own, "No other shall I have," as the example of determination to have nothing but the finest in ingredients and vowed to produce their chocolates for an elite and select chocolate public. They wanted their product to be judged by gourmet standards, and so their candies came to be appreciated by a discerning public throughout the world.

Corné comes from Belgium, and can be purchased there in any of its shops. They also have those regal Belgian gift boxes. I chose the velvet, which was decorated with feathers, since I am partial to soft fabrics; a tin of Corné was also shipped to me. It came through in perfect shape.

If you live near New York, you can enjoy Corné's candies at the Au Chocolat Boutique at Bloomingdale's. If I cannot have the pleasure of buying them in Belgium, I make it a point to buy them in New York. My own vows are devoutly chocolate, and willingly made to Corné.

BRUSSELS

12, Av. de la Toison d'Or
Tel: 512–89–47

53, rue Marché aux Poulets
Tel.: 512–23–60

24-26, Galerie du Roi
Tel.: 512–49–84

111, Bd. A. Max
Tel.: 218–70–42

T 8, Galerie du Cinquantenaire
Tel.: 733–95–55

11, Shopping Center Bascule
Tel.: 345–60–30

21, Chaussée de Louvain
Tel.: 218–66–75

67, Av. du Roi Chevalier
Tel.: 771–54–17

ANTWERP
78, Av. de Keyser
Tel: (031) 33–20–10

NIVELLES
20, rue des Vieilles Prisons
Tel.: (067) 22–36–28

LE ZOUTE
101, Av. du Littoral
Tel.: (050) 60–27–25

Wittamer Boutique

As I stood there watching the ultimate pastry chef, Marc Debaillevl, create chocolate marvel after chocolate marvel, it was all I could do to refrain from renouncing my life of travel, move onto the premises and remain forever. He is worth that kind of loyalty. He is a true high priest of chocolate confections. He convinced me—without much trouble, I might add—that it would be sinful to go a day without tasting one of his masterpieces, whether it is a gateau, a candy, or some promise of a chocolate vision yet to come.

Take his chocolate gateau, for instance, the one with Wittamer's "W" dusted on the surface. One doesn't bite into it, one dissolves into the creamy center with its hint of Grand Marnier, and then discovers the

A Wittamer chocolate delicacy. *(Adrianne Marcus)*

rich chocolate cake beneath that. Then there is his black forest cake filled with buttercream and topped with shavings of Callebaut milk chocolate. As if that weren't enough, he dusts the cake with cocoa and confectioner's sugar. A caloric overkill if ever I enjoyed one.

For those who feel they would like their chocolate cake on a smaller basis, try the Chocolate au Lait. It is a small square with the imprint of a coffee bean on top. Enough flavor, however, resides in that tiny morsel to make even an Englishman swear off tea forever.

For those who feel more spartan than I ever have, I think the true test of willpower is to purchase just one box of Wittamer's candy. I should warn you that the raspberry cream in the center of the molded chocolate is truly the ultimate test of that willpower. The freshly whipped cream, blended with puréed fruit, and all in a chocolate coating that provides a perfect counterpoint, makes me go back time and time again to embrace all these marvelous textures and flavors.

I did manage to bring some home, directly from Belgium. Double-wrapped and placed in my freezer, they have held up perfectly. I take one out now and then and let it thaw slowly at room temperature before I unwrap it. It tastes just as if I were there, or almost, depending on my power of imagination. It is true you cannot save them any other way, or hold them at room temperature for any length of time, but if you will wrap them just as carefully as possible before freezing, to make sure no air can get to them, I find they do not deteriorate to any degree.

The candies must *not* be placed near any substance with a strong flavor. Please do not put them in the refrigerator where they can pick up foreign odors, such as onions or cheese. I know of no chocolate lover who wants chocolates to taste much like those aforementioned flavors.

My other alternative is just as enjoyable: have as many as you can while there. If you do not have more willpower than I do, and cannot stop at just one piece, well then, you are my kind of person.

Wittamer Boutique
12-13 place du Grand Sablon
Brussels 1000
Tel.: 512–37–42

Paul Wittamer has told me these cannot be shipped. They would arrive inedible, even by airmail. So have someone bring you some back, or bring them back yourself, when leaving Brussels. And of course, be sure and have a dozen or so right there on the spot. The raspberry creams are my very, very favorite.

ZELLIK
Neuhaus

Just on the outskirts of Brussels, about a half-hour by car, the small suburb of Zellik is home ground for a chocolate factory, Neuhaus. From here, the firm ships candy to a few select countries, America among them.

In Belgium, these chocolates are readily available. Gift shops, delicatessen stores, department stores, and hotels feature the lovely gifts that Neuhaus packages. Such pieces as the Mandarinette, a milk chocolate coating with a mandarin cream inside, and Colorado, a milk chocolate and praline piece in an unusual triangular shape, are featured in the Silver Boxes. Baccara has a hard chocolate shell in which a hazelnut praline is centered. Sappho is a milk cover with a bed of hazelnut cream praline inside. I also recommend you try the Fripons, whose hard chocolate outside gives way to a praline and giandujas interior. It is a rectangular piece, featuring three waves of chocolate cresting.

Their Belgian Box has the same assortment, but the box doesn't look quite as elegant to some as the Silver Box. If you choose to select which pieces you'd like beyond the standard assortments, the shell molds include other pieces, such as the fragile Bouchon (cork), which is a dark chocolate, shaped like a cork, inside of which they feature a Benedictine cream. Neuhaus creams are not the whipped, fluffy ones that last only a few days; they are closer to fondant centers, the kind one finds inside a chocolate-covered mint. The center is treated to perfection in a piece such as Coeurs Grand Marnier, a foil-wrapped chocolate heart with Grand Marnier as the predominant flavor. The Canasta piece has a marzipan and almond chip interior, but I didn't get to try it because it wasn't available the day I was there.

One item I carried home, cradled quite gently in my bag all the way to California, is called Mademoiselle. This is a beautiful bottled spectrum of round fruits, from figs to grapes, all nestled in Cointreau. It makes a spectacular dessert, either spooned over ice cream (you can have your chocolates as a side dish with that) or chilled and served in a crystal goblet. Europeans adore fruits that have been preserved by such special means. After tasting this offering by Neuhaus, I can understand why.

BRUSSELS:
Gal. de la Reine 25-27
Tel.: (02) 512–63–59

Av. de la Toison d'Or 27
Tel.: (02) 513–15–47

Bascule, Shopping Center
Tel.: (02) 345–40–56

Rue Marie Christine 211
Tel.: (02) 426–70–79

Rue Au Beurre 44 (Grand Place)
Tel.: (02) 511–08–76

Av. de l'Université 2
Tel.: (02) 647–89–61

OSTENDE:
Rue Royale 6
Tel.: (059) 80–84–56

LOUVAIN:
Av. des Allies 78
Tel.: (016) 22–26–34

ZELLIK:
1. Crokaertstraat 21, 1730
Tel.: (02) 466–84–32

In the United States, they're available by mail from Neiman-Marcus in Dallas, Texas. You can write them for a price list. Or contact Mr. Borms, their marketing manager in Zellik, to see if they are available elsewhere.

WIEZE
N.V. Chocolaterie Callebaut
The week before Oktoberfest begins, the town of Wieze is almost ready to accommodate the thousands of tourists who will be arriving to celebrate. The main hall is decorated, but still deserted. It will be full, in

every sense of that word, when the festival begins. There will be an overwhelming indulgence of good people, good music, and superb beer. One of Wieze's major industries is beer; the other is chocolate.

We can get their chocolate in America, for some of our best candy makers use Callebaut coating over their centers, but I haven't found their beer in the United States. On that special September afternoon, beer was the first offering and indication of Wieze's crafts. Although I recommend the finest dry champagne—Roederer's, to be exact—is the beverage most worthy of chocolates, I think the beer that Wieze is noted for deserves a bit of praise all on its own, so let me digress for a moment.

Our host, Mr. De Ridder, who is with the Belgian Foreign Trade office, took us to a place he recommended for lunch, the Gasthof Brouwershius Wieze. He urged us to try a glass of the local product before eating our meal. Not much of a beer drinker, I declined. He persisted. So I tried a bit of that dark amber brew served to me in what looked like a cross between a wine and a champagne glass. What arrogance, I thought, until I tasted it. That was my first lesson: anything that spectacular deserves a special presentation. It bore as little resemblance to what I have called beer as carob does to chocolate. Wieze Royal was heavy and heady, and it held the whole taste of autumn in one glass.

When we sat down to enjoy our meal, we were overcome by more splendid offerings. Tender shoots of hops had been sautéed in a white wine and cream sauce; the tart, almost piquant taste of the thin green shoots gave the bland sauce a rich, biting quality. Under all of this rested the whitest, most tender veal imaginable. *Pommes Fritz,* the Belgian French fries, accompanied the veal. Consuming all this made for a leisurely lunch, and as the last bite was devoured, a contented smile. Mr. De Ridder insisted there was one more thing to try—the house specialty, dessert. It is listed as Saboyon on the menu, and it does resemble the traditional egg whip in looks, but finely minced orange peel is at the bottom, and homemade sherbet throughout. All of the above ingredients had been flavored quite liberally with Grand Marnier.

Even in memory, the description of that one meal satisfies me. From the first taste to the extravagant finale, a host of joys in the form of Belgian food were lavished upon more than willing Americans. I floated out of the restaurant like the sun in that Belgian afternoon, benevolent, full, ready to descend on the shining chocolate factory a few kilometers distant.

It looks very much like an American chocolate factory—spotlessly clean, the facilities all on one level. Giant hoppers are full of cocoa beans, the roasters are busily roasting various blends, and the grinding machines are turning the nibs into chocolate paste. The process was, by now, a familiar one, and we moved on to see some of the four hundred different coatings they make, each to a specific formulation, and each bearing the name Callebaut.

The firm obtains its cocoa beans from some fourteen different sources. When the beans have reached the proper stage after all the processing, the coatings are ready to be molded into five-kilo blocks. Callebaut has two molding lines, one for milk and the other for dark chocolate, and each one can process two tons per hour.

Having tasted Callebaut as coating on some of the finest Belgian chocolate candies, I find the dark fondant type of coatings to be my favorite. Now it was time to try some items I had not tasted before: Callebaut Candy Bars.

Out of the milk chocolate line, I like the Melk Noten-Lait Noisettes, the milk chocolate with hazelnuts. It is a good, moderate milk chocolate bar. Their bittersweet fondant bar, with its strong, rich chocolate taste has an unusually fine aftertaste, and suggests the particular cocoa beans that have been blended to create this taste have a good proportion of high-flavor beans added to the staple cocoa beans.

Their milk chocolates tend to taste blander, and, as you know, that is not the taste I gravitate toward. In chocolate, I prefer a heavier, fuller-bodied blend. So the bittersweet, or what is sometimes called bitter chocolate, is my choice. What I look for is the aftertaste, as one might in a fine red wine, for good chocolate leaves its aftertaste on the tongue. It is not the sugar I seem to require, but a blend that makes sweetness secondary in flavor and in taste. As such, their filled bars tend toward the sweet side, and I bypass these. They are strictly for those people who like a lot of sugar with their chocolate.

Do try the red bar Callebaut makes, the one called Bitter. It is not bitter. It is exceptionally good. Available at most places that carry chocolate candy bars in Belgium, the Bitter chocolate can also be found in Belgian grocery stores. I have not located any of them in America;

neither grocery stores that carry this bar nor the bar itself. Here, in the United States, I resort to finding a good candy maker who uses Callebaut's superb chocolate coating and convincing him or her to allow me to buy a five-kilo block. After all, with over four hundred kinds to choose from, the candy maker is bound to have one that is just right for my taste.

N.V. Chocolaterie Callebaut
B. 9380
Wieze

FRANCE

PARIS
French Chocolate

If chocolates were an alphabet, the French couldn't get beyond the letter D. For Disappointment. We arrived in Paris with all the expectations of the finest chocolates in mind, and certainly the Paris chocolatiers have mastered visual presentation. The candies looked unbelievably lovely. The cost, unbelievably dear, was immediately rationalized by my saying, "Well, you have to pay a lot to get the best." Then we bit in. Disbelief. Distress. Doubt. I turned to my companion, whose face mirrored my own, and said, "Have we erred?" But we are humans, so we went back and bought other samples, looking for the Divine. No. Not there. Our conclusions remain: grainy chocolate coatings, inferior in quality and texture, centers either awash with liquor, or, in the case of cream centers, bland, without distinction.

The creativity with which one associates the chocolatier's art is evident only in presentation. If there are good French chocolates, alas, we didn't discover them. Even their boxed variety, Poulain, was dull. Only one piece, the milk chocolate with the hazelnut embedded in it, was passable. My advice to chocolate travelers who find themselves in Paris with symptoms of chocolate withdrawal: go find an Italian, Swiss, or Belgian specialty store. Buy their chocolates.

SWITZERLAND

BROC
Nestlé, S.A.

In the worldwide production of chocolate, no name is more instantly recognized than Nestlé. Just over a hundred years ago, Henri Nestlé placed his name and trademark, "Little Nest," on the milk process he invented. Then, in 1904, Daniel Peter, the man who invented milk chocolate, and another Swiss manufacturer, Jean-Jacques Kohler, entered into an agreement with the Henri Nestlé Company. Nestlé would do all the marketing, while Peter and Kohler would produce the Swiss chocolate bars, bearing all three names. In 1911, they were joined by another man, Cailler, and to bring all this history closer to our time, in 1951, everything became known as Nestlé. By 1978, Nestlé is not only a worldwide organization with 297 factories on five continents and over 140,000 employees, it is also the largest food company in the world.

Now contrast that monolithic, impressive set of facts with the village of Broc, in Switzerland. There, nestled in the mountains, tucked against the side of a hill, six hundred people are busy making the products that bear the names Cailler (the top of the Nestlé Swiss chocolate line), Frigor, and a familiar one we all know—Nestlé. As in Nestlé Crunch.

Chocolate makes people happy, and the town of Broc is devoted to just this pursuit. It would not be too difficult to be happy here. I managed to visit twice, and went away each time enraptured with the town, the people who work here, and the chocolate.

In November, the whole village turns into a Swiss fairytale. The hills and mountains surrounding Broc are white as Christmas card scenes, and the tiny, intricate houses on the steep hills, the thin threads of smoke curling up from the chimneys, complete the fantasy. Gruyère, the nearby town noted for its fine cheese and rich cream, looms white and magical on a distant hill, then you round the curve and begin the descent down the steep hill into the white valley of Broc, where the factory is.

The day is white and crisp. A sudden wave of warm chocolate air drifts down from the factory. Then everything smells deliciously friendly. I walk inside the factory, which is neither tiny nor enormous. There is the ever-present Swiss efficiency coupled with a feeling of family pride.

The warm greetings and eager attention of the smiling workers are not staged. They are glad to stop and explain exactly what they are doing and why. On my second visit, they remember me by name. I am free to look at any part of the production and to ask any questions that occur to me. All my queries are answered graciously, no matter to whom I direct my questions, from workers on the assembly wrapping line right on to top management.

I note they are conching chocolate, not in the high-speed conches so evident everywhere else in Europe, but according to an older method. Here, granite rollers conche the chocolate, moving it in waves back and forth, rocking it to the creamy smoothness that takes days. This refusal to switch over to the newer, high-speed, higher volume production is part of the tradition that Nestlé maintains in making their chocolate. It is produced the same way it was years ago, a slower, more exacting method that requires long conching and continuous care. As I watch wave after wave in the infinite ocean of chocolate, I know it is literally being pounded into sweet, delicate submission.

This same care goes into the choice of ingredients they use—the finest cocoa beans, fresh Swiss milk. Nestlé uses fresh condensed Swiss milk in the making of their chocolates. Most other factories have long since gone to dried milk. The difference may not be crucial, but Nestlé thinks their way produces the best, and as far as I am concerned, the difference is apparent in the taste. The Swiss Nestlé is one of the best chocolate candies made anywhere in the world.

This creamy taste is immediately evident. Open a Femina box. This particular assortment was designed for women, and interestingly enough, does not contain any of the pieces which have alcohol in them. I hardly notice the omission, busy as I am with such chocolate candies as the Moka and the light Avelotte squares. The thin slivered almonds almost hidden away in the chocolate rectangles bearing the name Malakoff are morsels of exquisite taste. One silver-wrapped favorite of mine, Buche, is a miniature log in whose center resides the crunchiest, creamiest mixture of chocolate and nuts possible.

Once you have enjoyed a surfeit of these, go on to the Cailler assortments. Here are the famous chocolate and alcohol candies. Griottes

---

Nestlé's milk chocolate cow watches over the vast Swiss milk chocolate assortments from such firms as Tobler, Suchard, Nestlé, Confiserie Honold, Eichenberger's, and Arni. *(Fred Lyon Pictures)*

Swiss village and waterfall. *(Adrianne Marcus)*

One of Nestlé's antique chocolate labels. (*Nestlé Alimentana S.A.*)

A Cailler chocolate label. *(Nestlé S.A.)*

au kirsch are fine examples of cherries in kirsch, each one hiding under a dome of chocolate. The familiar red box marked Frigor, which the Swiss all know and love, defies overstatement. I think the inscription on the box says it perfectly: *"Chocolat fin fourré à la crème d'amandes,"* fine chocolate filled with the cream of almonds.

The usual assortments of miniature bars are available. They bear the name Cailler. Inside is the sweet Crémant and the Dessert Praline in its tiny gold and green wrapper. They are available anywhere in Switzerland. One other item I suggest trying is the Nestlé Crunch. If you are curious as to whether or not there really is a difference between Swiss milk chocolate and their American counterpart, open one and eat it. As much as I love the good folks in White Plains, New York, who are busily creating new chocolate products for us which bear the same name, Nestlé—and they do make many, many good things—the Swiss version of the Nestlé Crunch bar puts every other one to shame. It actually could be because of that fine Swiss milk, but whatever the reason, it is tastier than any other Nestlé bar from any other country I have ever had. So far, I have tried at least eight other versions, including the Belgian, German, French, English, Italian, and American bar of the same name. The package looks the same, but the Swiss bar is as exotic and lavish as any chocolate bar you have ever hoped to have. It is so good I brought back eighty of them.

But I did not slight any of the other assortments. I brought those home also. Now, all I have to do is open one of these lovely silver wrappers bearing the blue scripted name of the candy on its outside, and

I am right back there, in Broc. The surrounding mountains shimmer in white and silver, the blue sky makes it all stand out in relief. As I bring my candy up to my mouth, I can almost smell the warm, friendly chocolate air as it drifts down from the factory. My world dissolves into the sweetness and incredible taste of Swiss chocolates. Just as it should, thanks to the magic of Nestlé, S.A.

Chocolate production:
Nestlé, S.A.
Broc 1636
Tel.: (029) 6–12–12

Vevey 1800
Tel.: (021) 51–01–11

Nestlé's Cremant candies. *(Melanie Annin)*

Antique Nestlé candy wrappings.
*(Nestlé Alimentana S.A.. Switzerland.
Dr. Mueller)*

Mr. Müller is in charge of the Nestlé plant in Broc. Tours can sometimes be arranged if conditions (group size, well-in-advance queries) permit. Dr. Stutz is in charge of the overall operations at Nestlé's home office in Vevey. But you can buy their products anywhere in Switzerland, and if you are bringing some home from there, be sure and include extras for your chocolate-friends. Even a Crunch bar or two makes a marvelous gift for which you will be endlessly thanked.

WINTERTHUR
Confiserie Bosshard am Bahnhof

Since I couldn't get to Winterthur, I am quite happy it could come to me, via airmail. There is no mail in the world quicker, more expedient, and more trustworthy than Swiss mail, and so these chocolates arrived promptly, in perfect shape and were not only still edible, but incredible.

There are key words which are guaranteed to produce a response in the heart and mouth of a true chocolate addict. One word is "truffles." And if you want to try overwhelming a chocolate addict, say, "Swiss truffles," even though that is redundant. A word of caution at this point: if you do say both words, be sure you have some at hand, or the devoted chocolate addict will cast off years of conditioned civility and be furious with anyone who plays light and easy with such a subject of love.

Light and easy is a perfect description. The Grand Marnier consists of the finest dark chocolate, butter, and original Grand Marnier. Nothing could be better, unless you happen to have an entire box of truffles, such as the Truffles Maison, which is Bosshard's entire collection, and offers you twelve different types of truffles in dark and milk chocolate, and even a few in white coating. Be sure to have the Orangtruffe for a unique and lovely taste.

Chocolate goes hand in mouth with another of my favorite things, champagne. This time it is the Champagne Truffles, made of milk chocolate, fresh cream, butter, and the famous Pommery Champagne Brut Royal. See, you can have your favorite chocolate and champagne all together.

The Pralines Maison are a varied selection of fine chocolate moments, ranging from the pineapple in chocolate to the orange section encased in glossy, deep splendor. I suggest not choosing; have them all. Then, if you can, take back a specialty of the house, Eulach Forellen. It is a fish filled with fine butter and chocolate and, yes, it is a confection whose name reflects the little river that crosses Winterthur. "Forelle" means trout. Bosshard's means fine chocolate.

Confiserie Bosshard am Bahnhof
8400 Winterthur
Tel.: (052) 22–55–22

They will accept mail orders. If you write and request the catalogs they make available, you can see exactly which of their lovely items you would like to have shipped. Assortments of truffles, tiny chocolate mice, and the fabulous chestnut-truffle pieces are all shown, with a convenient postcard included on which you can list what you would like air-mailed. The descriptions are all in German, but the pictures make the contents abundantly clear.

NEUCHATEL
Suchard

I was a terrible disappointment to Suchard. There we were, busily touring the factory in Neuchatel, and I was making all the appropriate comments, asking all sorts of questions, when Mr. Chopard, the man in charge of all this, reached over onto a rack of what looked like translucent white candies. Innocuous candies. "Try this," he offered, handing one to me.

Well, to make a long story horrid, I bit in, not sure what I was biting into (the daring of chocolate addicts extends in all directions) and gin burst onto my tongue. But not for long. I opened my mouth wide, all the liquid spilled out into my hand, including the sugar casing in which it had been residing. I rushed over to a convenient washbasin to unstick myself from my own reaction.

After I'd washed up, come back over, and joined the others, Mr. Chopard asked, "You don't have chocolates with liquor in them available in the United States, do you?"

It was that evident. I had just destroyed one prior to its final chocolate coating. So I replied, "No. We don't." We both smiled rather weakly at one another and I went on to items that my tongue might accept at this early hour of the day: the various bars Suchard makes. Candy bars, that is.

Now, thinking back on this minor tragedy, I do realize that I'm probably in the minority as things go with chocolate and liquor. I've been told countless times since then that most Americans just love these items. And I can believe it. There's something about the idea of an unavailable item that makes us delight in it. I do know people for whom gin, vodka, cognac—even scotch—encased in sugar shells and then in chocolate is the ultimate candy. For them, there is the assurance that these candies made by Suchard are the recipients of the finest liquors available, and believe me, I have a healthy respect for Swiss kirsch.

Suchard makes Easter eggs a seasonal excitement. Under the huge bows, enormous hollow chocolate eggs are filled with tiny candies. These

Huge air-conditioned rooms allow for the wrapping of the almond candies at Suchard. *(Fernand Perret)*

In long files, the candies pass by an employee of Suchard who paints them chocolate. *(Fernand Perret)*

From the Suchard private collection, an example of an antique chocolate gift box. *(Suchard of Switzerland)*

cellophane-wrapped extravaganzas are elaborate. The only other country which makes them more lavishly is Italy.

I was fortunate enough to visit Suchard's museum where they have over a century of chocolate artifacts, posters, and packaging displays in a locked room of the factory. In this surrounding, I was able to understand more about Philipp Suchard, the founder. He must have been quite a surprise to the Swiss, as he set sail in 1824 for America, something few people did at that point in history. He wanted to study American technology.

When he returned to Switzerland, he built the first mixing apparatus for chocolate. It was driven by water power. Unfortunately, the whole thing proved a disaster when a tailor shut the floodgates one evening, bringing the waterwheel to a complete standstill. The tailor had no malevolent reasons behind his act. He simply wanted a good night's sleep without any noise. He was not thinking about what might happen to the chocolate paste, which of course hardened. When the gates were opened the next morning, the wheels disintegrated and the transmission snapped.

Antique Suchard label. *(Suchard of Switzerland)*

Suchard, being persistent and inventive, tried again. There was the steamship which he commanded on the lake. Then there was the silk. He had three thousand mulberry bushes planted in the vineyards of Serrieres. These produced enough to warrant silk being spun and woven. However, when the epidemic came, it destroyed the silkworms and ended his idea of a silk industry on the Lake of Neuchatel. The shipping company he founded could not hold its own because of the competition with the railways. Philipp Suchard was a man who had the misfortune to be ahead of his time in too many ways. In chocolate he managed to reverse this and to be at the right time in the right place. His business flourished. His son joined him in the business, then his son-in-law and eventually he registered his trademark, first in Switzerland, and then in 1893 with the International Patents Office. Suchard's trademark bore the number 1.

From those initial thirty kilograms of chocolate per day that Philipp Suchard produced and distributed by hand, the firm has grown to such a vast size that the automatic warehouse, run by one person, is capable of handling up to five thousand pallets. It is all computerized and the computer directs even the forklift trucks. The firm has managed to merge Philipp Suchard's original love, his early dream of chocolate, with his other great love, technology, bringing both dreams to fruition, and chocolates to a great deal of the world.

Suchard of Switzerland
Ch. 2003
Neuchatel
Tel.: (031) 58–44–41 (Multifood Ltd.)

Most of Suchard's candy bars, such as their Milka line, which includes milk chocolates with raisins, nuts, and nougat, are available throughout Switzerland and Europe. Their solid bars are Swiss favorites, and the only bar I have not seen available to us, here in America, is the one they produce with Cointreau. Their assortments and chocolate liqueurs are readily available throughout Europe, but the only chocolate assortments I have found in America are the miniature bar assortments. The chocolate liqueurs are never shipped to America.

BERNE
Eichenberger Confiserie and Tea Room

If there were Academy Awards in the field of chocolate, Eichenberger's would be presented at least two of them. The first would be for a confectionary shop in a starring role on the longest continuous basis. That translates to the oldest confectionary store in Switzerland. Though it's been called Eichenberger's for only the past eighteen years, it's been in that location, just five minutes' walk from the train station, for longer than any of us have been eating chocolate.

The second award would have been given for the Truffle Cake. Its fudge exterior (almost a candy coating) gives way to a dry milk chocolate interior held together by a mousselike chocolate cream. I said would have, but a new entry presented itself recently and this cake, as yet unnamed (I call it overwhelming), is causing the chocolate statue in my hands to melt as the jury attempts to reach a decision. As much as I love the Truffle Cake, I'm afraid Daniel Eichenberger's new creation has to be it, forks up! It's a small, square cake made without flour and the closest description upon first taste might be a mousse au chocolat until you get down toward the bottom with its rich pastry shell. There's also a hint of honey mingled with the thick creamy taste, but it all slid down so easily, who could stop and name all the nuances? You can recognize it by the pink stripe on top and the bear, the symbol of Berne that graces one corner.

In late October or early November, as the gray wind sweeps through the arcades of Berne, Eichenberger's is busy making their seasonal items. One of them, a chestnut candy, looks as if it were a real chestnut. When you bite through the thin exterior of chocolate, you discover the thick, sweet puree of chestnuts.

The Florentines, a cross between a cookie and a candy, are as delicate, as wafery-crisp, as any I've encountered anywhere. These are a filigree of almonds and pistachios, half coated in chocolate.

Of course, there are the regular assortments of candies. Their caramel nougat, with overtones of sesame, is a three-sided moment of chocolate delight. The marzipan candies are as perfect as marzipan should be, when handled properly: a creamy indulgence of almond paste.

On the minus side, I am not fond of the pistachio candies in chocolate, but their champagne truffles, those smooth, moist blends of chocolate and champagne, are perfect. The cognac truffles are another

Desserts in the window of Eichenberger. *(Adrianne Marcus)*

after-dinner pleasure. The rich cognac taste permeates but doesn't completely dominate the chocolate.

It is a tribute to Daniel Eichenberger and his master touch that any chocolate creation he makes is eagerly consumed by a knowledgeable Swiss public; they stand in line to buy his cakes and candies. His insistence on quality is a constant, and it does contribute to his reluctance to ship these truffles to America. Some candies, he points out, will travel, and these he is willing to ship, but I can still hear his firm voice saying "No" when asked about the more delicate, perishable ones. "Come here and enjoy them," was his reply. As replies go, it is a weighty temptation.

Eichenberger Confiserie and Tea Room
Bahnhofplatz 5
Berne

You can write to Mr. Eichenberger and he will ship some of his candies, but not the perishable, fragile ones.

Tobler

In the chocolate traveler's world of plus and minus, a plus experience is to go somewhere new and to recognize, buy, and taste something familiar. Like Toblerone. In Berne, that city of marvelous shopping arcades and sweeping wind, I found a kiosk just outside my hotel, and, since it was a bit early for lunch, I bought a Toblerone, broke it apart to taste the pure milk chocolate, almonds, and honey I had tasted so many times before, thousands of light-years away, in California.

Only now, from my hotel window, which faces the mountains, can I fully understand why in 1908 Theodor Tobler and Emil Baumann conducted that series of experiments in Mr. Tobler's kitchen. They took an idea from an Italian confectionary product, Torrone, and decided to give it the distinctive triangular shape with its handy serrations. It was a masterful touch and a perfect Swiss conclusion: the shapes of the mountains surrounding Berne.

Having consumed my bar, satisfied, I know this taste by heart. All of the Tobler line exported to the United States is made in Switzerland. My favorite, the triangular green bar of bittersweet chocolate with its almonds and honey nougat, tasted exactly as I remembered it tasting. Great.

Later that day, at the factory, I discovered the true problem of the chocolate traveler. How to taste all twenty-five or more of the Tobler goodies? The spirit is willing, but the flesh is full by the fifteenth sample bite. Solution: save and have. I carefully carted back those few candies Tobler makes that I cannot buy in America. One of these, the Griottes, is milk chocolate with a brandy-flavored fruit pulp filling. I also brought back some other after-dinner delights in the form of the Grisette box. These are bonbons with liquor in them. Of course, these were to be shared with friends, and generous chocolate dealer as I am, I do love sharing them.

Even as gifts, Tobler makes it easy. You can bring home a book of chocolates. It comes complete, leather binding and all. After eating the chocolate candies hidden away on the inside, you can then use the cover for an actual book. This gift comes in various sizes, from small book up to telephone cover dimensions. There is also a beautiful wicker basket with its contents of chocolate; it becomes a perfect picnic basket after you consume your chocolate gifts which graced its interior. Tobler also makes

(Tobler)

a jewel box, suitable for family heirlooms, once the three drawers of chocolate have been emptied of their dark jewels.

My daughter has in her possession another item available only in Switzerland—a box of Berne chocolate bears. The box itself is what makes it so special to her that she refuses to part with it. As she slides the cover forward, a hidden mechanism slides the bear across the box and up into a tree. I did not buy her the racing box on which the car moves across the front as the box is opened, but I did bring home those Tobler chocolate bars which feature the Paddington Bear. Again, these are not available in places other than Switzerland, owing to copyright agreements.

What can be purchased here in America are the miniature bar assortments with Swiss scenes (how dull that word "scenes" is compared to the photographs that grace the boxes and bars). I have one of the Matterhorn that is all Heidi. Others, showing pictures of white mountains and blue skies, green trees thrusting up through meadows of snow, castles on the shores of unbelievably blue lakes, feature Swiss landscapes in enough detail to make me wish I were there once again.

No matter what Tobler products you buy, they are all made in Switzerland. So I open the last bar of chocolate, and think of Berne, of Jean Tobler, and how in 1877, just over a century ago, he moved his confectionary business to Langgasstrasse, to have room to grow. I taste this chocolate and I congratulate him, in memory, as do most chocolate lovers, for now it is possible to buy a Tobler bar or two anywhere in the civilized world. Somewhere, at some airport, Swissair is bringing more. I am grateful for the benefits and continuity of modern technology. It brings the taste of Switzerland that much closer to all of us.

Chocolat Tobler Ltd.
Berne
or contact

Multifood Ltd.
Tiefenaustrasse 2
P.O. Box 35
Worblaufen
Tel.: (031) 58–44–41

Mr. M. Gerber was my kind and informative host who took me through all the Tobler facilities. Tours of the factory may be possible if you write far enough in advance, but it depends on whether or not there is a group situation which they can accommodate. Their products are easily obtainable everywhere in Switzerland, and in most other countries as well. Mr. M. Baumann is in charge of handling your queries and will be happy to answer your questions about their various products.

GENEVA
Rohr

The Swiss are to chocolate truffles what the French are to champagne: the best. But Henri Rohr takes his truffles one step further: he produces a truffle with a sense of humor. Where else would you find a truffle in the shape of a tiny chocolate garbage can? A Geneva garbage can, if you will. It is filled with that rich, moist, sensual chocolate-truffle mixture. So much for the myth that the Swiss have a delayed sense of humor. Anyone

La Petite Marmite made by Rohr. *(Adrianne Marcus)*

who could turn a joke as delightful as that one into a tasty profit deserves applause.

He makes a wide assortment of novelty confections. His tennis balls are not just chocolate tennis balls. These have a meringue interior, covered with a hazelnut mixture, and then coated in chocolate. The final touch is added when he gives it a grayish-white coating and indents the surface to resemble an actual tennis ball. It is a perfect gift to serve to anyone.

You could also make a present of his champagne bottle (in chocolate, naturally) filled with truffles, or his griottes, which are the cherries marinated in kirsch, then covered with chocolate. For the more conventional gifts, there are the regular assortments he makes and packages in his distinctive red velvet box.

What I particularly suggest you buy is only available in mid-November. Mr. Rohr begins to produce Marmites at this time. This is a specialty of Geneva, and if the story I was told held up in translation, it commemorates an occasion in Swiss history when the natives dumped hot soup on the heads of invaders. The historical past is now captured in chocolate, in the form of three-legged chocolate soup pots filled with an assortment of chocolates.

I carried a Petite Marmite home with me. They cannot be shipped, since the three-legged chocolate kettles would probably be broken in transit.

They come in all sizes from the smallest (about four inches high) to one well over three feet in diameter, done completely in chocolate, with a ribbon and seal attached to hold the lid in place. I'd suggest the smaller versions, if you happen to be bringing one home.

Then all you have to worry about is how to explain these chocolate items to customs, as they stare in delight and disbelief as you unpack what a chocolate addict manages to accrue on a chocolate trip: soup pots, tennis balls, champagne bottles, spools of thread, all done in chocolate and all produced by Mr. Rohr and his seventeen helpers. It will prove to any officials that the novelty of chocolate goes beyond mere words.

Rohr
Rue Vautier 6
Geneva
Tel.: 21–63–03
43–32–72

They will be glad to accept mail orders. Their chocolates are expensive, but one of a kind items.

ZURICH
Confiserie Honold
Despite the fact that Madame Honold insisted these truffles would not keep more than ten to twelve days, I urged her to wrap them

carefully, since I fully intended to take them back to California. And I did. How could I possibly not share these spectacular Swiss chocolate creations of butter and cream? Or to be more truthful, share the guilt and allow others to convert their desires into kilos, as I had—about two kilos, to be exact. I blame it all on Switzerland, and I would do it again in an instant.

It wasn't completely the fault of the truffles, however. There were those marvelous glazed orange slices, quartered, which had the zesty bite of a Seville orange, complemented to perfection by their rich chocolate dip. Again, the pistachios didn't intrigue me, since the Swiss manage to do something to them that does not please my palate. The walnut creams with their smooth nut paste and blend of chocolate outside added a few grams of weight to my total. The lemon jelly, covered with chocolate, is also responsible, in part. But the true joy of consuming has to take into account all those marvelous truffles Honold makes, and one kind in particular—the grape truffle. It is a whole grape with cognac surrounded by a velvety chocolate cream, then dusted with sugar. There is no way to pass these up.

How marvelous to be able to point an exact finger at one's sins with complete surety! It was the truffles that led me down the chocolate path. If I could have figured out any way to take home the ornate gingerbread house Honold produces for the holiday season, I would have. It had a bit of chocolate trim, but what really made it impressive was the decoration, plus the fact that it came complete with witch and children. Sweet menace as it was, I had to settle for the truffles in place of it. The truffles could be hand-carried and consumed much more easily.

Confiserie Honold
Rennweg 53
Zurich 8001
Tel.: 211–52–59

They do some mail-order upon request, but will not ship the truffles since these do not hold up in the mail. You can however, hand-carry them, although it is illegal to bring into the United States liquor chocolates. Eat them on the plane, if you feel as if customs is going to take them away. But I have never known anyone who wasn't able to bring truffles into this country, if the amount was small enough that it was obvious it was for their own consumption. I am not sure if Customs just didn't ask, or if they simply thought these were without liquor.

ITALY

Talmone; Ferrero

To travel from Switzerland to Italy is a journey that involves more than merely changing geography. We leave Zurich late afternoon on the train. Although it is only September, the weather has turned cold. As we cross the Gotthard Pass at twilight, the mountains, a series of white, spectacular peaks, catch the last light. These are our final moments in Switzerland. The darkness settles and we arrive in Italy.

In Milan, we disembark and wait for the train that will take us to Torino. The station is one mass movement of people walking back and forth, back and forth. Chaos. If chaos ever walked anywhere, it began in Italy. Here, our sense of punctuality that delighted the Swiss becomes a liability. We finally board the correct train, the right car, and arrive in Torino.

After a night's rest, it is time to begin work again. And what better work could one ask for than looking for chocolates? I'd like to recommend Torino for at least two places: Ferrero's and Talmone's. At Talmone, try a Crostata Cioccolata, which is a cross between a tart, a torte, and a coffee cake, all with a macaroon crust. It features a fine macaroonlike topping, a dense chocolate filling. The whole thick adventure rests on a crust of heavy, yet flaky, macaroon pastry. Enjoy it with a cup of espresso there at the sidewalk cafe. It is about three blocks from the train station and an easy, interesting walk to Piazza C. Felice 36, Torino.

Ferrero's, the restaurant bearing the same name as the firm visited the next day, is about the same distance from the train station, but on another street. It is easy to find, and you can enjoy pastries, candies, or a meal inside the premises. Since I was going to Alba the very next day, I didn't eat there, but the patrons who had and were leaving looked quite pleased. We bought a few candies, however, and I must admit, this was priming the pump. By next morning, I was more than ready to find Alba, the headquarters of Ferrero's chocolate production.

An overview of Italian boxed chocolates, with a few chocolate bars adding their touch of sweetness. *(Fred Lyon Pictures)*

ALBA
Ferrero

Eating chocolates with liquor in them used to strike me as something akin to trying to make love while wearing seventeen layers of crinoline. I hasten to explain. It is not the fault of the liquor or of the chocolate, but rather of what keeps the two apart—the sugar casing. That is what most manufacturers use to hold the alcohol in place. The sugar casing keeps the alcohol from leaking through the chocolate shell. My unfortunate reaction has been that the sugar casing leaves a residue on the tongue, and this residue has all the subtlety of sandpaper. Whatever loving or delicate thoughts I should be having about a particular chocolate as it combines with a particular liquor is all but lost in the crunching.

Well, Ferrero could have laid all my doubts to rest some years ago, if I had but known. Mon Cheri, the item for which they are justly famous, combines a cherry that has been properly steeped in rum, cherry, or curaçao and then all of it is placed inside a chocolate shell. Ferrero does it very, very well. Subtlety, not sugar casings, are the flavors that linger.

In their factory at Alba, I watch as, layer by layer, chocolate is poured into molds, the excess shaken off, then perfect cherries are lovingly placed to rest, one in each candy center. The cherries receive a blanket of chocolate, then another, and the process is repeated until each tiny rectangle is ready to be wrapped in pink foil, then paper, and sent out into the wide world of waiting chocolate lovers.

Ferrero's philosophy was to attack the chocolate market in a creative way, and considering the fact they have only been in business since 1946, they have done admirably, both with their philosophy and with chocolate. According to them, Mon Cheri is the biggest selling item of its type in all of Europe, and Ferrero employs over eight thousand people. The firm concentrates on producing a few highly specialized items and high-volume sales. Before they enter an item into the competitive market, they have already done extensive consumer research to find if that proposed item will be well received, and how well. The best example of their thoroughness is an item available in America at almost every supermarket checkout counter: Tic Tac, the tiny mint candies in the plastic box. If you look closely, you will discover they come to you from Ferrero's plant in Alba, Italy.

It is the Mon Cheri that impresses me. The box with its three liqueurs/cherries has been an instant success with my guests, as I offer them after dinner. If you should tire of such luxury, there are all those other chocolate trinkets Ferrero makes with which you can amuse yourself. Under the Mon Cheri label are chocolates with almonds and hazelnuts, although my favorite hazelnut and milk chocolate confection is the wedge-shaped Giandujot. These are obviously the favorites of Italians as well, for each firm in Italy makes its own version of this candy. The hazelnuts are grown in and around Alba, for this is the Piedmont section of Italy. Of course this makes it even easier for Ferrero. They can practically walk out their front door and obtain all the fine hazelnuts they need. For that matter, the cherries are also grown here. I tasted them, prior to their immersion in alcohol, and the only other cherries I have tasted that match the Alba ones are those grown in the Bitterroot Valley of Montana. The cherries are a cross between a pie cherry (tart) and a Bing cherry. A remarkable fruit!

By late afternoon we had toured the factory, eaten our share of chocolates, and felt as if we could not hold one more bite. Ferrero then proceeded to provide us with a lasting example of Italian ingenuity. They have taken espresso coffee, a beverage beloved by the natives for its ability to banish sleep after only one sip, and, in a deceptively innocent-looking small candy called Pocket Coffee, Ferrero produces a combination chocolate/espresso confection. No, not a blend, but an envelope of rich chocolate in whose center is a pure, dark espresso. Bite into this and what you receive is instant energy. Three of these little jewels will bring anyone around to a state of keen alertness, ready to go at least two more chocolate rounds.

So I hereby retract any and all statements I have heretofore made that might be disparaging about chocolate and liquor. I know exactly what kind of person would mix these two flavors. I would. Just as I now mix chocolate and coffee. Thanks to Ferrero, the people who took a fine Italian tradition, that of putting cherries into alcohol, and went it one step beter, to cover the whole luscious idea in fine chocolate.

P. Ferrero and Co. S.p.A.
Alba
Headquarters: Pino Torin, Italy

Their candies are available in Italy, Germany, France, Belgium, Luxembourg, the Netherlands, Great Britain, Switzerland, and Scandinavia. The Mon Cheri is not exported to America; liquor/chocolates are not permitted. Mr. Fink-Jensen, the assisting general manager of the International Division of Ferrero is the gentleman to whom questions can be directed. He will be glad to inform you of exact places in which all Ferrero products are sold in Europe.

Rigoni Aldo

There's La Scala in Milan, the Medici chapels in Florence, and Rigoni Aldo in Alba. I can see you flipping the pages of your tour books frantically, for it is easy enough to locate Milan and Florence, but unless you are visiting Ferrero, few people visit Alba. And fewer know of Rigoni Aldo.

The magic answer should take you to northern Italy, and Alba should be visited. It is where those famous white truffles bearing the same name, Alba Truffles, are found, the ones gourmets prize so highly. After tasting them, you will know why it is worth a trip there. During the months the truffles are available, September through December, those lucky enough to have them one time never forget Alba. As truffles go, these are unlike any others in the world, for they taste "earthy"—and that is a bad description, but Alba truffles seem to defy description. They are pungent and heavy with an aroma all their own. If you are fortunate enough, have them as we did, sliced paper-thin, over a cheese dish or on a veal creation. Slice by slice they add a voluptuous flavor that hints of garlic, heady wine, musky aphrodisiacs.

But there is also another Alba truffle which you should have, and this one is the creation of Rigoni Aldo. It is a confectionary truffle that Mr. Rigoni makes in his shop. He blends chocolate, sugar, fine spices and sometimes a bit of rum into a creation that is part candy, part cookie. They are also unlike any truffles, of chocolate nature, you have tasted anywhere else in the world. When you unwrap one from its waxed paper, and then bite into it, for that moment time is suspended. The light, tantalizing mixture of textures and flavors literally floats on the tongue and then dissolves. Then it is just a memory; that is, until you reach for another.

For just as his father and grandfather did before him in this very same shop, Mr. Rigoni makes these the old way, slow and exact, and whatever comes out of his shop bearing the family name is more than enough reason to find Alba. And to want to go back again.

Rigoni Aldo shop. *(Melanie Annin)*

I could spend hours praising his tiny cream puffs, each one filled with the richest cream possible, or his finger-sized eclairs, which are held down only by the chocolate glazing the top. Otherwise, I am sure they are so light they would float up and out of that shop. If Mr. Rigoni refuses to participate in the various "blessings" of modern technology, eschewing chemicals, shortcuts, premixes, and artificial flavors and preservatives, I guess it simply means he is just old-fashioned. He is part of that cultural heritage that takes the finest raw materials and transforms them into art. His art is transient, but no less a major feat of creation.

Rigoni truffles last for a week or two. During that length of time, each is as light and desirable as a lover's first kiss—and equally unforgettable. Like the perfect note sung at La Scala, the fine hand of Donatello on the ceiling of the chapel in Florence, the true artist must be praised for his refusal to be anything but the best.' And Aldo Rigoni, that master artist, is that. By whatever means one gets to Alba, by all means get to his shop. This one bakery in the heart of Alba is all richness beyond mere pastry or candy. These are true confectionary miracles one searches for. The tour books sometimes forget we need something to remember, something that says we have had the good taste to find this, the good fortune of the discriminating traveler.

Rigoni Aldo Pasticceria and Confetteria
Corso Italia 6
Alba
Tel.: 22–11

I don't know if he can ship his truffles, but you might write and ask if it is possible. Airmail, Italian style, is not necessarily quick, however, so I recommend going there. And even bringing them back on the plane.

NOVI LIGURE
Pernigotti

I enjoy traveling, and when there is chocolate at the promised destination, few things can deter me from my goal—not even an entire train system that has decided to go out on a modified strike plan. Armed with my useless train schedule, I went out to explore the intricacies of the Italian train system, and arrived at Alessandria, the closest stop to Novi Ligure, and Pernigotti chocolates.

There I was met by Stefano Rosso, who provided transportation and interpretation, and thanks to him I can say that Pernigotti is worth all the effort it takes to get to their doorstep. Indeed, it is an exquisite embellishment, all Italian, of any and all chocolate adventures. Pernigotti, is to my taste, a sparkling constellation in a heaven of chocolate. Cremini, that small blue star, unwraps in my hand easily, and I feast on the strata of chocolate, in between which a cream layer has been sandwiched.

The Italian favorite, milk chocolate and hazelnut, has its own name here, Giandutto. The hazelnuts from the Piedmont section of Italy are blended with fine chocolate and milk until they achieve a smooth, consummate flavor and disposition. Just to see them improves mine, for each chocolate candy is a gift of visual delight. Wrapped in gold foil, the triangles of chocolate lie in geometric splendor in their box. They promise a host of goodness, and they exceed their promise.

Other chocolate candies are beautifully presented, wrapped in foil with floral motifs, or in the case of the walnut piece, wrapped to resemble

Pernigotti reveals a small selection from their vast choice of chocolates.
(*Adrianne Marcus*)

an actual walnut. Each tastes as good as it looks. Under the blue foil is a
mocha of impeccable virtue.

When we finally reach the room in which the Easter assortments are
displayed, the Easter eggs alone are works of art. These hollow chocolate
eggs eclipse any I have ever seen. They are wrapped in intricate, pleated
foil, and are flowery, glittering, delicate. I am not sure if I could bear to
see one broken open, though this is what happens to them. For inside
each is a prize for a lucky child.

For over a hundred years, Pernigotti has made the finest candies one
could hope to find. From the very beginning, when the firm made only
one item, Torrone, that honey, almond, sugar, and pistachio favorite, to
today, when that same item can be bought in a bar, coated with
chocolate, everything they put their hand to comes out perfectly.

Their assortments are beautifully packaged, and the contents memorable. My only regret is that Pernigotti is not available in the United
States as yet. One item that would make Valentine's Day perfect is the
box they make with its twenty or so chocolate hearts resting in individual
niches. Each is wrapped in gold foil with tiny red hearts sprinkled on the
wrappings. I would think there is no nicer way to give one's heart to a
loved one than this. And twenty times over, at that.

Pernigotti
Stefano Pernigotti and Figlio S.p.A.
Viale della Rimembranza, 100
Novi Ligure
Tel.: 77–63–1

Dr. Rosso is in charge of the chocolate production in the factory, and thanks to his son, Stefano, was glad to show us all the products they made and share these exquisite Italian chocolate candies with us. They might be willing to mail you some of their chocolate, if you write to them, and they are chocolates worth writing about and waiting for.

PERUGIA
Perugina

I now know the meaning of the phrase, "the crowning touch." It describes Perugia, which sits high on the hills, as well as Perugina chocolates. Perugia is the home of the University of Perugia, so the streets of the town were filled with students, just returning to their studies. The scenery in this part of Italy is splendid. The shops have a great many beautiful clothes; since Italian knits are made here, they are quite reasonably priced. Every corner of Perugia is within walking distance, and the view from each corner brings another spectacular vista to delight you. Perugia is also the best place I know to enjoy a copa, that cup of Italian ice creams (at least three different kinds) over which marinated cherries are liberally ladled.

Perugina, the crowning touch of Italian chocolates, is made here. These candies are available in the United States, of course, and any Italian delicatessen worth its weight in olive oil usually carries one of their best-known items, Baci. Since *bacio* means kiss in Italian, this is the story behind the naming of this candy:

The candy used to be named Cazzotti, which means punch. One day a pretty girl walked into the store where Mr. Buitoni, the owner of Perugina, happened to be standing. He heard her ask for a Cazzotti. Mr. Buitoni quickly concluded that this was not right. No lovely young lady should be asking for a punch. He promptly renamed his candy Baci, kiss. Not only were his intentions correct, but Baci was a kiss of good fortune for Mr. Buitoni, since it became the cornerstone of that company, the candy from which every other item grew.

Only in France is it possible to have your Baci made of milk chocolate. Everywhere else the hazelnut is embedded in chocolate perfection in its usual dark chocolate form. Perugina also makes the familiar wedge-shaped piece of candy that features hazelnuts ground up in chocolate they call Giandioutto. The name varies according to the company that makes it, but the candy remains uniformly Italian and marvelous. Perugina is busily turning them out by the thousands, all in glittering gold wrap.

If I ever had anything I wished packaged, I would make sure to have the Italian chocolate manufacturer decide how to do it. Gift box after gift box, Perugina places its candies in the most lavish boxes possible. I still cannot bring myself to tear apart one in which row after row of exquisite multicolored foil pieces hold their chocolates in an inviolate state. I did manage to unwrap enough of them there to convince myself that what is beneath all that glitter is fine chocolate, in every form.

Their purple-wrapped Glassato is a chocolate wafer with vanilla. Their Canasta is a chocolate-covered cherry, which is without peer, unless

Perugina's foil-wrapped chocolates nested in their box. *(Adrianne Marcus)*

you happen upon the Tartufis, the denser chocolate miracles with their overtaste of cherry. You might also enjoy the Pomona, which is a mixture of candied perfection and fruit.

It all begins with the fine chocolate Perugina makes. They use both the longitudinal conches (the old-fashioned way) and the newer types. Either way, they produce exceptional chocolate in their coatings and a well-above-average chocolate bar. Try the Louisa, which is the favorite of most Italians (and mine) with its bittersweet chocolate taste. It is almost drab in appearance, compared to the bright wrapping that the smaller candies wear, but its taste is a reminder never to judge chocolate by its cover alone.

The bars they make are available most places in Italy. What was most interesting to me was the number of gift boxes of Perugina that are sold daily. I was told it is the custom to bring a box of chocolate to someone's house when you are invited as a guest. Wine would favor the man, flowers, the woman, but chocolate favors the entire family. Certainly, Perugina chocolates favor everyone, on every occasion. In New York, they operate their own store at 636 Lexington Avenue. In Italy, no city is left unsavored, or without its Perugina candy shop.

PERUGINA-OWNED SHOPS

FIRENZE 50122
Via Por S. Maria, 68
Tel.: 287–111

MILANO 20123
Corso Buenos Aires, 77
Tel.: 803–816
Signora Leda Baraldi

NAPOLI 1° 80121
Piazza Martiri, 55
Tel.: 392–937
Signora Eleonora Gastaldello

PERUGIA 06100
Corso Vannucci, 85
Tel.: 21–896
Signora Evelina Castellano ·

ROMA 1° 00187
Via Condotti, 82/83
Tel.: 6792–250
Signora Ornella Savonelli

ROMA 2° 00192
Via Cola di Rienzo, 225/227
Tel.: 350–462
Signora Guiliana Piccolo

ROMA 3° 00183
Via Appia Nuova, 110
Tel.: 7578–588
Signora Michela Pomposini

TORINO 10121
Via Roma, 104
Tel.: 535–453
Signora Maria Martina

VENEZIA S.L. 30124
Campo S. Luca, 4586
Tel.: 25–613
Signora Franca Lachin

VENEZIA LIDO 30126
Viale S.M. Elisabetta, 43
Tel.: 760–138
Signora Franca Lachin

VENEZIA MESTRE 30170
Via Rosa, 22
Tel.: 59–646
Signora Isabella Seeman

VERONA 37100
Via Mazzini, 66
Tel.: 23–641

NEW YORK 10022
636 Lexington Ave.
Tel.: Pl. 5–5365
Signora Fare Stelle

YUGOSLAVIA

ZAGREB
Josip Kras

I was lucky enough to taste these Yugoslavian chocolates, thanks to that country's trade commissioner in Chicago, who got them for me. Having already heard how marvelous the Kras chocolates were from a reliable source, namely, another chocolate addict who had tasted them in Yugoslavia, I was eager to try them. Having done that, I fully concur—they are splendid.

They make an item called Bajadera, which can fulfill any and all chocolate lovers' fantasies. It is a creamy chocolate three-layered production. Each bite is a sensation of delectable taste. The dark top layer gives way to a whipped nougat center, and the bottom layer is a repeat of that dark top chocolate.

Their fruit and nut bar, as well as the red-and-white-wrapped plain chocolate bar, are equally worth having. There is a good chance the candy is being considered for import into this country, and I hope by the time the word gets to you, the chocolates Josip Kras makes will be available.

Kras
Industrija Cokolade
Bombona I Kepsa
Zagreb

I don't know if they will ship these to you, but it would be worth the time and effort to try and convince them to.

HUNGARY

BUDAPEST
We did not get to Budapest, but a chocolate aficionado gave me these notes. These are her recommendations and I pass them along in case

anyone happens to be in Budapest and wants to hear the place suggested by someone who has eaten chocolate there:

Vörösmarty

She tells me this one is close to the airline terminal and the Danube, at Ter 7. "For almost fifty years Vörösmarty was called the Gerbeaud, after a French pastry cook who settled in Hungary. He developed a line of chocolates packaged in wooden boxes that became world famous. Today these chocolates are manufactured in Rio de Janeiro. Although the name has changed, the place remains the same."

Ruswurm

Ruswurm's Rigó Jancsi is a moist marvel of a cake, according to my source. "Mousse and whipped cream that out-chocolate all rivals." She also suggests Kugel Torta, chocolate and poppy seeds which combine perfectly to produce a pastry with an unusually good taste. She tells me the combination sounds unlikely, but it really works. You should have your treats right in shop, since you can enjoy the view of the Pest and the Danube from Ruswurm, at Szenthéromsag Utca 7.

AUSTRIA

VIENNA
Demel's

In a setting as gracious and ornate as a Viennese opera, Demels, this monument to exquisite moments of gastronomic pleasure, creates a variety of lavish chocolate delights. From the tiniest Rum Nuss Pastillei, with its chocolate counterpointed by marzipan and dusted with white sugar, to the individual chocolates boxed in tiny art forms, Demel's is to chocolates what Santa is to Christmas.

Their Gypsy Cake, for instance: five layers high with a heavy Paris Cream between each layer is no one's idea of a light repast. You cannot stop to worry about being full; you simply want more.

As you approach the vast array of desserts displayed in all their opulence, the temptation continues to try one of each. The desserts are beyond description and almost beyond belief. If you happen to be there on a splendid fall afternoon, and Demel's has just made their fabulous Annatorte, begin with this one. Named after Anna, the last Demel, this delicacy's dark chocolate and slight hazelnut exterior gives way to a bittersweet, incomparable filling. The whole surprise is not that it is delectable, as it is, but that its taste is matched by its beauty. The frosting—if, indeed, such a crass word can be used to describe the covering—has been overlapped, chocolate sheet by chocolate sheet, until it mounts up in the center of the cake in high waves of chocolate which have been lightly dusted with confectioner's sugar.

If you are not there on the day the Annatorte is, take heart. Their version of the Sachertorte or the Truffletorte is more than an acceptable substitute. Each of these chocolate moments in time can be enjoyed as you sit in the marble and crystal splendor of the Demel's rooms. Having pointed to the chocolate of your desire, you will be served by the "Demelinerin"—the women who work at Demel's.

The desserts will vary on a given day (Demel's makes some 260 different cookies as well as 35 different cakes); it would be impossible to try them all. Aside from the chocolate ones, you should have some of their tiny Dattels, which are dates rolled in marzipan and baked. I gathered up at least a pound of these to eat along the way, and I have also discovered they ship well. Since the Dattels are impossibly rich, consider freezing some when you get them. They do freeze well, with no loss of flavor or magnificent texture, if properly wrapped.

One dessert you can only have while at Demel's is their Milchramstrudel. If it is available that day, do have it. It features a custard of impeccable lineage with plump raisins embedded in the custard; it all rests on the flakiest, lightest crust of all. Milchramstrudel demands prompt attention. And yes, I did manage to eat an entire piece.

For two days, we attempted to balance ourselves between gorging and tact. Gorging won. Everything Demel's makes is a true Viennese splendor, and so the gods of heaven must forgive all our excesses, but never has so much been prepared with such exquisite care. Demel's is reason enough to go to Vienna, and the confections they create make it impossible not to wish to return time after time.

Ch. Demel's Söhne Gesellschaft M.B.H.
Kohlmarkt 14
Vienna 1-1010
Tel.: 63–55–16–0

Perhaps you could convince Jurgen Meinghast of your authentic desire for the Dattels and he might be persuaded to airmail some to you. I do not know what this would cost, but I assure you it is worth any amount and then some just to have them.

Hotel Sacher

"It's too sweet for me," the imperious young man at the Hotel Sacher replied, as he was questioned about Sacher Torte. After tasting other versions of this chocolate delicacy, I can only agree with his appraisal of his own hotel's confectionary efforts. Yet the Hotel Sacher, with its hunting-lodge-cum-kitsch decor, still maintains an effort at Viennese affluence with this item and sells two to three hundred of these cakes daily by mail. Plus all the others that tourists line up to buy.

The secret, according to our young authority of Vienna's confectionary cuisine ("I *am* an authority, madame"), is the blend of four Austrian companies' chocolates over a rather nondescript chocolate cake. ("A cake anyone can make," he announces haughtily, when questioned, "if you have a German version of—what do you call it?—the *Encyclopaedia Britannica.*")

Here is the recipe as he told it to us on that rainy afternoon:

10 decagrams chocolate
10 decagrams sugar
10 decagrams egg whites
10 decagrams egg yolks
10 decagrams butter

Take the butter, add the yolks, add the chocolate, sugar, flour. Then add the beaten egg whites. Bake at 180° c. for ¾ hour. Cool and remove cake; slice once, spread with apricot preserves, put together again, and spread with apricot preserves again. Then pour melted chocolate over it all.

I hasten to add that I prefer not to take the blame for this cake or this recipe; he's the authority, after all.

Now then, as to the Sacher Torte itself, I will venture this appraisal. It is a moderately inoffensive chocolate cake which is divided into parts by an apricot glaze. It is reputed to keep three weeks, and has been said to have made the round trip to Australia and returned edible. Edible, I must remind the cautious reader, is a relative term.

Fresh, as we had it that day, the cake is almost wet; three weeks in a good Vienna sanitarium would dry it out. The grainy chocolate covering, otherwise known as "the chef's secret," should remain so. For Viennese Sacher Torte of an infinitely finer texture and taste, do yourself a favor: go to Demel's.

Hotel Sacher
Vienna

I wouldn't order this under any circumstances, and I would suggest it is not a gift any chocolate lover I know would appreciate. On the contrary.

Café Konditorei L. Heiner

Vienna has the privilege of containing more crown jewels in the chocolate kingdom than any other city. After the priceless treasures of Demel's have been enjoyed in all their brilliance, there is yet another place to capture your attention—Heiner's. As you walk through the front door, case after case holds chocolate jewels of such magnificence that the impossible task of choosing one or two requires a restraint few visitors exhibit.

Their Truffletorte is the finest you will have anywhere. Although my German leaves more than a bit to be desired, I believe we were told that their chocolate is made by an Austrian firm, Knäbchen. I did get the name of the cake right, Truffletorte, and Herr Meinbeck nodded no as I pointed to the Sachertorte, for we had asked for the Hope Diamond of chocolate desserts, and he indicated that the Sachertorte was only a supporting jewel in their diadem. I was to try the Truffletorte first. There is no way to attempt to try anything afterward, for it would be sheer folly to think you could hold another bite beyond that miracle of elegance and decadence. Start with the cake, which is as chocolate rich as anything you can imagine, then drift down through the layers of Paris Cream, whipped until it has reached a deceptive lightness, then you can slide down into the taste of orange and back into chocolate again. They make their cake not only with fresh orange juice, but also with orange curaçao liqueur. When you get to the last bite, it is all you can do to lift the final forkful into your satiated mouth.

Therefore, I must only tell you my companion raved equally over her Nuss Dessert, a walnut paste over which rich chocolate had been poured.

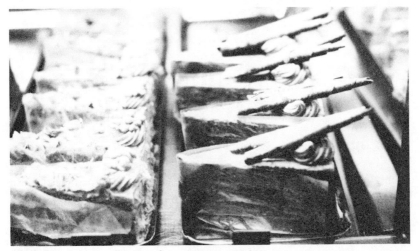

A bit of Austrian confections from Heiner. *(Melanie Annin)*

I will have to take her word for it. I could not eat one more bite of anything.

Heiner's will not export their chocolate candies, which are made on the premises, but are much too fragile to ship. If you are there (and where else should you be?) have them pack you some in their flowered boxes, which will become a beautiful memory after you have finished all your chocolates.

Heiner is not for the faint of heart. None of their marvelous desserts could be considered a light snack. No, they are excessive, in the best sense of the word—extravagantly tasty, notable, textured, as lavish a promise as was ever made.

Café Konditorei L. Heiner
Wien, i, Wollzeile 9, or

Wien 1, Kärtnerstrasse 21
Vienna
Tel.: 52–68–63

They will not ship, but you might be able to convince someone who is going to Vienna to have them pack you a box to bring back. The chocolates will hold up for a few days, while in transit, if your friend doesn't eat them.

DENMARK

COPENHAGEN

Toms/Anton Berg

We would have spent more time in Copenhagen, researching candy stores and chocolate resources, but October arrived in Copenhagen at the same moment we did. We came from Vienna. October came from the Arctic.

We did manage to see the new factory of Toms, of which Anton Berg is part. This huge, modern (Danish modern, of course) plant produces both labels of chocolate. What they make is what many Europeans have told us is the finest Danish chocolate anywhere. Having gone through the factory and tasted a wide range of their chocolate production, I can recommend them quite highly. Some of my favorites are now available in the United States, in specialty food stores, where I have found their marzipan fingers (pink foil wrapped), which have a fine marzipan center covered with chocolate.

If you happen to be in Canada or Europe, you will probably have less trouble locating Toms and Anton Berg candies. The firm ships throughout the world, but the items that contain that forbidden substance, liquor, are not permitted entry into America. That is a pity, for their Queen of Denmark tin contains chocolates filled with Grand Marnier. In America, we are able to buy their other Queen of Denmark tin, which contains strawberries in liquid, but not an alcoholic liquid. I feel that I should let you in on one other secret, one I discovered by accident. No matter which of these chocolates you try, here or abroad, the Grand Marnier or the strawberry, be sure to put the whole piece of candy into your mouth. Do not bite in. If you do, you will have a problem. The liquid spurts out, and you will stand there as I did, with the filling everywhere but where it belongs: in your mouth.

Once you have mastered that, go on and taste their marvelous miniature chocolate bottles that contain Cherry Heering, or whiskey, or Grand Marnier. The all-in-one thrust into the waiting mouth is ever so rewarding. Believe me.

They, just as Ferrero, the Italian firm, have found the secret of putting a liquid (usually alcoholic) filling into a chocolate without

Toms/Anton Berg's chocolate assortment. *(Adrianne Marcus)*

resorting to my old nemesis, the sugar casing. Again, however they manage it, it is a trade secret. The taste is no secret. It is purely good, from chocolate shell to liquid inside, a blend of the best ingredients.

You should also try some of their chocolate assortments. These are usually packaged in Anton Berg boxes (particularly in America), but under that name or the name Toms, be sure to look inside the box and find the triangular-shaped piece, a chocolate-covered apricot. Not a jelly, nor a jam, but somewhere in between. It is the first piece I reach for.

I am not fond of their Copenhagen Thins. These slivers of chocolate are shaped into rectangles, but they are not to my taste. I do like Toms Guld Barre, which is a chocolate crunch number. It bears the label "Toms" on it, and I found it in many stores throughout Europe. All of their bars are above average in taste. The Guld Barre rates even higher. The real rave review has to be for their marzipan pieces, chocolate-covered disks with apricot brandy added. I have not tasted marzipan treated this beautifully before. The one with Plum in Madeira is smashing. Each luscious combination works perfectly, and everyone who has tried them returned for seconds. Then thirds.

I am sure if I looked long enough, I could probably find someone who would not like these, but who wants to be around anyone like that? My

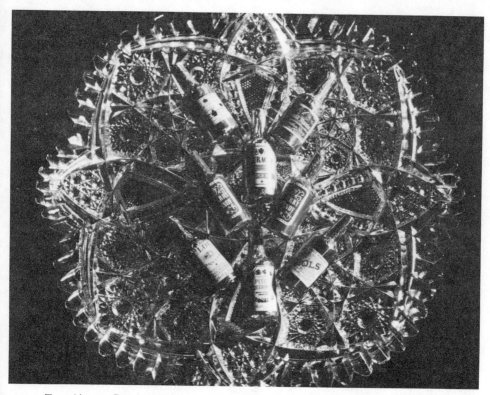

Toms/Anton Berg's miniature chocolate bottles filled with liqueurs. (*Adrianne Marcus*)

motto is and has always been: trust no one who won't eat chocolate. Under or over thirty.

Better to put my trust in such places as it is warranted, and Anton Berg, Toms, have returned that investment, chocolate candy by chocolate candy. With interest. Even if I decline their chocolate thins, or an occasional chocolate pretzel, I can show you my loyalty and dedication to all their other chocolates. Just hand me that tin of Queen of Denmark strawberries or Grand Marnier-filled candies. I will not only show you loyalty and devotion, but an empty tin as well.

Toms/Anton Berg
DK 2750 Ballerup
Copenhagen
Tel.: 2–9721–22

Their products are easy to find in Denmark, as well as other parts of Europe. In the United States, their products are handled by Mr. Malcolm Newberg, of the firm of Direct International Ltd., 50-10 69th St., Woodside, New York. You can write and ask him where you can obtain these candies (those which are imported into America) or phone (212) 426–4000, and perhaps he can give you a few sources near you.

HOLLAND

ZAANDAM
Verkade

Everything about Holland says to the visitor, "Stay here," from the friendliness of the people to the nature of the place, which radiates a sense of joy, of welcome. The glass windows, front and back, in their houses are left open at all times to let the light in and out. It is a country with a remarkable energy one wishes to bring back. The light in Holland is internal and external. Even when it is raining, Holland is bright and alive.

We wanted to stay, but we did the next best thing, we brought a bit of Holland back with us in the form of Verkade candy bars. Droste chocolates are easy to obtain in America, but if I were to choose only one example of a chocolate that reflects the character of a country, it would have to be Verkade. The Zartbitter is magnificent, a bittersweet of such goodness you do not expect to find it in a simple candy bar. Smooth and lustrous, it has an unforgettable taste. For a bittersweet chocolate bar, you cannot find anyone, anywhere else in the world any better than this one.

Equal in taste and just as outrageously good is the Chocolat au Lait Avec Raisins Mit Secs, which I guess translates out to Milk Chocolate with Raisins and Nuts. That is too easy a way to describe this light-textured, crunchy, fruit-filled bar. This bar is as good as the Flemish food, and that is saying something.

I have not been able to locate these bars in the United States, but you can buy them in a great many countries in Europe—Holland, of course, but they are also easy to find in Germany and Belgium. Once you have tasted them, you will know why. Everyone wants Verkade. I wish I had brought more Holland home with me. I do miss it.

Verkade
Koninklijke Verkade Fabrieken V.V.
Zaandam

I don't know if they'll ship these, but I intend to ask them anyway.

GERMANY

TRAVELING THROUGH
Sarotti, Gubor, Ritter Chocolate Bars

I didn't have much luck finding German chocolates. The few places I tried in Frankfurt were not memorable, so we bought chocolate bars. My first attempt with Sarotti led to these words: grainy, sweet, awful. I gave it another try, and reached into a box of Sarotti. Truthfully, the graphics on the outside had sold the box to me. Inside the slick and dreamy package were some nice-looking candies. Better to leave them that way. I cannot imagine anyone eating them with any degree of pleasure. None were of lasting quality. I do not know if they were stale, or if they really were supposed to taste like that. Let me believe the former.

Now that I've dispensed with the bad news, here's the good news. You can buy good Ritter bars on any train, at any newsstand, in any number of places. Called Pocket Chocolate, Ritter bars' square shape fits into a pocket easily. My particular favorite is the one that combines chocolate with fruits and nuts. It resembles the Nestlé Fitness bar (my other favorite), but Ritter calls it the Sport bar. Whatever you call it, call it yours—it's a treat worth buying and enjoying. I wish we had brought at least a dozen back with us, for their taste matches what we believe is the best of German chocolate taste: a bittersweet, smooth-textured chocolate.

More good news, since it ought to outweigh the bad beginning: Gubor makes great chocolate bars, also. Their Grand Marnier Truffel is a smooth filled bar without too much sugar added to its orange filling. With a refreshingly tart taste, it contrasts superbly with an unusual milk chocolate exterior. Or, as the label states, "Feinste Gubor-Vollmilchschokolade mit köstlich abgestimmter Tüffel-Füllung auf der Basis des original französchen Grand Marnier Liqueurs." I could not have put it better myself, since I just call it milk chocolate with Grand Marnier filling.

The Gubor Schwarzulderli is a packaged candy bar that contains a whole series of thin-as-veneer, wood-grained chocolate slices. Each one looks as if it came straight from the lumber mill, and panel by panel melts into an instant chocolate mouth-warming delight. There is a slight smoky aftertaste which is nice, and lingers a bit. They call it their specialty, and my companion added, "It tastes like I want a Black Forest cake to taste, but has never been this good."

We both agree that Gubor's restrained packaging is a perfect example of what good candy bar packaging ought to imply: good taste outside means (at best) better inside. You can enjoy the time between trains at the Frankfurt train station a great deal better with one of these in hand. Gubor's helps to pass the time the way it should be, in good company.

ENGLAND

BOURNVILLE
Cadbury Limited

Cadbury's is the world's largest producer of chocolate. Not the largest food company, for that honor belongs to Nestlé, but as a chocolate firm,

Cadbury Limited makes more chocolate than any other single firm in the world.

The history of Cadbury's goes back over 150 years, to 1824, the year twenty-three-year-old John Cadbury opened his coffee and tea business right next door to his father's draper's shop in Birmingham. As a sideline, he carried cocoa beans, which he would grind by hand with a mortar and pestle. With a distinct flare for showmanship, John displayed his products behind plate glass and introduced window displays into merchandising, while inside his store he had hired a Chinese servant, in full native costume, to help sell his teas.

As business expanded, John's brother, Benjamin, joined the firm as a partner; a larger factory came about, and in 1860, the partnership dissolved. The following year, Cadbury's sons, Richard and George, were handed the factory. By 1866, they were doing it so well they introduced a new process to the world, and called it Cocoa Essence. The process produced a better chocolate beverage by removing part of the cocoa butter from chocolate. The powder that remained with its smaller percentage of cocoa butter made a creamy-bodied chocolate drink.

With business continuing to prosper, the brothers took another gigantic step forward in 1879 when they bought the Bournbrook Estate, four miles north of Birmingham. It had good rail and road facilities. Here they built the Bournville factory. By the turn of the century, the original staff of 231 employees had grown to 3,000.

Bournville Chocolate was introduced in 1906, about the same time that Cadbury's Dairy Milk was offered to the public. It was a chocolate beverage produced in England for English tastes, and it broke what had been the Swiss monopoly on the milk chocolate market in England.

When J. S. Fry and Sons Limited joined with Cadbury Brothers Limited in the year 1920, the merger marked a move to overseas factories. Shortly thereafter, factories were opened in Tasmania, Canada, Dunedin, New Zealand, Ireland, South Africa, India, and Nigeria. These factories are now part of Cadbury Schweppes (Overseas) Limited.

In 1927, chocolate molding machines increased Cadbury's chocolate output by double. By the time the final merger with Schweppes took place in 1969, Cadbury's Bournville factory covered three million square feet, or sixty-five acres of floor space.

Today, Americans consume their share of Cadbury's products, which are also produced in Connecticut. There is another Cadbury factory in Canada just for that market.

Cadbury's antique candy box (1889). *(Cadbury Limited)*

A full line of chocolate bars, as well as boxed chocolates and specialty items, is made by Cadbury's. Not all are available in the United States. The Bournville, a bittersweet chocolate wrapped in bright red, can be bought in England, but it does not sell well enough to warrant producing it in America.

Another item, one I wish we could purchase here, is the Cadbury Flakes. This light crumbly tube is thin curl after thin curl of the lightest milk chocolate. The Flakes taste is so distinct, so light (just as their name suggests), that I have never found it successfully imitated by another chocolate manufacturer.

Cadbury has a great many standard assortments for sale in England. Their Bournville Selection is more for the English than it is for me; it is sweet. We have grown so unaccustomed to seeing a lot of food colorings in our candy centers that to bite into a piece of these chocolates and find a bright orange or almost Dayglo pink center is rather unsettling. I find their Rose Chocolate assortment to be oversweet and overcolored also. Their bars are quite good, however, and a bit above the ordinary. Try the Fruit and Nut bar, which is milk chocolate with raisins and mixed nuts. It is considerably sweeter than Nestlé's Fitness bar.

I still go with two of their products out of the wide range they make. The Flakes and the red Bournville bar are my favorites. I wish I could convince Cadbury's to give us another chance, that our chocolate tastes deserve these two fine products. They would have to change their formulations to conform to our standards if they were to be made here in America. Cadbury's is permitted in England to use up to 5 percent other vegetable oils in their chocolate and still call their products "chocolate." In this country, any product labeled chocolate must contain only cocoa butter, no other vegetable fats. If it does contain anything other than cocoa butter it must be labeled chocolate-flavored. When you buy a bar of chocolate or a chocolate product labeled chocolate-flavored, all that is usually different about it is that substitution of oil for cocoa butter. American chocolate purists claim nothing tastes exactly like cocoa butter. European tastes disagree. That may be the reason my favorite two items are not produced in this country. I still like them and wish I could get them here.

Cadbury Ltd.
A Division of Cadbury-Schweppes. Ltd.
Bournville

The visit to the factory was an education in itself, and a combination of British ingenuity and technology. A great many of Cadbury's candy bars are available wherever you are in the world, but the original ones still come from England.

6
THE CARE
AND FEEDING
of your
CHOCOLATES

Now that you have some of your favorite chocolates at hand, the question comes up: how to take care of these fragile beauties? Chocolates are delicate, and should be enjoyed as soon as possible, but if you are planning to keep them for a bit, to share with others, the first rule concerning their care is to keep them out of the refrigerator.

Chocolate candies should be kept cool and away from moisture or strong odors. The average refrigerator is too moist and contains too many other foods to guarantee your chocolates will remain in prime condition. I recommend a cool, dark place if you plan to save them for a week or two. Longer than that, I suggest you freeze them.

If exposed to sunlight or heat, the candies will, as flowers do, "bloom." When chocolate is exposed to sunlight or excessive heat, the cocoa butter, which is in suspension, rises to the surface, producing that familiar grayish film on top. It many not ruin the chocolate at first, but it certainly makes it less appetizing. Prolonged exposure to either element will eventually affect the taste.

If you do not have a humidity-free environment or a cool room in which to store your candies, try freezing them, after first double wrapping the box or container in two layers of foil or plastic wrap. This will keep the air and moisture away from your candies. Once you bring them out, follow the suggestions of the chemist John W. Vassons, a consultant to the chocolate industry, who says:

"Condensation usually occurs when the centers or chocolates are cold and subjected to warm air. When a box of candy is removed from a freezer at − 5 degrees, it should remain wrapped in foil or plastic and subjected to a room of 60 to 70 degrees for about twenty-four hours before opening. . . ."

The important thing to remember is not to open the wrappings before twenty-four hours have elapsed. This permits the chocolate to reach room temperature slowly. Of course, you must take the precaution of allowing them to reach this temperature without sunlight striking them.

If you are bringing chocolates back from Europe, or from another part of the country, by air, he offers the following reminders: "On most planes the pressure in the freight department is equivalent to five thousand feet, or five-inch vacuum. Many aerated candies such as marshmallow, nougat, and light cream centers will expand and split the chocolate."

Having flown a great many miles with my chocolate candies, I have not experienced this problem, but I have had a few of the candies with liquid centers leak through their chocolate shells. Again, this is a problem that concerns altitude, and it will not invariably happen. Most chocolates travel well, but I have known friends who have lost part of a box of "not quite legal" liquor-filled chocolates. It seems to be more a matter of luck than anything else. It is cool in the freight compartment of a plane, so heat is not the problem.

Taking them by car from one destination to another does mean you should have a proper cooler. I have invented my own way of dealing with that problem, and I am glad to pass it along. I place my chocolates in the bottom of a large cooler (which is in the trunk of my car), and then I place layers of newspaper over them. On the very top, I put dry ice. Then

I shut the whole thing up. This method keeps the chocolates in perfect condition for up to twenty-four hours. They are cool, but they do not freeze, since the newspapers provide adequate insulation. Regular ice does not work very well. It melts fast, and moisture is chocolates' enemy. I tried regular ice only once, in plastic bags, and found it too wet for my chocolates. When I arrived at my destination and opened the cooler, I discovered that half my chocolates had lost their sheen. The moisture had dissolved some of the sugar in the chocolate, and when the sugar recrystallized, it did so in small diamonds all over the surface of the candies, much to their detriment. Perhaps plastic-wrapping them two or three times might have prevented some of the major damage, but in any case, there was an inch of water (from condensation) on the bottom of the cooler, and who wants a chocolate candy float?

If you have trouble finding a place with dry ice, try an ice-cream store. That is where I have located dry ice in strange cities when I could not find a place listed in the yellow pages.

Good chocolate candies should be enjoyed promptly, or frozen, to enjoy later. Fruits dipped in chocolate will not hold up at all. Freezing turns the fruit centers into mush. So fresh fruit coated in chocolate is a seasonal enjoyment to be eaten right away. In fact, during the summer, it is easy to make your own. Buy a block or piece of coating from a local candy maker. Then melt it *slowly* in a crock pot (set at *low*) or in a double boiler. When the chocolate becomes liquid, take your whole-stemmed strawberries, grapes, or whatever (be sure they are dry), and dip them piece by piece into the warm chocolate liquid. This is the only time I suggest you use the refrigerator for chocolates: it permits the chocolate to harden if the weather is warm. Be sure nothing of a nature and odor stronger than a carton of milk is anywhere in the vicinity, unless you wish to have onion- or cheese-flavored chocolate-dipped fruit. But done right, the fruits dipped in chocolate in the morning can be served that evening, and to great exclamations of delight as a stunning dessert. Sometimes I just bring the crock pot out and let my guests dip their own pieces of fruit in chocolate. They love that.

Wherever you are, there is probably a good candy maker within reaching distance. Obviously, you may know of some particular place or candy maker I have not found as yet. There is no way I could reach all of them, nor could I hope to in only two years of travel and tasting. So if you know of a place that produces a candy you think extraordinary, I would like to know all about it. Just drop me a few lines % Putnam's, sharing the name of the place and those candies you have found that make that place special. I am always eager to share the best of all chocolate experiences.

There are always new chocolate candies being created for us and new places to enjoy them. Such information is a special gift one chocolate lover shares with another. Wisdom consists in being prepared to enjoy an unexpected adventure, and fine chocolate candies are an adventure in taste. A chocolate addict is more than prepared to leave for such an adventure at the chocolate drop of a hat. Or a name.

Having searched for as many of the extraordinary chocolate candies as time and energy allowed, I have been helped in my quest by many authorities. The late L. Russell Cook bestowed an accolade when I picked up a cocoa bean (this was after a full year of instruction), broke it open, tasted the nib, and identified the bean's origin—a Ghana bean. He looked pleased at the fact I had managed to identify its particular taste and said, "I see I have taught you properly." I remember feeling quite special at this moment.

On another level, this discrimination is exactly what each of us looks for when we compare the differences of one piece of chocolate from another. This is why we have our favorites; a particular taste is what we are looking for. There are candies and chocolates I will not touch. Others are worth going miles out of my way to procure. Good chocolate is its own reward. For centuries it has been lauded as a bromide, a stimulant, an aphrodisiac and a source of enjoyment. Chocolate is called "the gift of love," best served by those who love, appreciate, and enjoy sharing the best.

ACKNOWLEDGEMENTS

Chocolate is a great attraction. And a great deal of chocolate in one place attracted a great many people. I want to thank them, for this book is due to their efforts in making sure I always had enough chocolate and enough help to keep me going.

To my parents, Edith and George Stuhl, who first led me down the chocolate path, I wish to acknowledge their help with my project. They can now safely enjoy their own chocolates. I finally have enough of my own. Since I have learned to read the "signature"—the line on the top of a piece of chocolate that indicates what flavor is inside—I am sure they are grateful that my habit of delicately punching in the bottoms of various pieces in a selection of chocolate, and leaving the ones I did not want, right side up, seemingly untouched, has ended.

My immediate family has also been a tremendous help. They willingly gave up their time to taste whatever came into the house. It was their devotion to this duty that assured all chocolates received prompt and complete attention. My husband, Warren, is now a veritable authority on bittersweet chocolates. My youngest child, Sarah, has proved her chocolate palate beyond a doubt by refusing my generous offer of a certain American crunch bar in preference, as she put it, "No! I want the foreign one." A ten-year-old authority is not to be denied, and she has convinced me that even a child is aware of the differences in taste between chocolate bars. My middle daughter, Shelby, proved herself by selecting the "leftover" portion of a ten-pound Callebaut bar. She removed it from the chocolate cellar to the wider world of collegiate testing, and reported that it got an A + and high honors. And of course, my eldest, Stacey, maintains her authority as milk chocolate expert, with preferences toward the Swiss varieties.

Thanks to my sister, Judy Lewis, who led me to the Fannie May counter in Washington, D.C., and brought those candies to my attention.

Everywhere Melanie and I went, our friends offered to help us taste their regional delights; in Boston, Larry and Jane Fogg placed their New England palates at our tasting table, and in New York, our friend Sheila Tschinkel was always ready and willing to help.

To my editor, Diane Matthews of Putnam's, I can only offer my complete respect and thanks. Since she does not eat chocolate, this book was truly a labor of love. Her suggestions were always helpful, and I think she has consumed great quantities of chocolate, at least metaphorically, during the course of this book.

For her enthusiasm and efforts, Betty Anne Clarke, my agent, should receive a chocolate accolade. Since we have already shared an entire chocolate cake together, her appreciation of chocolates has been tested and noted.

I thank Margaret Albanese, and Pat and Kenneth Woeber for the gracious use of their facilities in preparing some of these photographs. I also thank the photographers who made their time and talent available to us, Fred Lyon of Fred Lyon Studios, Richard Steinheimer, and Alonso Gonzales. And finally, my thanks are due to Swissair and British Leyland for their help in transportation.

None of this would have happened, however, without the people in the chocolate industry. Candy makers and manufacturers made time, energy, and chocolates available to us. They are listed by country, although chocolates cross geographical boundaries. In various ways, each has contributed to the completion of this book, and certainly helped keep me in chocolate.

In Belgium, Karel Ossieur of Côte d'Or; J. De Ridder of the Belgian Foreign Trade Center; Madame Francis Giardi-Corné of Corné; Antoine F. M. Borms of Neuhaus; A. Vanderkerken of Manon; Paul Wittamer of Wittamer; Mr. Vermeers of Callebaut; Mr. E. Sinclair of Godiva-Belgium; and Mike LaSalle, who escorted us and acted as interpreter, our thanks.

Switzerland found us first in the good hands of Markus Gerber of Multifood-Tobler, with help from Mr. M. Baumann, also. Jurgen Chopard of Suchard; Daniel Eichenberger of Eichenberger Confiserie; Madame Honold of Confiserie Honold; Henri Rohr of Rohr Confections; and the generous people at Nestlé S.A.: Dr. Stutz in Vevey, and Martin Müller, the Direktor at Broc, as well as his assistants, Hans Moos, Heinz Adler, and Gerard Tiedemann; must be noted. Our guide, Veronique Dugoud, was of inestimable help in taking us through the factory.

In Italy, we were grateful for the help of the following people: Ejner Fink-Jensen of Ferrero; Stephano Rossi and Dr. Rossi of Pernigotti; Peter Gilbert at Perugina, as well as Mr. Rossi of Perugina.

Austria, with its fantastic chocolate reputation, was made available to us thanks to Jurgen Meingast of Demel's. Mr. Meinbeck of Heiner's was also most helpful.

Hans Rysgaard and Ole Kieler of Toms introduced us to the Danish chocolates, for which we are grateful.

In England, we were in the capable hands of S. B. Ross, the public relations officer of Cadbury-Schweppes, Ltd., and Dr. L. Bradford, the head chemist.

I would also like to thank the various consulates in San Francisco that we contacted prior to leaving for Europe, who set up our appointments in their countries: Giovanni Zuccarello of the Italian Trade Commission; and Adeline Simones, the consulate general of Belgium; and M. J. Writer, the consulate's trade analyst.

In the United States, we were helped by almost everyone in the industry. Special thanks are due to these people:

Hank Bornhofft, Jr., and John Unger at Merckens; Malcolm Blue and William Savel at Nestlé, Inc.; Hank Blommer and Dod Boldemann at Boldemann; Dan Wing and Jay Guittard at Guittard; Jerrold Tellier and Gene Hollenberger at Ambrosia; Henry Bloomer, Sr., at Blommer; Malcolm Campbell and Ted Van Leer at Van Leer; and Jim Eldris at Hershey. John and Penny Buzzard at Wilbur Chocolate Company also helped in every way they could. John Vassos gave expert answers on questions involving the chemistry of chocolate.

The National Confectioners Association was most cooperative. With Tom Sullivan's help, the Retail Confectioners' International became aware of our needs. We wish to acknowledge those members who responded with chocolates, advice, and most of all, pride in their products:

Doris and Ralph Skidmore of Sydney Boggs; H. Schmid of Edelweiss; Art Preston of Preston's Candies; Allen Wertz, Jr., of Allen Wertz Candies; Charles Huggins of See's Candies; Hank Barner of Lileds; Gordon Hooper of Hooper's; June Mendell of Fun-in-the-Sun Candies; Peter Lojkovic of Princess Delight Confections; John Prongos of Alhambra Candy; Peter Bolanis of Bolan's Candies; Bud Kolbrener of Karl Bissinger, Inc.; Will Gregg, Jr., of Bissinger's; C. Kay Cummings of C. Kay Cummings Candies; Paul Cummings of Cummings Studio Candies; Georgianna Lundgren of The Candy Factory; Michael De-Benedictis of Cape Cod Candies; Nick Phillips of Critchley's Candies; Georges Huwyler of Echo Chocolate Boutique; the Helen Elliot Candy Company; Frank Benson and Carol Gamache of Fanny Farmer Candy Shops; Denton Thorne of Fannie May Candy Shops; Ben Strohecker of Harbor Sweets; Tom Hammond of Hammond's Candies; Bernice's Fine Candies; Fred Hebert of Hebert Candies; Donald Kilwin of Kilwin's Candy Kitchen; Laura Secord Candy Shops; Cedric Waggoner of Harry London Candies; John Marzalino of Mackinac Island Fudge; Bill Malley of Malley's Candies; Tom Wotka of Mavrakos Candy Company; Jim Nixon of Whitman's Candies; Bob and Marie Munson of Munson's Candies; Robert Nagel of Harry C. Nagel and Son; Gust E. Tassy of New Garden of Sweets; Roy Lee and Art Mayland of Nut Tree Candy and Foods; Robert Flesher of Pease's; John Moon of Godiva; Peter Meliotes of Peter's Chocolate Shoppe; Spyros Marcris of Philadelphia Candies; Tom and Diane Kron of Kron's; Achilles Pulakos of Pulakos Candies; John Booe of Rebecca Ruth Candies; Charles Elliot of Regina's Candies; Leon Ricelli of Ricelli Candies; Nick Vlahakis of Lee Sims Chocolates; John Poulos of Stephany's Candies; Louis Ward of Russell Stover Candies;

Alison Schanz of Va Lora's Candies; Kelly Westrom of Van Duyn Candies; Dick Odabashian of Liberty Orchards; Brown and Haley Candies; Alland and Maxine Levy of Milton York Candies; Irwin Witte of Chocolaterie Callebaut; Ruth Morrison of Ruth Morrison Agency; Thelma Lu White of Mrs. J. G. McDonald's; Hy Becker of Cella Confections; Steve Hegedus and James Oletzke of Abdallah, Inc.; Franklin Wyman, Jr., of Bailey's; Gladys Ronsvalle of Ronsvalle; Thomas Zahars of The Candy Shop; Gale O'Malley of the Plaza Hotel; Colette's; William Greenberrg Jr. Desserts; VernaLee Cook; Galo Emerson, Jr. of Putnam Pantry; Frank and Mary Vukmanic of Jo's Candy Cottage; Dick Amandoli of Carl's Pastry Shop.

Finally, I want to thank all the friends who made sure I knew about their special candy places. Without everyone's help, I would not have enjoyed this book as much as I have. It has been, as a friend suggested, the perfect answer for a chocolate addict: for I managed to have my chocolates and eat them also.

ADRIANNE MARCUS
San Rafael, California
September 1978